D0285892

Highland
CALL

Highland
CALL

Sharon Gillenwater

ALABASTER

B O O K S

This is a work of fiction. The characters, incidents, and dialogues are products of the author's imagination and are not to be construed as real. Any resemblance to actual events or persons, living or dead, is entirely coincidental.

HIGHLAND CALL
published by Alabaster Books
a division of Multnomah Publishers, Inc.
© 1999 by Sharon Gillenwater

International Standard Book Number: 1–57673–275–4

Cover design by Brenda McGee
Cover photo by Michael Hudson

All Scripture quotations, unless otherwise indicated, are taken from either *The Holy Bible,* King James Version or *The Holy Bible,* New International Version © 1973, 1984 by International Bible Society, used by permission of Zondervan Publishing House.

Printed in the United States of America
Alabaster Books and the colophon are trademarks of
Multnomah Publishers, Inc.

ALL RIGHTS RESERVED
No part of this publication may be reproduced, stored in a retrieval system, or transmitted, in any form or by any means—electronic, mechanical, photocopying, recording, or otherwise—without prior written permission.

For information:
MULTNOMAH PUBLISHERS, INC.
POST OFFICE BOX 1720 • SISTERS, OREGON 97759

Library of Congress Cataloging-in-Publication Data
Gillenwater, Sharon.
    Highland call/by Sharon Gillenwater.
        p.   cm.
    ISBN 1-57673-275-4 (alk.paper)
    1. Napoleonic Wars, 1800–1815—Fiction.   I. Title.
PS3557.I3758H54   1999
813'.54—dc21   99-11747
                                                                                  CIP
99 00 01 02 03 04 05 06—10 9 8 7 6 5 4 3 2 1

To my brother Bill.

Thank you for going the extra mile…and ten thousand more.

I love you.

Trust in the Lord with all your heart
and lean not on your own understanding;
in all your ways acknowledge him,
and he will make your paths straight.

PROVERBS 3:5–6

Prologue

London, England
Spring, 1810

GABRIEL MACPHERSON HAD DANCED with a dozen ladies during the evening. He had been noble and charming to each and every one, prompting pleased smiles from a lofty duchess down to a shy country miss. But no one interested him enough to ask for a second dance, not even those who clearly hoped he would.

Only one woman had caught his eye. They hadn't danced. Hadn't even spoken. He'd simply glimpsed her during the last reel. But something about her had struck him and he couldn't get her out of his mind.

Working his way through the crowded ballroom, Gabe searched for her, scanning the dance floor. She was not there. Perhaps his imagination and the candlelight had played a trick on him, endowing a pretty lass with an ethereal beauty.

Then he saw her: hair black as a Highland night, violet eyes sparkling like precious gems, and a face too perfect to be imagined. She took his breath away.

Gentlemen surrounded her, all vying for her attention. She joined in their banter, laughing and teasing, but it seemed she favored no one. Gabriel listened intently, hoping to hear her voice, but the music and noise of other conversations made it impossible.

Bad form to be caught staring.

Looking away, he considered approaching her, charming her with a witty comment. Pity his mind seemed to have gone blank. It was a rare and discomforting occurrence.

Gabriel glanced back at the woman, then frowned. True,

she was smiling at her entourage, but he detected something in her expression, in the set of her shoulders. He had the distinct impression of…what? Sadness? Sorrow? She sighed as if weary of the noise, the commotion, and the crush of people.

You would find peace in the Highlands, lass.

He shook his head. He was more homesick than he had realized and was letting his imagination run amok.

Just then she looked up, gazing slowly around the room. Before he could look away, her sorrowful gaze met his, and it was as though he'd been pierced through. Gabriel bowed slightly and smiled. For a heartbeat, time stood still. Gentle warmth lit her eyes, and when she smiled at him, he felt the whisper of angels' wings brush his soul.

Then a gentleman offered her his arm, escorting her onto the dance floor. She politely focused her attention on the other man, never looking back in Gabe's direction.

He took a deep, ragged breath and knew he would never be the same.

CHAPTER  One

Worcestershire, England
Summer, 1811

HOW COULD A LASS WITH SUCH AN ANGELIC *smile be a spy?*

Gabriel was not personally acquainted with the lady under discussion, but he had noticed her the previous year at a London party. Time and time again, Selena Delaroe had unknowingly drawn his gaze.

The son of a viscount, Gabriel had grown up confident of himself and his place in the aristocracy. He had easily charmed some of Society's most enchanting women, yet he had never worked up the courage to approach Selena. Beauty such as hers rendered men speechless.

Or loosened their tongues.

Irritated by the unexpected thought, he frowned and glanced around the billiard room at his companions. He trusted no one more than these three men: Kiernan Macpherson, the earl of Branderee; Dominic Thorne, Kiernan's brother-in-law; and Major William Cameron, his and Kiernan's former commander in the Gordon Highlanders.

Cameron presently served his country in a civilian capacity as an agent in the espionage section of the Foreign Office. Of course, other than his current companions, few knew his true occupation.

Gabriel and Kiernan had fought alongside the major against Napoleon's forces dozens of times before they left the army two years earlier. Gabe had never questioned the man's judgment.

Until now.

Kiernan walked around the mahogany billiard table to line

up his shot. "Why do you believe Miss Delaroe might be working for the French?"

"With her wealth and beauty, she could easily catch a marquis or duke, but she remains single at four-and-twenty." The major's smile was wry. "Her single state is no concern to us, of course. What is troublesome is Miss Delaroe's sudden preference for military officers, especially those home on a short leave from the fighting or those soon to depart on a new assignment. I was a soldier too long no' to notice officers' conduct. During this year's Season, I soon realized she favored their company above all others. Casual questioning of my acquaintances revealed that such has no' been her habit in past years."

He paused, taking a sip of port, and stretched his long legs out in front of him. Like Gabriel and Kiernan, he wore a kilt. The shades of red, green, and blue in the material were similar, but the tartan of his was different than theirs—Clan Cameron rather than Macpherson. "I mentioned it to an undersecretary at the home office, since they are supposed to handle possible counterespionage." Cameron shook his head in disgust. "They are too busy worrying about labor unrest to investigate a potential spy. I have been given permission to look into it."

Kiernan took the shot, hitting his ivory ball against the side cushion so it moved back across the table at an angle. It knocked Gabe's ball close to the pocket, but not quite into it. Frowning slightly, Kiernan stepped back from the table.

Gabriel chalked the end of his cue. Why was he in such a turmoil? He didn't even know this woman. *But I want to.* Her lovely image had lingered in his thoughts more than he cared to admit.

At the end of the room, Dominic added another log to the small fire in the fireplace. Thornridge belonged to him, as did several other English holdings and a Scottish estate. He adjusted the log with the poker, then straightened, glancing thoughtfully at Gabriel before he turned to Cameron. "I have known Selena for many years. Some English openly admire the French and Napoleon, but I have never heard her praise them. Given that her brother is a captive in France, she probably hates them." He glanced at Gabriel again. "Nicholas is a détenu."

Gabriel's frown deepened at that bit of news. When the long war between France and England ended with the Peace of Amiens in October of 1801, a broad cross section of Britons flocked to France. Merchants and tradesmen rushed across the channel, but the aristocracy and gentry led the way. Unfortunately, Napoleon did not abide by the terms of the treaty, and England declared war in May 1803. Many British citizens traveling in the French empire were caught unaware and had no chance to flee.

Less than a week later, Napoleon issued a command previously unknown in the history of European war. He ordered the arrest of any British males between the ages of eighteen and sixty who were then on French soil—civilians as well as those in the military. Because men between those ages might conceivably serve in the British militia, no exceptions were made.

Of the several hundred detained, approximately half were members of the aristocracy and gentry. Some of the wealthiest and most influential gained their freedom rather quickly and returned to England. The others were later sent far from the coast to the walled town of Verdun. If they had money—or someone at home to send it to them—they usually lived well, much as they would in Britain, though they were confined to the city. Many, even titled lords, were still held. Some managed to escape. Others tried but were caught and wound up in French prisons, where their lot was much worse than in Verdun.

Since all of these men had been traveling with French-approved passports, the British viewed their arrests as a breach of international law and common decency, but Napoleon lived by his own rules. He declared that the détenus were prisoners of war. They could only be exchanged for French prisoners of equal importance—a nobleman for a high-ranking officer, and so forth. Britain refused, unwilling to allow the French emperor to set such a precedent. Negotiations had been at a stalemate for eight years.

Cameron nodded slowly. "In all likelihood, she does hate them. Still, since the name *Delaroe* comes from the French *Delarue*, a few in the Foreign Office question her family's loyalty to England. They think there might be a possible family tie of which we are unaware, and that Nicholas has remained in France of his own accord."

"Balderdash!" Gabriel was almost as surprised as the others at the vehemence in his tone. "Half the names in England came from France through the Norman conquest."

Cameron looked at him, eyebrows arched. "No need to be testy. I dinna lend any credence to the idea myself. But her brother is her twin, and I am told that they were quite close. It is certainly no' above Napoleon to threaten grave harm to him if she does no' cooperate with them."

"How much damage could she do?" Dominic asked, sitting down in a red tapestry and mahogany armchair.

"We do no' believe she has passed on anything substantial. At worst she may have confirmed news that Napoleon gleaned from other sources. But someday she might truly learn a secret and relay military plans that will cost the lives of British soldiers."

Gabriel's hand slipped, and the cue came close to tearing the smooth, green felt covering of the billiard table. He glared at the ball, which he had missed completely, then carefully composed his expression before turning toward Dominic and Cameron. His former commander had an uncanny ability to read a man's thoughts. "I dinna believe she would do such a thing."

"You know her?" Kiernan looked at him, his eyes wide and curious.

"No, but I've seen her." Realizing how foolish he sounded,

Gabriel shrugged, moving out of Kiernan's way. "And I have heard a great deal about her."

"Nothing but praise, I daresay," Cameron said. "I would have had a similar reaction six months ago." He studied Gabriel carefully. "You have never talked to her?"

"No."

A knowing grin lit Cameron's face. "Yet you instantly defend her. I do believe you've been smitten from afar."

Despite his best efforts, Gabe felt his cheeks grow warm. *Blast and thunder!* He had not shown embarrassment since he was a green-as-grass youth. "I'm four-and-thirty. Far too old to do something so foolish."

Kiernan paused in the process of studying his next shot and glanced at Gabe. Straightening slowly, Kiernan stared at him. "You're blushing."

"Merely the exertion of the game."

Kiernan nudged him with an elbow. "What a plumper."

The others laughed, and Cameron jumped up, patting Gabe on the back. "Poor laddie, I never thought I'd see the day when a woman made you tongue-tied."

"I simply never had an opportunity to speak to her. She was always surrounded by admirers."

"That never stopped you before," Kiernan said with a chuckle. "When was this?"

"At the Altbury ball last year."

"A night permanently etched in my memory." At Dominic's quiet comment, Cameron looked at him expectantly, and he continued. "It was the first time I saw my Jeanie." Dominic met Gabriel's gaze. "You are not too old to be intrigued by a woman from a distance. I'm older than you and I was halfway in love with Jeanette before I ever spoke to her."

Gabriel smiled at his friend, who had been a notorious rake before he met Kiernan's gentle, godly sister. Dominic was living proof of God's grace and forgiveness. "That is because the heavenly Father had already chosen her for you."

"Perhaps you are drawn to Selena for the same reason."

Gabriel had no ready response. God knew he longed for a wife and family. And yet, though he had met many unattached women since he left the military, he had no inclination to pursue any of them. The only one who interested him was Selena. Was it possible Dominic could be right?

Cameron moved back to his chair and sat down with a sigh. "I truly hope no'. If she is working for Napoleon, she is guilty of high treason. Traitors hang."

Gabriel winced. "No' if she is innocent."

"It does no' look promising."

Gabriel doubted Selena had any inkling of the government's suspicions. Too often, guilty verdicts were rendered based on questionable evidence. In all fairness, she needed someone on her side. "Then I'll prove it."

"Always ready to be a lady's champion," muttered Kiernan, putting his billiard cue away. He had obviously decided there was no use in continuing the game.

Gabe met his friend's gaze evenly. "You're one to talk. You were bent on protecting Mariah from the very first." He followed Kiernan's lead and slid his cue into the empty slot on the rack.

"She didna have a feather to fly with and no one to help her."

Gabriel shrugged. "Selena may no' be penniless, but who can she turn to?"

"Just because you are bored is no reason to involve yourself in this mire. You canna walk up to her door and say, 'Pardon me, miss, but I'm here to save you.'" When Kiernan settled his fists on his hips and scowled at him, Gabriel almost laughed in spite of the seriousness of the situation. He had seen that determined stance more times than he could count.

"That's no' exactly what I had in mind."

"How are you thinking of handling it?" Dominic's question was more curious than a challenge.

"He has no' thought. Never does," Kiernan said. "Jumps into the thick of it, then tries to find a way out."

That wasn't true. Gabe usually tried to formulate a plan. Though he silently admitted there had been occasions when he had no time to do so. Rarely had he run into trouble by acting on his instincts. He knew Kiernan only made the comment because he was afraid he might be hurt.

"We'll come up with something." Gabriel looked at Cameron. "There must be a way to learn what you need to know without tipping your hand."

"I'm relieved to hear you dinna intend to warn her. What will you do if she is guilty?"

"There is no need to question my loyalty to my country," Gabriel chided Cameron quietly. "You know I will tell you the truth."

"Could you lie to her?"

"What do you mean?" Gabriel sat down, hoping he did not appear as tense as he felt. Lying was something he strove to avoid, even in a society where prevarication and falsehoods were commonplace. He tried to live a godly life, though he knew he was far from perfect. He absently ran his fingertip over the intricately carved foliage at the edge of the armchair, suspecting he would not like Cameron's answer.

"Miss Delaroe's grandfather left her an estate near here. She and her aunt, the countess of Camfield, have taken up residence there for the summer. I spent a short time in the village before coming to Thornridge this afternoon. It seems our lady is in need of an estate manager. Since you have accomplished minor miracles with your own holdings, you should be more than qualified for the position."

Kiernan frowned at Gabe again. "It's foolishness. You're bound to run into someone you know—"

"No' necessarily." Cameron broke in. "Contact with the *ton* would be far more limited at a country house than if you were in London. If Miss Delaroe or her aunt have company, you stay out of sight. And even if you were spotted, well—" he studied Gabe for a moment—"You've changed since I last saw you, Gabriel. I suspect only a close acquaintance would recognize you."

Gabriel knew it was true. He'd spent long hours working outdoors on his newly acquired estate during the past year, and his once auburn hair had faded to a light reddish blond. The addition of a mustache, grown on a whim during the winter and now the same color as his sun-bleached hair, also altered his features.

Cameron continued. "If we had passed each other on the street, I'm no' sure I would have known you."

Gabriel frowned, doubting it would be as easy as the major made it sound.

Cameron drummed his fingertips against the arm of the chair, thinking, then shook his head. "There is a problem, though. The kilt would have given you away, even if your features did not. If you are to succeed with the masquerade, clothing more common to England will be required. It will have to be pantaloons and trousers, laddie."

Gabriel had worn the kilt practically every day of his life, not just when he was with the Gordons. He started to tell Cameron that he would not go through with the mad scheme, until he spotted Kiernan's grin. His friend's smugness gave him pause—but it was that unforgettable moment in time when Selena's gaze had met his across the crowded ballroom that made up his mind. Her smile had been for him alone and her gentle sweetness had captured a piece of his heart.

He straightened, squaring his shoulders. "Dominic, I trust you can recommend a tailor in Worcester who is fast and will do good work." When Kiernan groaned and started to protest, Gabriel held up his hand. "Save your breath. I know the risks. Whether the end be good or ill, I must do this."

CHAPTER *Two*

GABRIEL MACPHERSON WAS NOT AT ALL what Selena had expected. Three of the others who applied for the position of estate manager had been boastful of their accomplishments and arrogant in their attitude. Though admiring her appearance, they clearly thought little of her intelligence or business ability. The other two men had been overly solicitous, quickly agreeing to even her most outlandish suggestions.

The man who now sat on the other side of the large satinwood desk was every inch a gentleman. The fine tailoring of his buff trousers, willow green striped waistcoat, and dark green coat bespoke excellent taste. The coat was cut slightly looser than those worn by men of fashion, probably so he could work freely, and possibly because he did not have a valet to help him put it on. The material was not the most expensive, but it was nonetheless well suited to a country gentleman—and it emphasized the rich olive green of his eyes.

Tall and lean, with light reddish blond hair and mustache, he was far too handsome for her peace of mind. Though she usually did not care for mustaches, Macpherson's was actually attractive.

He met her gaze directly, answering every question with ease or measured consideration. When she tested him with one of her more ridiculous suggestions, his eyes twinkled merrily as though he knew exactly what she was about. His respectful response, though, was that he thought such an endeavor would be unwise.

At first she had the faint impression she might have met him before. After hearing his deep voice with a trace of brogue, she was certain she had not. His appearance and that almost musical voice made a potent combination a woman did not soon forget. Still, those remarkable eyes prompted the vague feeling that she had at least seen him before. The memory was too elusive to pursue, however, so she did not mention it.

He spoke and moved with the quiet assurance of a man confident of his abilities and his place in life. The only hint of self-consciousness was the way he occasionally pushed his spectacles up on his nose. With some men, she might have been irritated by the action. With Macpherson, it seemed mildly endearing.

He asked a few questions about the estate, ones she suspected were meant as much to test her business aplomb as to gain knowledge of Fairhaven. Since his manner was respectful and not condescending, she did not mind. In essence, he treated her as an equal.

And that posed a potential problem. An estate manager needed to command the respect of the farm laborers, servants, and those with whom they transacted business. She had no doubt Macpherson would succeed well in that area. But Fairhaven belonged to her. If her wishes ran contrary to his on a matter, she wondered if he would acquiesce. He did not strike her as a man who would take orders easily, especially ones with which he disagreed.

Selena glanced at his references. "You come highly recommended, sir. None of the other applicants have references of the caliber of Dominic Thorne or the earl of Branderee." She frowned and met his steady gaze. "If I remember correctly, the earl's name is Macpherson also. Are you related?"

"Perhaps in the distant past. Traditionally, Macphersons are said to be descendants of Muirich, a priest or parson of the Culdee church at Kingussie." One corner of his mouth lifted in a slight smile. "The priests of this church were not bound to celibacy, and Macpherson means 'son of the parson.' I have known the earl all my life. He introduced me to Mr. Thorne."

"This is an impressive list in Mr. John Macpherson's letter regarding your accomplishments on his estate." She glanced up to see him shift uncomfortably in his chair.

"It is merely a statement of facts," he said briskly, seemingly embarrassed by the other man's praise. He again fussed with his spectacles.

"Still, it appears you turned a neglected estate into a profitable venture in less than a year's time. That is certainly nothing to take lightly."

"It merely needed some judicious management and the investment of a large sum to set things to rights."

"I am surprised you did not remain there to keep it running smoothly."

"I still serve in an advisory capacity and receive regular reports from the man now in charge." He hesitated. "Since the owner is no' presently residing in Scotland, I might occasionally be required to return to the Highlands for a short stay. However, I do no' anticipate the need for such a journey anytime soon. I would, of course, no' expect any wages while I am away. Nor would I leave if circumstances here prevented it."

"Have you managed any other farms or estates?"

He shook his head. "I spent many years traveling from place to place." His grin held a distinct trace of mischief. "No' exactly a vagabond, but at times my ragged appearance might have caused some to think so. Still, I learned much along the way."

No doubt he had, not the least of which was how to charm a lady. "Why do you wish to work for me, Mr. Macpherson?"

He straightened minutely and pushed up his spectacles, meeting her gaze. "I need more income. Mr. Thorne told me something of your situation—that the estate is in dire need of improvements. Though my experience has been in the Highlands, he assures me that I might seek his advice anytime I need it." He smiled ruefully. "I dinna think the work here will be all that different, but if I'm proven wrong, he may wish he had never made the offer."

Selena chuckled softly. "You both may wish to reserve judgment. My grandfather bought this estate fully intending to

21

bring it up to modern standards. Of course, he also had hoped to turn a tidy profit. Other interests preoccupied him, however, and he never gave Fairhaven more than token attention. When he died two years ago and left the lands to me, I basically relinquished the running of the property to the man in charge at the time. Then I made an extended visit here last fall—"

She broke off, glancing away briefly. The memory of what she'd found still raised her ire. "I was unaware of how poorly he handled estate affairs. He let Fairhaven fall into a shameful condition." She looked back at Macpherson. "I replaced him with someone recommended by my London solicitor, but he was no better. That prompted me to establish Fairhaven as my permanent residence and oversee its gradual transformation. My aunt, Lady Camfield, is staying with me, both for the pleasure of her company and to occasionally offer advice."

She paused, studying him silently for a moment. "I assume you like a challenge, Mr. Macpherson?"

A glint lit his eyes. Or was it merely a reflection off his spectacles? "Yes, I do, Miss Delaroe."

Had she imagined that flash of masculine interest simply because she saw it in practically every man's eyes? Or because, fool that she was, she *wanted* to see it in his? Gabriel Macpherson might be seeking employment, but everything about him proclaimed him to be at least a member of the gentry, if not on the fringes of the *haut ton* itself. Impoverished perhaps, but willing to work for his keep. It was an unusual trait for a member of the aristocracy, but one she found appealing.

The thought crossed her mind that he might be a fortune hunter, but she dismissed it immediately. Dominic Thorne would never have given him his blessing if he were such a man.

Selena reminded herself that he was her employee—or would be if she offered him the position. Yet she had never been so drawn to any other man. It would be safer not to hire him. But she could not bring herself to turn him away. There could be no deep or lasting relationship between them, though not because she was rich and he wasn't, or because she was part of the aristocracy and he might not be. She could allow no strong attachment to develop with him, or any man, for she had no future.

Still, she would like to have this man's friendship, though even that might last all too short a time.

He removed his spectacles and rubbed the bridge of his nose before folding the earpieces close to the lens. Sticking the glasses in the inside pocket of his jacket, he shrugged lightly. "Annoying things. Canna see any better with them than I can without them." His penetrating gaze met hers, causing her heart to flutter like that of a girl still in the schoolroom. "I would like to help you, Miss Delaroe…in any way I can."

Selena caught her breath. Coming from another man, a similar statement might have been shaded with impropriety. But she could discern nothing provocative or unseemly in his manner. Then why, as he intently searched her eyes, did she sense his words held a much deeper meaning than merely setting the estate to rights?

"I would like to help you…"

The words, and the sincerity with which they were spoken, echoed through her mind. A sudden wave of anguish rocked her. Turning away from his gaze, she barely controlled the cry of despair that burst from her heart.

No one can help me!

A web of treachery, deceit, and lies held her firmly in its grasp, with no hope of escape or redemption. According to Scripture, there was no greater love than if a man lay down his life for his friends. In essence, she had forfeited her life for her brother's, but there was nothing honorable in the act. A shiver whispered down her back. How many others had she sacrificed to save Nick?

Rising with far more composure than she felt, Selena walked over to the window, putting her back to Macpherson.

She toyed with the frill at the throat of her dark pink dress, reminding herself to be strong and not let her emotions betray her. When her brother was safely home, she would pay for her sins, no matter the cost. Until then, she must guard her secret with all diligence.

She took a deep breath and turned to face him, only to find him right behind her. Her breath came out in a little squeak as she jumped in surprise, almost losing her balance.

He steadied her, resting his hands on her arms at the edge of the short sleeves. "My apologies," he said quietly, lowering his hands to his side with seeming reluctance. "I didna mean to startle you."

He stepped back, and a twinge of disappointment nudged her. *You're vulnerable to this man. Hiring him could be dangerous. To you. To Nick.* Then she looked up, noting the tiny frown between his brows, the concern in his eyes.

"Are you unwell, miss?"

"No." She supposed sick of one's self did not count.

"Did I offend you in some way?" His frown deepened.

"No." The concern on Macpherson's face unsettled her. Why should he care so for one he scarcely knew? She gave him a self-deprecating smile. "For some reason, I suddenly thought of my brother. He is a détenu."

Macpherson nodded. "Thorne told me. He said Nicholas is your twin."

Selena sighed heavily. "And my dearest friend. I have greatly missed him all these years." She forced a smile. "Perhaps you and I can turn Fairhaven into a model farm. Then when he returns to England, he will be astounded that his little sister could accomplish such a thing."

Macpherson grinned. "Little sister?"

This time her smile came easily. "He's three minutes older and never lets me forget it."

He chuckled softly. "I too have an older brother. Whether the difference in age is measured in minutes or years, they like

24

to lord it over us." Moving aside, he gave her a slightly lopsided smile. "I gather I am hired?"

"You are, sir. Would you like a tour of the estate?"

"I could wander around on my own, but it would be much more pleasant if you are my guide. More beneficial, too, since you could tell me what changes you are considering."

"And will you make an instant determination as to whether they are good or bad?" She didn't think there would be a problem, but she needed a bit of banter to lighten her mood.

He deftly took up the challenge. "Of course. With my vast knowledge of farming here in the Vale of Severn, I am undoubtedly an expert. My gig awaits if you care to accompany me."

"It seems wise. Who knows what atrocities you might decide to plant."

"Neeps and tatties, of course." When she sent him a questioning look, he grinned. "Turnips and potatoes."

Though both were eaten in England, she had read that in the Scottish Highlands potatoes were the main food of the poorer classes. The use of potatoes, and especially turnips, as winter fodder for livestock was even more prevalent in Scotland than in England.

"Not too many, I hope."

"Only half the estate." He opened the door for her, and they strolled from the room. "What else would we eat?"

She wrinkled her nose. "Almost anything. I do not care for turnips."

"Alas, then we'll have to give them to the cattle."

"I only have a small herd."

"Perhaps we can increase it with some fine black cattle from the Highland estate where I last worked." The teasing had left his voice as he gave her a considering glance. "I believe I could persuade the laird to give you a fair price."

They paused in the hallway for a few moments while a maid fetched Selena's hat. "Then John Macpherson has a title?"

He shook his head. "Nothing impressive such as an earl or viscount. In Scotland, *laird* is used in several ways, particularly in the Highlands. Most often it means the landlord of an estate, but it also is a beloved title for the chief of a clan."

"Is John the chief?"

"No." He smiled patiently. "That is Duncan of Cluny. His father was Ewen, the Cluny Macpherson who fought valiantly with Bonnie Prince Charlie in the '45. After the war, his home was burned and his estates forfeited, as were those of many others involved in the Rebellion. There was a price on his head. Cluny hid in caves in the mountains and among his people for nine years. To avoid detection by the army during that time, his wife gave birth to Duncan in a kiln used for drying corn."

"His people must have loved him very much." Selena smiled at her maid as the young woman handed her a wide-brimmed straw gypsy hat.

"Yes, they did. None were ever tempted to betray him despite the offer of a large reward. He eventually escaped to France. The forfeited estates were returned to Duncan in 1784, and he now lives at Cluny Castle. Like his father before him, he is much admired and respected."

"So John is called the laird because he owns an estate?" She glanced up as she tied the hat's pink ribbon beneath her chin. A spark flickered in Macpherson's eyes, warming her from head to toe.

"Simply that." His reply was even, giving no hint of the emotion she'd seen a moment before. Had it really been there?

When he offered her his arm, she tucked her hand around it and allowed him to escort her out the front door. He carefully helped her into the gig, a two-wheeled, two-passenger vehicle drawn by a single horse. The top had been folded down, likely so he could enjoy the sunshine.

"Do you wish me to raise the top?" He sat next to her, taking the reins from the footman.

"No. It's a lovely day. My hat should keep the freckles at bay."

He flicked the reins, driving the horse down the lane toward the orchards. "Even freckles could not mar your lovely skin." Glancing down at her, he grinned impishly. "Unless it was a single one on the tip of your nose. Then it might prove a distraction."

"I could always develop an affectation and cover it with a beauty mark as they did in years past."

When Gabriel laughed, it occurred to her that somewhere between the study and the front door, she had begun to think of him in terms of his Christian name rather than his surname. It was highly improper so soon after meeting him. Many women did not even call their *husbands* by their Christian names. But propriety notwithstanding, Gabriel he was—in her mind, at least.

Like the angel...

The thought brought her a tiny smile. Then she remembered that in the Bible, a heavenly visitor was not always the bearer of glad tidings. Sometimes they were harbingers of doom.

When Gabriel returned to Thornridge later in the day, Cameron practically herded him into the study. Kiernan and Dominic trailed behind them.

"Well, did she hire you?" Cameron sat on the edge of the desk, his eyes bright with anticipation.

"Of course. How could she resist?" With a smug grin, he collapsed on a chair. "I just came back to collect my clothes— my English clothes," he added dryly.

"She didn't recognize you?" Dominic sat down in a chair across from him.

"She gave no indication of it. It seems I didna make as much of an impression on her as she did on me." Gabe couldn't help but wish he had, even though it would thwart their whole plan. He was already starting to question the wisdom of their scheme.

"So, does she have a high, whiny voice? Or some other annoying flaw?" Kiernan tapped his fingers on the mantel.

Gabe didn't miss the trace of hopefulness in his friend's expression. Kiernan's stubborn dislike of Selena—sight unseen—annoyed him. "Her voice is beautiful, like the rest of her. She is perfect in every way."

Kiernan glared at him and shook his head. "You canna go into this being blind to her faults. It could get you killed."

Or break my heart. Gabe was not foolish enough to dismiss either possibility. "I know. Dinna worry, I'll be careful. I'm no' a lovestruck fool."

"Yet," Kiernan muttered.

It was a troubling thought, one Gabe had considered many times. What would he do if he fell in love with her and then learned she was a spy? *That's no' going to happen. She's too good and gentle to do something so despicable.*

Still, he couldn't shake the nagging feeling that he was doing something wrong. Did God condone deception in a situation such as this? Gabe doubted it, but how else would they go about it? How else could he prove her innocent? He had prayed about it but received no clear answer. So for now, he saw no other way than to muddle through on his own.

Gabe remembered the anguish on her face when she thought of her brother, and it again tugged at his heart. "I have to pursue this, Kiernan. For my own peace of mind, and perhaps for hers. She suffers greatly because of her brother's detainment."

"Enough to do anything to possibly gain his release?" Cameron's piercing gaze set off a warning bell in Gabe's mind. The major was not interested in protecting Selena or comforting her. He wanted to catch a spy.

"That's what I'm there to find out. So I'd better get on with it." He rose and headed for the door. "I want to learn the layout of the grounds before dark."

"Dinna forget your objective, Gabriel." Cameron stood, assuming the commanding air Gabe knew so well. "Befriend Miss Delaroe. Court her if you must. Use whatever means necessary to discover if she is working for Napoleon."

A shiver raced down Gabriel's spine as he caught Kiernan's dark frown. Could he be so callous?

He fervently hoped not.

CHAPTER *Three*

GABRIEL QUICKLY SETTLED INTO his new role. Fairhaven had excellent potential, but a great deal of work needed to be done to make it self-supporting, much less turn it into a profitable venture. He estimated that the account ledgers would show a deficit for at least another year. It was a pity he would not be there to see the final results.

While Gabe took stock of the estate, Selena was busy redecorating her home, one of the few buildings that did not need a major repair of some kind. He had a nice house to himself on the grounds but often worked in the office in the manor. He and his new employer saw each other every day, usually for only a few minutes at a time, as one or the other hurried off to tend to some task.

He had been at the estate for a week, and though he'd watched her actions carefully, he found nothing to indicate she was involved with the enemy. She was as beautiful, charming, and kind as he'd ever imagined.

Cameron was wrong. He had to be.

Late one afternoon, Gabriel trotted up the steps of Dominic's home, nodding a greeting to the footman who opened the front door. From beyond the house, a lively bagpipe tune drifted across the countryside.

"Good afternoon, Mr. Macpherson."

"Good afternoon. They are in the garden?"

"Yes, sir."

Gabriel hid his amusement at the man's slightly pained expression. Some Englishmen had no appreciation for the pipes. He handed his black top hat to the footman. "No need to show me the way."

The servant bowed, his expression relieved. "Thank you, sir."

As Gabriel walked through the large house, he thought of the days so long ago when Kiernan first learned to play. Imagining the footman's reaction to the screeching pipes and the dog's howls, he laughed quietly. Kiernan's mother had not wanted to discourage him, but finally even she had had enough and sent him partway up the mountain to practice.

Gabriel was closer to Kiernan than he was to his own brother, Neil. Ten years his senior, Neil had been sent to school in England about the time Gabe was born. They'd only seen each other during Neil's visits home each summer. Their relationship was cordial, but they were not at all close. In actuality, they scarcely knew each other.

Gabriel and Kiernan, on the other hand, had grown up together in the Highlands, near Loch Laggan. Though his father was a viscount and Kiernan's had been a forester, the two boys had been inseparable until Gabriel headed for Oxford at eighteen.

A good student, he managed a reasonably proficient classical education. Like most of the young men at the university, Gabe had tried a bit of gambling and drinking, but found no pleasure in it. Indeed, he'd tired of it quickly, which helped him avoid squandering his time and fortune like so many of his classmates. Instead, he'd focused on learning. And on acquiring much of his Town polish at his father's side whenever that gentleman visited England.

While Gabe was at school, Kiernan stayed in the Highlands. He worked with his father in the forest and practiced the bagpipes for hours, hoping to fulfill his long-held dream of being hired by some Scottish officer as a military piper.

After a year and a half at the university, Gabriel grew restless. He left Oxford, purchasing a commission as a captain with the Gordon Highlanders. By that time, Kiernan had honed his musical skills to perfection. From the beginning Gabriel had intended to take him along when he left with the Gordons. Upon hearing him play, he did so with great pride.

Now, as Gabe walked down the hall at Thornridge, he listened to the music with a smile. He passed through the French doors leading to the terrace and paused, taking in the happy scene before him. Playing a Scottish reel on the great Highland bagpipe, Kiernan stood away from the others, who sat in brown wicker chairs beneath a huge oak. He wore a white shirt, red hose, and black shoes, along with his normal Highland garb of kilt and plaid—which was made in a predominately red tartan shaded with blue and green.

The tartan was a pattern favored by the Macphersons, and one that Gabriel often wore as well. At least, he'd done so before he had been coerced into donning trousers in a fool's masquerade. He was slowly growing accustomed to them, though he wondered if he would ever consider them as comfortable as the kilt.

The spectacles were another story. He tried wearing them in Selena's presence, but though the lenses were plain glass, they drove him to distraction. Keeping a clear head around her was difficult enough without having to constantly adjust the cursed things on his nose. So he gave up on them.

Kiernan was a large, strong man with black hair and eyes—the embodiment of a great Highland warrior. It was a fitting image, for Gabriel did not know a braver man. Kiernan had fought in Minorca, Egypt, Copenhagen, Sweden, and finally in Portugal as part of the Peninsular campaign, but he never carried a musket into battle. Though he was usually armed with a couple of pistols and a dirk, his principal weapons against Napoleon's tyranny were sheer courage and the pipes.

The sound of the pipes stirred a sudden swell of emotion, catching Gabe off guard. Tears stung his eyes. Images from the war swept over him. He and Kiernan had fought in almost every battle together, with the exception of a few when one or the other was wounded. Gabriel did not discount his own valor and abilities. He knew he had served honorably and well. But when he charged into battle, it was at the head of a company of men. Kiernan walked onto the battlefield alone, before everyone else. His music led the men into the fray and roused them to fight. As they rushed past him, still he continued to play. No matter how fierce the fighting, Gabe's heart had been attuned to the haunting, stirring notes of Kiernan's pipes. And on the rare occasions when they fell silent, Gabriel fought like a madman to reach him, to protect him, and, a few times, to save him.

In 1809, Kiernan's father died after a sudden illness. Gabriel sold his commission, and they went home to the Highlands. A few months later, Kiernan unexpectedly received an inheritance from a distant cousin—vast wealth, an estate on the northern Scottish coast, and a title, earl of Branderee. The change in social and financial status had been uncomfortable for his friend, but Gabe did what he could to ease the way.

Last year he had accompanied Kiernan, his mother, and his sister, Jeanette, to England for their entry into Society. The visit changed Gabe's life yet again. The other three each found love and were married after they returned to Branderee.

Seeing everyone else in love only emphasized Gabe's loneliness, and he left a few days after Kiernan and Mariah's wedding. There were times when he did not know which was worse—living so far from his closest friend, or being near him as the odd man out in the midst of so much marital happiness.

He had visited his parents, thinking of attempting to purchase land overlooking Loch Laggan from a neighbor. He soon decided the land was not suitable, nor was the notion of living right next to his parents particularly appealing. Though he had a good relationship with his father, Viscount Liath, he discovered his parents had grown rather overbearing. Gabe had no trouble asking for advice when he chose, but he would not tolerate being told what to do every step of the way. His choices— and his mistakes—were his to make. Not another's.

Still, he wanted to settle in the Highlands of his youth, close enough to easily visit his family but not have his father constantly hovering over him. He'd found the perfect property at Inshirra, a large estate twenty-five miles to the north on Loch Insh. Bordered by the River Spey and the Cairngorm Mountains, it had forests and meadows, a view of the river and Monadhliath Mountains in one direction, and the Cairngorm Mountains in the other. The tenants and employees were pleasant and hard workers. The house was large and in good condition, though the furnishings were somewhat out of style.

He could reach his parents' home in about three hours, close enough to visit when he wanted, but far enough away to keep his father from dropping by too often. It generally took a day and a half to reach Branderee, Kiernan's estate, stopping at an inn along the way. If necessary, however, the trip could be made in one day of hard riding on horseback.

Though Kiernan had chided him about becoming involved with Selena's investigation out of boredom, Gabriel had not left Inshirra due to monotony. He loved the place, but as he rambled through the house on stormy days or sleepless nights, the silence of its halls echoed the emptiness of his heart.

At times he regretted not buying a home closer to Kiernan's estate on the coast, but the call of the Highlands had been ever present during the twelve years he fought in the war. It grew stronger in the months after they left the regiment, until one day he realized that the Highlands, especially the mountains, were a part of him, an integral piece of the puzzle that was his life.

His gaze drifted to Mariah, the lovely woman who had won Kiernan's heart. Wearing an apple green gown that complemented her red hair and gray eyes, she smiled at her husband. They'd recently learned that she carried their first child, and she fairly glowed with happiness.

Jeanette, dressed in a poppy red, short-sleeved gown, sat beside her, laughing as Dominic gently bounced their two-month-old son, Donald, on his knee, keeping time to the music. The little boy giggled and reached for Dominic's head but missed, his tiny fingers clutching the lapel of his bright blue coat. The child seemed fascinated by the silver streaks in his father's blond hair.

The baby's features resembled those of his father, but beneath his little white ruffled cap, his hair was light brown like his mother's. His eyes were currently blue, but Jeanette told Gabe the color was fading. Dominic insisted his little boy would have topaz eyes like Jeanie's. She countered that they should be emerald green, like her husband's.

Gabe wished he had a love like theirs and a wife who would playfully argue over things that neither of them could control.

Amid his friends' happiness, a deep sadness filled him. He was known for his carefree, teasing ways, yet his heart ached. For over a year, even before Kiernan's marriage, he had secretly asked God to bring him a wife, chosen by the Master's hand. Now, constantly near the one woman who fascinated him above all others, he prayed that God might guard his heart and direct his path.

Taking a deep breath, he pushed aside his worrisome thoughts and put on a smile as he strolled out to join the group.

Kiernan finished the song and laid the bagpipes on a nearby wicker table. "It's about time you paid us a call. We decided you had forgotten all about us." He dropped into a chair next to his wife, his concerned expression belying his teasing tone. Other than a quick visit to pick up his new English-style clothes after Selena hired him, Gabriel had stayed away from Thornridge.

"I didna think it wise to come too soon. I had to see what improvements are needed at Fairhaven before I could come up with a reasonable excuse to seek the local expert's advice." He smiled at Dominic. "I have a whole list of things to ask you."

"I'll be pleased to help if I can," Dominic said.

Kiernan glanced around, and Gabe restrained a smile at his

friend's caution. Dominic's employees knew Gabriel was their master's friend, though it was not likely they were aware of his wealth. Even if they were, Dominic had one firm, long-standing rule that should stop the knowledge from being bandied about elsewhere. It was too much to expect the servants not to gossip among themselves, but anyone who spread tales about his guests beyond Thornridge would be instantly dismissed. Still, Kiernan spoke quietly and discreetly. "Have you discovered anything?"

Gabriel shook his head. "Selena is involved in redecorating her house and concocting all manner of things to do to the estate." Thinking of her sparkling eyes and animated features as she explained her plans brought a smile. "She has new ideas almost every day. She has no' gone out socially since I've been there."

"That is unusual." Dominic turned little Donald around, leaning him back against his chest, and steadied him with his hand. "There are several members of the *ton* with country houses in the area. Many more rent lodgings in and around Worcester for the summer. We receive two or three invitations to dinner or parties every week. Add afternoon visits, a stroll along the walks, the theater, assemblies, and concerts in Worcester, and there is something available every day. Though Selena has not resided at Fairhaven in the past, she often stayed on the other side of the city at another family home. Both here and in London, she has always been quite active socially."

"Given that she is so involved with the changes on the estate, it doesn't seem too odd that she would forgo the regular amusements for a time," Mariah said.

Jeanette wiped some drool from the baby's chin. "Perhaps she simply needs a rest from the social whirl. I easily tire of the noise, crowds, and late nights."

"True enough." Dominic glanced at Gabriel with a frown. "Or her self-imposed isolation could be because there are currently no officers in the area. If one arrives, and she suddenly resumes her normal social schedule, it will look incriminating."

Frowning, Gabriel nodded. "I canna help but hope none come within a hundred miles of here. Though I would like to prove her innocent of Cameron's suspicions, I regret my involvement in this scheme more every day. I canna believe the Lord approves of my deceit."

"Is there another way to find the answers Cameron needs?" Mariah's doubt was clear in the tone of her voice.

"None that I can think of."

"Nor I," Kiernan said. "And believe me, I have tried to come up with something."

"Have you been forced to lie often?" Mariah's question held only understanding and concern.

"No' outright, though I fear shading the truth is the same thing. I never thought there would be a cloudy line between honoring God and honoring country. Thankfully, I've managed to avoid even that most of the time, though I did squirm when Selena was so impressed by the letter of recommendation from John Macpherson."

Kiernan smiled. "Boasted of your own accomplishments, did you?"

Though troubled, Gabriel could see the humor in that particular situation. "Others might think so, but I merely stated the facts—as I see them, anyway. I just hope nothing arises where I must include my full name in my signature. If she notes that my middle name is John, she will likely see through the pretense."

"It is a common name. She might no' connect the two."

Mariah leaned forward, her eyes bright. "What is Selena like? I haven't been going out so I have not met her yet."

Gabe turned to his friend in concern. When he'd moved to Fairhaven, Mariah had been plagued with morning sickness from the pregnancy. "Are you feeling better, then?"

"Much better. Not perfect, yet—"

"Yes, you are." Kiernan leaned over and dropped a kiss on her cheek.

Mariah laughed. "Hardly. Tell us about Selena. Is she all you hoped she would be?"

Gabe couldn't hold back a smile. "Aye, so far, but we have no' spent much time together. She seems kind to the servants and is more patient with the workmen than I. Most of our conversations have been short and about estate business."

"You mean she hasn't fallen into your arms yet?" Mariah shook her head. "Whatever happened to the irresistible man we all know and love?"

Gabe didn't hesitate. "He suddenly turned shy."

The other four laughed.

"That will be the day!" Jeanie's eyes danced with amusement. "Invite her for a moonlight stroll in the garden."

"Or for a drive around the estate." Mariah winked at Kiernan. "In the smallest cart you can find."

"I canna believe my ears," Kiernan said, laughing. "'Tis almost like giving Casanova suggestions on how to woo a lady."

"Quiet, you scoundrel. You'll make the ladies think I'm wicked. Truly, I'm no'."

"We know you are God-loving man, Gabe," Jeanette said gently. Then she grinned. "But you *are* a charmer, laddie, and you canna deny it."

He grinned and shrugged. "I do well enough when I have the opportunity."

"Sometimes you have to create opportunities," Dominic said, with a hint of a knowing smile. "Though I admit being your ladylove's employee complicates matters somewhat. You may have to be patient." He wagged his finger at Jeanie and Mariah. "And you do, too. Stop bamming him."

Jeanie glanced at Mariah. "Perhaps we can do a little matchmaking. Help out his cause."

Gabe held up his hand. "No, thanks. I'll sink or swim on my own."

"Then start paddling faster." Mariah smiled gently at him. "You need a wife so I have someone to spend time with when we visit Inshirra."

"I dinna think I should be too obvious about my interest."

"Be yourself, Gabriel." Dominic looked at Jeanie, his love in his eyes. "Let her see the man you are. Then it won't matter if you are working for her."

Little Donald began to fuss and leaned toward his mother. Jeanie took him, cooing softly. "Come, my wee laddie. Time for your supper and then off to bed." She cradled him comfortably against her with his head resting on her shoulder.

"You're spoiling the bairn," Gabriel said with a teasing smile.

"All wee ones should be so loved." She kissed the baby's forehead. Jeanette had a special love for children. She was always giving those who lived on their estates gifts for their children. Before Donald was born, she often visited the tenants so she could spend time with their little ones.

"If I bow to your wisdom, will you invite me to dinner? I grow weary of eating alone or in the company of Selena's housekeeper and butler."

Jeanie grinned. "I didna think you were so high in the instep."

"I'm no', but they are. To hear them tell it, the other household servants are no better than peasants and constantly grumble. From everything I've seen, they are all competent and seem to like working there. The coachman confided that he lasted less than a week dining in the company of Mrs. Pool and Hardwick. Has his meals sent to his room. Selena's maid does the same."

"Mercy, she has her meals sent to his room?" Mariah feigned horror.

"No, minx." Gabriel laughed, glad he had decided on the impromptu visit. "You know that is no' what I meant. She takes her meals in her own room." Though he had seen the lady's maid and the coachman walking together in the garden late in the evenings.

"Good. I feared you might be led astray," she said, her eyes twinkling.

"I'm too old and wise for such foolishness." A maid could not tempt him. As for the mistress of Fairhaven…well, best not to ponder that temptation too long. He glanced at Kiernan.

As though reading his thoughts, his old friend nodded. "Let's take a walk."

"We keep country hours," Jeanette said. "Dinner is at six, and of course, you will stay."

Gabriel smiled his thanks, standing when she did. The others rose also.

"I'll go inside with the ladies." Dominic rested his hand against Jeanie's back. "I see that my steward has returned from town. There are a few matters I should discuss with him. After dinner, we'll see what I can do to answer your questions."

Gabriel nodded, though he suspected Dominic wanted to give him time for a private talk with Kiernan. Dominic had always been rather intuitive, but he had grown more so after his marriage to Kiernan's sister. Jeanie was one of those rare people who seemed in constant communication with the heavenly Father, and God often gave her knowledge and wisdom unknown to others.

Gabe and Kiernan meandered across the lawn, with no particular destination in mind.

Finally, Gabe broke the silence. "Mariah looks wonderful."

"She is doing fairly well. She assures me the sickness will pass. Tomorrow willna be too soon for me."

Gabriel smiled at him and clamped a hand on his shoulder. "You never were good around someone casting up his accounts."

Kiernan shuddered. "Dinna remind me. How are you?"

"Tapsie-turvie. I grow more attracted to Selena every day, but I fear I am destroying my chances by my deception."

"If you clear her name, she canna be too angry with you."

"I fear she willna believe that is my purpose. It is more likely she will be convinced I am on the government's side."

"You are."

"And that's the coil. I am on both sides—for now at least. You were right when you said I was jumping into the thick of it without thinking. I acted on impulse without considering all the ramifications. If she is indeed a spy, I am honor bound to put an end to it if I can. I suppose I thought I could resolve the situation in a few days."

"Before you became too attached to her. I know Cameron is intent on being thorough, but his parting words to you have deeply troubled me." Kiernan's brow creased in a deep frown.

"And me," Gabriel said bitterly, remembering Cameron's orders. *Befriend Miss Delaroe. Court her if you must. Use whatever means necessary to discover if she is working for Napoleon.* "Having him state my mission in such a cold, unfeeling manner wipes away all my carefully contrived reasoning, all my excuses for doing this on her behalf. Logically, I know she must be stopped if she is a traitor. But even if I am helping my country and possibly saving lives, I find it far harder than I ever imagined to create a trust, then possibly break it."

"And does she trust you?" Kiernan studied him closely.

"No' yet. Other than the drive around the estate that first day, we have no' spent much time together. We see each other every day but only for a few minutes at a time. She does no' seem to be avoiding me, but I certainly didna sweep her off her feet."

Kiernan grinned. "And you've had a whole week. Hard to believe, but it was bound to happen sometime."

"Stop gloating." Gabriel gave his friend a slow smile. "I'm no' ready to give up yet. No' on myself nor on her."

CHAPTER *Four*

SINCE THEY WERE ALONE, Selena and her Aunt Augusta, the countess of Camfield, generally preferred to take their meals in the breakfast room. The oval rosewood pedestal table, which was built to seat eight, lent an intimate air to the sunny, pleasant room. Even if Selena were to have a houseful of company later on, not everyone would come to breakfast at the same time, so a bigger table was not necessary.

"You really should have gone to the assembly with me last night, my dear. The music was fine and the dancing lively. Everyone asked after you, of course. The gentlemen were quite beside themselves because you abandoned them yet again." Augusta cut a bite of cold chicken, adding a leaf of pickled cauliflower to the fork before lifting it to her mouth. At five-and-sixty, the countess was still a striking beauty with silver hair and dark brown eyes.

Selena regarded her aunt with a small smile. "I doubt even one of them spent the evening pining away. Surely there were more than enough females present to fill every set and flirt with the men between songs." She took a bite of cherry tart.

"Of course there were. And I daresay the young ladies were not troubled in the least by your absence. Gave a few of them a chance to shine."

"Which is as it should be. I've been center stage far too many years as it is."

"Are you having a fit of the dismals, pet?" Her aunt frowned and dabbed her lips with a white linen napkin. "It is because we have workmen coming out our ears. All the noise and questions and the smell of paint. You have not left the house for days. It is more than enough to give you the headache. I insist you attend the Copeland dinner with me tonight."

"I have declined the invitation. I cannot simply show up.

They already will have made other arrangements." Selena laid her fork on the plate and met her aunt's piercing gaze. "Aunt Gussie, I am weary of parties and being constantly on display. I am not up to tolerating the attention of some dunderhead just because he is a duke."

Augusta laughed. "We do have a few dunderheaded dukes, as well as madcap marquis." She flicked the lace ruffle on her white mob cap for emphasis.

Selena smiled at her aunt. Though she spoke in jest, there was much truth to the comment. It did little to lift her mood.

A light knock on the open door to the breakfast room drew Selena's attention. Gabriel stood there, regarding them with a charming smile. "Good afternoon. May I intrude?"

Selena's pulse quickened at the sound of his voice. When she met his twinkling gaze, she knew he had overheard her aunt's comment. The warmth in his smile and green eyes made her feel as though they shared a private joke. He stepped into the sunlight, threads of gold and dark copper shining in his hair, matching the colors of his quilted silk waistcoat. In his biscuit-colored trousers and chocolate brown coat, he seemed taller, his shoulders wider, his presence even more commanding than usual. She thought he must surely notice how he took her breath away.

"And an enticing estate manager," Aunt Gussie mumbled.

Selena lightly nudged the older woman's leg with the toe of her slipper. "Good afternoon, Mr. Macpherson. Please join us. Would you care for something to eat?"

"No, thank you. I've already had luncheon. The tarts are delicious." He pulled out a chair across from her and sat down. "I was hoping I might take you for a drive, Miss Delaroe. We've begun some of the projects, so you can review our progress. And I would like your opinion on a couple of other ideas." He captured her gaze, causing her heart to skip a beat. "It would do you good to get away from the paint fumes. You have no' gone out all week."

"Noticed that, did you?" Augusta grinned at him, then wagged her finger at Selena. "You see, I'm not the only one who thinks you are becoming a hermit."

"Such a fair lady could never become a hermit. But you have seemed a bit pale the last few days. The fresh air should put the roses back in your cheeks."

The countess shot Gabriel a sly smile. "So would a light flirtation."

"Aunt Gussie!"

Gabriel glanced at Augusta, then turned his attention back to Selena. A smile played about his lips even as a spark flashed through his eyes. To her grateful surprise, he ignored her aunt's outrageous remark. "Shall I have the gig brought around, then?"

Selena nodded. "I'll need a few minutes to fetch a bonnet and change my shoes."

"I am in no rush. I'll see to the gig and meet you out front." Gabriel stood and bowed slightly. "Or should we take the landau so you might join us, Lady Camfield?"

Augusta raised an eyebrow as though suddenly questioning the man's intellect. "I do not have the energy to be interested in Selena's projects. I intend to escape to the garden and curl up with the latest issue of *Lady's Monthly Museum*. There I can read and doze in peace. The best thing you could do for Selena, young man, is to keep her away from here the rest of the day. It will take that long to clear the fog from her brain. Finish up your business and escort her to Worcester for the afternoon."

Gabriel moved behind Selena's chair, scooting it back as she stood. "If that is what the lady wishes," he said quietly, stepping aside.

"It is not." Selena looked at her aunt instead of him. "I have no interest in going to town today. I am not in the mood for crowds and hustle and bustle." A board clattered to the floor in the drawing room, followed by muffled grumbling from one of the carpenters. "Peace and quiet will suit me nicely. Enjoy your reading."

A plague on Aunt Gussie's meddling! Selena swept from the room, pausing a good distance down the hallway to wait for Gabriel. A few minutes later, he stepped from the breakfast room. Surprise flickered across his face when he saw her. He walked quietly down the hall, stopping in front of her, his expression guarded.

She wondered yet again at the effect he had on her. Her mood had brightened the minute he stepped into the room. She reacted the same way now, though moments before she had been so annoyed she was almost shaking. "I wanted to apologize for Aunt Augusta. She has no qualms about speaking her mind. I love her, but she can be somewhat trying."

Gabriel glanced toward the breakfast room with a chuckle. "Reminds me of my grandmother, though the countess is younger. I like her."

"I'm glad. She truly is a dear in her own way."

"When I saw you waiting, I feared you had changed your mind about our drive."

"No. I would be pleased to have your company for as much of the day as you can spare. But other than a brief visit to the village, I do not want to leave Fairhaven."

A slow smile spread across his face. "I canna see any reason no' to take as long as you wish." His gaze skimmed over her lilac floral print cotton frock, and he lowered his voice. "You look very nice today. That color becomes you."

"Even though I'm pale?" She sniffed in feigned affront.

He leaned a little closer. "But you no longer are, dear lady. A delightful pink shades your cheeks. Perhaps your aunt is right." With a wink and an impish smile, Gabriel turned and sauntered toward the back of the house.

Certain the pink had bloomed to full red, Selena barely held back a giggle. Shaking her head at her own foolishness, she started toward her bedchamber. Still, she was glad she had chosen that particular dress for the day. The round neckline was low enough to be comfortably cool while remaining quite modest. The lightweight, full sleeves, gathered at a band at the wrist, would protect her arms from the sun. The lilac color intensified the violet in her eyes.

And most of all, Gabe liked it.

She exchanged her shoes for black kid walking boots and added a straw poke bonnet. The yellow of her kid gloves, parasol, and the ribbon on the bonnet all matched the tiny flowers in the print of her dress.

With a sense of anticipation, she waited on the front portico until Gabe brought the gig around the house a few minutes later.

His eyes sparkled when he saw her, but his attitude changed subtly in front of the servants. There was no hint of teasing or of anything that might be construed as forward or too familiar. She wondered if this was his way of reminding her—and perhaps himself—that he worked for her. He assisted her into the carriage, removing his hand from her arm the second she was situated, then took his place beside her, sitting as far as possible to the left.

There's enough room between us for Aunt Gussie, for heaven's sake!

Selena turned her head away from the disgruntled thought—and the man at her side.

He handled the horse with ease, sometimes driving with one hand and pointing to an area on the property with the other. When they came alongside an overgrown hop field, he slowed the gig.

"I dinna think it would be worth the expense to try to grow hops here again. I'd wager it has no' been tended for over seven or eight years. The poles were no' taken up, which should be done at the end of each season. Nor was the bind cleared away."

"The bind? What is that?"

He glanced at her. "The shoots, or stems. When they grow up they are attached to the poles. They dry up at the end of the growing season. Normally, after the hops are picked and the poles removed, the bind is gathered. Sometimes the landowner gives it to the laborers to burn in their own homes. Or the owner has it gathered and stored in sheds to burn in his house or other houses on the estate."

Selena studied the area beside them. "The grass has taken over."

Gabriel nodded. "Few of the hop plants even send up shoots anymore. According to Thorne, raising hops is expensive and uncertain. I think the land could be better utilized for grazing. We would need to clear out everything but the grass before we turn cattle into the field."

"If the binds are still usable for fuel, let those who clear the fields have them. I can easily afford to heat my home comfortably. Others are not so fortunate."

"They will appreciate it." Approval and perhaps admiration warmed his eyes.

She liked that look—and the feeling it gave her.

"Do you still believe I should purchase some black Highland cattle?"

He pursed his lips, thinking. "With the addition of this field, the land could easily support another fifty head."

"Then do it."

"I'll contact the laird right away. By the time the cattle arrive, it should be ready for them."

They drove past a pear orchard where workmen were clearing out the last of the weeds and grass that had covered the ground. "The trees were covered with blossoms in May." Selena clasped her hands, remembering the beauty that had been all around. "At the time, I told the manager to have the undergrowth cleaned up, but he did not bother to follow my directions on that or anything else. He was of the opinion that women have inferior intellect."

"He is an idiot. Given the same opportunities for learning, I've found women often outshine us." Gabriel smiled lazily. "Since men desperately need to feel superior, we often try to make up for it by brute strength."

Selena laughed. "There are times brute strength is a bonus. I cannot imagine trying to dig the new well myself."

"Nor should you have to. May you never be forced to do hard labor."

His voice held an oddly somber note. Selena searched his face, but his expression revealed nothing of what he was thinking. Still, it was vaguely unsettling. She knew prisoners, even women, were sometimes forced to do hard labor, especially if they were transported to New South Wales. It was not something she liked to think about—though she did, since it might be her fate.

Gabriel glanced around. "All those blossoms must have turned into fruit. The trees in all the orchards are covered. You should have a good crop of pears and apples for eating, and abundant fruit for perry and cider."

Selena followed his gaze. "Do you think I'm wrong not to lease the farm to someone else?" Some landlords might lease the Fairhaven lands to a tenant or two, letting them run the farm as they saw fit. But she wanted to be in control—perhaps because it was the one area of her life where she was free to make decisions, good or bad. Still, she was anxious to hear what he thought. His opinion mattered a great deal to her, though she was at a loss to say exactly why.

He considered the question carefully. "No. If it were larger, that might be a wiser thing to do. With the expanding market, rising prices because of the war, and cheap labor, tenants are willing to pay a high rent. They will still make a good profit. But tenants often have their own ideas on what they want to do and how they want to do it. You have a good plan for Fairhaven. As long as you have a competent manager to carry it out, there is no reason to change."

Her heart sang at his words of affirmation. "I'm glad you agree with me. I trust you to tell me if you don't." At various times, they'd briefly discussed improvements she wanted made, such as repairing the cottages on the estate. But they had not had time for any lengthy conversations. "I believe we were interrupted a few days ago when we were talking about the cottages. Did I say why I wanted them repaired?"

He shook his head. "I assumed you want homes for the farmworkers." He glanced at her. "You do intend to hire more permanent laborers, do you no'?"

"Yes. That is another reason I do not want a tenant. After I decided to make Fairhaven my home, I visited several other farms and estates to see how they were run. On some, particularly those leased by tenants who were farming large pieces of land, I discovered that they have done away with housing for the farm laborers. It seems to be a growing trend to hire men to do the work but not to provide any place for them to live. The men work at the whim of the farmers or landlords. Too often, their wages are not sufficient to provide a decent living for them and their families."

"True enough. 'Tis a sad thing."

She smiled at him, grateful for his understanding. "Indeed. I discovered just how sad when I followed a laborer home from a nearby farm. He and his family live in a single room in Worcester. At one time they had lived in a small cottage near a village. They'd kept a cow on the manorial common and had a strip of land in the parish field for a garden. Then Parliament passed enclosure acts regarding that land. First they lost their part of the field, then a few years later, the common pasture. Now they have to purchase everything to feed the family. With today's high prices, the money simply does not go far enough. It is terribly unfair for the laborer to see the abundance of his creations all around him and be unable to partake of it."

"You canna change the world, lass." The gentle words swept over her, warming her.

She nodded. "I know, but I can help a few families. At least they will have warm, dry houses, a place for a garden, and some pasture for a cow or two. They can grow vegetables and raise chickens and have eggs, milk, and butter and still earn a decent wage."

Gabriel looked at her, his expression thoughtful. "This is an increasing problem as men seek to make a profit and greatly improve their own lot without thought for those who do the work. It is also a problem few see, or if they do realize it exists, they do nothing about it. You impress me, madam."

"That was not my goal." She smiled at him, though his praise was vastly pleasing. "There are still many landlords and farmers who kindly provide for their workers and others in the vicinity. They are the ones I seek to imitate. Dominic Thorne is my best example."

Gabriel nodded. "He is a good man, and his wife is the most generous of souls."

Selena glanced at him. She could read nothing unusual in his expression, yet there had been tenderness in his voice when he spoke of Jeanette Thorne. Did he harbor a secret affection for Dominic's pretty young wife?

She bit her lip, dismayed at just how unpleasant that thought was. *Gabriel Macpherson is your manager, nothing more! It shouldn't matter one whit to you what he feels for another woman.* A valid reminder. Pity it did nothing to lift her suddenly drooping spirits.

When they arrived at the first cottage, workmen were busy on the roof. "This one only needed a small section repaired. We'll replace the two broken windows and clean it up thoroughly. It should be ready for a new occupant in about a week. The other houses will take longer."

"Do we necessarily need this one for a laborer?"

"No. Whom do you have in mind?"

"A young woman in the village, Becky Goodhew. She lost her husband a few months ago in the fighting. He had only been in the army a short time. They were renting a cottage in the village, but she can no longer afford it. I knew she had planned to stay with a sister in Manchester, but Mrs. Pool informed me this morning that Becky intends to take a job at the wool mill. Staying with her sister because she needs comfort is one thing. Staying with her so she can do hard, dismal work is another. She has a young son, so it is not practical to hire her as a maid. A free place to live would be more beneficial."

"I agree. Though she will still need to earn money in some way."

"I'm sure we can come up with something. For now, she needs rest and comfort."

There were seven cottages on the estate. Five of them were empty, partly because they were not currently habitable and partly because there had been no work for additional people. "We should not have difficulty finding new farmworkers."

"Once the houses are put in order, I expect we can have our choice. I told the villagers to spread the word that Fairhaven is undergoing a transformation. Those who already work for you needed no such prompting." He looked down at her and smiled. "They are so excited about the changes, we can have our own hiring fair in the meadow."

He pulled the gig close enough to speak with the workmen for a few minutes, making certain all was going well, then drove on. "We will have to hire additional outside labor during the fruit harvest. Even with a good crop, you willna see a profit the first year. The cider mill should work fine once the millstone is dressed, but the press must be replaced. The largest expense will be a new cellar house to store the perry and cider."

Selena nodded. "The Bareland pear trees are over fifty years old. I'm told that variety makes some of the finest perry available. We also have two kinds of pears for eating, both excellent. The great blanquet pear ripens in August."

"Otherwise known as the bagpipe of Anjou," he said with a grin.

"Do you know why it is called that?"

"No. It does no' look anything like a bagpipe to me. The little lard pear ripens in December, does it no'?"

"Yes. We had some last year at Christmastime. They are quite fine, with very sweet juice. You can send some to your friends in the Highlands."

"Perhaps."

At the sadness in his voice, she laid her hand lightly on his arm. "Forgive me if my comment caused you discomfort."

"You did no'. I was merely thinking that the weather at that time of year is often too harsh for travel. It will be difficult to send any gifts home."

His explanation didn't quite wash, but she saw no benefit in pointing it out.

"I noticed a row of mulberry trees along the edge of the apple orchard," Gabriel said. "In Devonshire, they mix mulberries with apples when making cider. Gives it a wonderful taste. I'm thinking of trying mulberries with a batch of the perry."

"It might overwhelm the flavor of the pears."

"True. And we would have to change the name."

When she looked up at him, she noticed that his eyes twinkled mischievously. "To what?"

"Replace the *p* with an *m*. Then, though we were working, we'd be making merry."

Selena laughed, briefly lifting her face to the sunshine. Aunt Augusta had been right this time, both about getting away from the house and about her charming companion. The gig hit a bump, jostling them on the seat until their shoulders touched. Selena did not move away from the contact. Neither did he.

He glanced at her. "As I predicted, the drive has already put the roses back in your cheeks."

"I enjoy your company, Mr. Macpherson."

His smile warmed her heart. "And I yours, Miss Delaroe."

They drove around the estate, sometimes in comfortable silence, sometimes discussing ongoing or potential projects. They stopped for a few minutes to watch the progress on the new well at Mr. O'Conner's house. The middle-aged man and his large family had worked at Fairhaven for ten years. He raised wheat and tended the cattle. Then they went by another cottage for a short visit with young Mrs. Altby and her new babe.

When they left the Altby home, Gabriel turned at the crossroads, heading toward the village. Selena directed him to the small house on the edge of town. The grounds were well tended, with a nice flower garden as well as a thriving vegetable garden.

Becky Goodhew sat on the front stoop, shelling peas into a bowl. Upon their arrival, she set the bowl aside and came out to the road to meet them. "Good afternoon, Miss Delaroe." She looked weary and pale and did not even attempt a smile.

"Good afternoon, Becky. How are you?"

"Somehow, I get through each day. It helps to tend the garden, do common things. And Robby keeps me busy, though I welcome the rest when he takes a nap, like now."

"How is he?"

"He misses his father. He's only three and don't understand that Dave won't come home." The woman blinked against the moisture in her eyes and glanced away. "I have to leave the cottage in a few weeks. Mr. Bell let me stay here this month even though I couldn't pay him the rent. It wouldn't be right to ask him for another month."

She glanced around sorrowfully. "I have a sister in Manchester. She says I can stay with her a while until I earn enough at the mill to find a place of my own."

"You do not have to do that." Selena spoke gently. "Becky, this is Mr. Macpherson, my new estate manager."

The young woman bobbed a shallow curtsy. "Good afternoon, sir."

"I'm pleased to meet you, Mrs. Goodhew." Gabriel smiled kindly.

"Mr. Macpherson is overseeing some repairs at Fairhaven. He informs me that one of the cottages should be ready for a new occupant within a week or so. We would be pleased if you would live there as long as you wish. You would not be charged rent." Becky's eyes widened. "That would allow you to stay here among your friends and raise your child in a way that would please your husband. You would not be able to have a garden this year, of course, but you may share the produce from the kitchen garden at the manor house."

"Miss Delaroe, I don't know what to say."

"'Yes' would do for a start," Gabriel said with a smile. "Unless you truly wish to live with your sister and work at a loom all day."

"Oh, *no,* sir. I mean, I would much rather stay here." She paused, half a dozen expressions darting across her face. "'Tis a truly generous offer, miss, but I still need a way to provide other things for myself and my babe. I might find work at the porcelain factory in Worcester." She frowned. "But I'd have to leave Robby with someone, and it's too far to walk every day."

Selena did not want to offend Becky by offering too much. She was well aware the woman would refuse anything that seemed like charity. "Or you could work for me. As I recall, you are a fair hand at sewing."

A faint smile touched the other woman's face. "I do well enough with simple things, but I'm no great seamstress."

"The maids at Fairhaven would beg to differ. So do I. The dresses you made for them were as nicely stitched as anything the seamstress in Worcester did. I could not keep you busy sewing only for Fairhaven, though in a large house there often seem to be linens in need of repair. However, the vicar's wife always knows of others in need and has use for clothing of all sizes and types. I have no knack for stitchery myself, but do have the means to purchase the cloth and pay you to sew.

Together, we might help others less fortunate. I would pay you by the piece, so you could set your own schedule."

Tears welled up in Becky's eyes. "Miss Delaroe, I can never thank you enough for your kindness. It would mean the world to me to raise my son in the place Dave loved so much. He had such dreams for a good life here."

"As long as Fairhaven belongs to me, you shall always have a home here, Becky." A chill brushed across Selena's heart. What would happen when Fairhaven was taken from her? "Should the estate ever pass into another's hands, I promise you will receive an adequate provision."

A child's sleepy cry sounded from inside the small house, and Selena smiled at the sound. "We won't keep you so you can go see to Robby. I'll send word when the cottage is finished."

"And a wagon and some men to help you move when you are ready," Gabriel added.

Selena glanced up at him gratefully. He seemed to know exactly what to say to help most. When the little boy's cry turned into a wail, she looked back at his mother. "You had better go."

"Thank you ever so much, miss!" Becky's voice was choked with emotion.

Tears stung Selena's eyes as well. "Nothing can replace what you have lost. But perhaps we can help ease your hurt."

Becky gave them both a watery smile before running into the house.

Gabriel guided the horse and carriage around in a half circle. Within a few minutes, they were on their way.

"You are a kind and generous woman."

At the quiet comment, Selena shook her head. "It is a small way to make amends."

He frowned slightly. "What do you mean?" He glanced at her, his penetrating gaze unnerving her.

Trust him not to let the slip pass. *Fool! Your carelessness could cost Nick his life! You must guard your tongue—and your heart!*

Selena shrugged, trying to act nonchalant. She doubted she fooled him. "For being rich. It has never seemed fair that I should have so much and others so little."

She looked away, hoping he would say nothing more. Thankfully he kept silent, though she felt his glance often as they traveled back to Fairhaven. Her thoughts dwelled on other widows, those who had lost their husbands in a horrible war. Old, young, English, Scots—faceless men who haunted her dreams. Her chest ached. Her throat and eyes burned with unshed tears. If not for the man beside her, she would have wept in grief and shame.

How could she ever make amends to them?

CHAPTER *Five*

GABRIEL GUIDED THE HORSE OFF THE ROAD and drew the gig to a halt near the small stream that meandered through Fairhaven. Beyond a cluster of trees, he caught a glimpse of a grassy stretch lying along the bank. "Would you care to sit in the shade for a while?"

Selena followed his gaze. "That would be nice. I haven't been down to the stream right here. The ground slopes steeply on the other side of the trees before it flattens out by the bank. The drop is too far to try on my own."

Gabriel grinned as he climbed from the gig. "That is why I'm here." He hobbled the horse, who promptly began nibbling on the grass at his feet. She laid her parasol on the seat, leaving it there when Gabriel lifted her down in his most polite manner. As they strolled toward the stream, he felt a twinge of misgiving. If anyone saw them, it could cause gossip. "Are you certain you would no' prefer to go back to the manor?"

"Quite certain. We might as well be having a house party for all the people underfoot." She was silent for a minute before adding softly, "It is much more pleasant here with you."

Gabriel caught his breath, sending her a quick glance. A hint of pink shaded her cheeks as she avoided his gaze, concentrating too intensely on the ground in front of them. He looked at the spot he had chosen, a place almost hidden from the road. Was she accustomed to being alone with men in secluded settings? Army officers, perhaps?

Or was it simply that at four-and-twenty, she did not feel the need to adhere strictly to the constraints of Society? Constraints that dictated a single woman, especially a young one, rarely go anywhere without a chaperone. The rules allowed a couple to drive about in an open carriage, but to stop along the way was greatly frowned upon.

Her aunt, however, had encouraged him to spend the day with her. Perhaps neither the countess nor Selena considered him to be of any consequence, therefore no danger to her reputation or her person. He was, after all, merely the estate manager. The thought irritated him.

They came to the edge of the embankment. "Wait here." He jumped down the slope in two long strides, then stepped in front of her and silently held out his hands. Selena paused, searching his face with a tiny frown before she leaned forward and rested her hands on his shoulders.

Holding her gaze, Gabriel put his hands around her waist and lifted her down the slope, setting her within inches of him as her feet touched the ground. Surprise flickered across her face, but she did not move her hands from his shoulders or step away. He slid his arms around her, gently pulling her closer. Her rose perfume had teased him all afternoon. He breathed deeply, inhaling her intoxicating, sweet fragrance.

Her gaze dropped to his mouth, her lips parting slightly as she drew a trembling breath. She wanted him to kiss her—perhaps almost as much as he wanted to. His pride soothed, common sense told him to release her. But he didn't. He needed to see the invitation in her eyes, to watch her eyelids close as he lowered his head to taste her sweetness. "Selena, look at me," he whispered.

She complied, longing and uncertainty clouding her eyes. Her confusion brought him to a halt, and he slowly released her. "Forgive me, Miss Delaroe." *Idiot!* He shook his head. "I overstepped—"

She touched her fingers to his lips to silence him, then lowered her hand to her side. "No, you did not. You have done nothing I did not encourage. I will not deny that I am attracted to you, for you would know it to be a lie. You are handsome and charming, but it is the inner man who draws me even more. You are a good, kind man, and being with you makes me happy."

Her words warmed his heart yet chilled his soul. When she learned the truth, she would not think him good and kind. He feared she would hate him. "It is no' wise to become too cozy with the hired help."

She shrugged and turned toward the stream. "I do not think of you as an employee."

He followed her. "But I am. At least I hope you intend to pay my wages."

She laughed softly. "Of course I do. But you share my dreams for Fairhaven. I consider you a partner and a friend."

Gabriel removed his coat and spread it on the grass beneath the shade of an oak tree. With one hand bracing her back and the other at her elbow, he eased her down to sit. "I am honored."

She smiled faintly, curling her legs beside her and tucking her feet beneath the hem of her skirt. "Don't esteem me too highly. I have my flaws."

Gabriel let his gaze skim over her. Sitting a few feet away, facing her, he laughed softly. "None that are obvious."

"Ah, but there are a few. I conceal them well." At his expression of disbelief, she laughed. "For one thing, my hair is as straight as a board, much to the frustration of my abigail. When short hair became the fashion, I'm not sure which one of us was happier. Long or short, a mass of curls is totally impossible." She untied the bow on her straw bonnet and removed it, setting it on the grass. Her shiny black hair, cut in a sleek style, framed her face perfectly.

Gabriel had not realized how the intricate cut gave the appearance of wispy curls around her face when there actually were none. Perhaps it was because his attention was usually drawn to her incredible eyes. In making them the exact color of sweet violets, his favorite flower, God had given him a special gift. "You canna possibly count such beautiful hair as a flaw."

"Thank you for the compliment, though I was not casting about for one." She stuck one booted foot out from beneath her skirt. "But even you cannot say that I have tiny feet."

He looked at her foot and grinned. It was by no means small, but neither was it particularly large. "No, I canna say that. But I count that as an advantage."

"How so?"

"More room to tickle."

Selena laughed, even as a soft blush stole across her cheeks. "I'm not ticklish, though I'd wager you would give it a try."

"Perhaps." He shrugged lightly, doubting he would ever have such an opportunity. More was the pity. They sat in silence for a few minutes, enjoying the comfortable breeze. At the trilling song of a bird overhead, they both looked up, searching the tree for the wood warbler, a pretty bird with a lemon yellow breast and green back.

"There he is," Selena said softly, pointing high in the tree. The little bird sang with its head thrown back, looking up at the sky. "I always wonder if they are singing praises to God."

Gabriel smiled at the thought. "If they are, he hears them." He indicated another small bird with a gray back, black throat, and rusty breast and tail. "There is a redstart, too. We have both of them at home."

"Home?"

Uh-oh. "The Highlands." He spoke rather curtly and looked away, hoping she would take the hint that he did not want to discuss it. When she asked nothing further, he breathed a quiet sigh of relief.

His mind returned to their conversation when they first sat down. He knew she was not thinking of outward imperfections, but inward ones. He hesitated, uncertain as to whether or not he wanted to venture into such potentially treacherous territory. If he hoped for her to reveal anything telling about her character, he had to be prepared to do the same. He suddenly realized she was staring at him. "Do I have dirt on my face?"

She smiled and shook her head. "No. I was trying to decide if you have any visible flaws."

He raised an eyebrow. "And what did you conclude?"

"I don't believe you do. Your nose is a little crooked, but that enhances your features instead of detracting from them."

Either she meant it, or she should be on the stage. He decided to accept the admiration in her expression as genuine— and bask in it for a few minutes. "You are kind." He broke off a blade of grass and twirled it between his fingertips. "My legs tend to be skinny unless I take frequent walks."

"No one would ever notice."

"They do when I wear a kilt." When she frowned thought-fully, he wondered if he had let something slip. Had she noticed him last year after all?

"Do you often wear a kilt?"

"Always when I'm in Scotland. But no' in England." *At least not now.*

"Why not?"

"I'd feel too conspicuous." Only because he was trying to hide his identity. "People make such a fuss about it." Remembering some of the parties he and Kiernan had attended the previous year evoked a smile. "The men jest, and the women stare."

"I would expect so. Still, I would like to see you in your Highland clothes."

"Perhaps someday I will be brave enough to wear them."

"You do not strike me as a man afraid to do what he wishes."

"Sometimes it is more prudent to compromise. It is easier to wear trousers than to be the center of attention. I suppose we all have something we truly fear." He watched an iridescent blue-green kingfisher speed along the stream bank, then dive into the water. "I love the outdoors and could no' bear to be shut up in a small space." He met her eyes, holding her gaze intently. Might as well stir up the waters a bit. "To me, being in prison, especially locked away in a dungeon, would be more horrible than anything I can imagine."

Selena caught her breath. Could this man see into her mind? Only the gallows would be worse than what he'd just described. She feared both fates awaited her. She picked up her bonnet. "Do you mind if we take a walk? The path runs beside the stream all the way through Fairhaven."

"I would enjoy it." He pushed himself to his feet, then held out his hand to help her stand. Retrieving his coat, he shook the grass from it while she put on her bonnet. He slipped on the coat and glanced at the path. It was just wide enough for two. "It would appear many couples have passed this way."

"Likely more cows than people." When he held out his arm, Selena curled her hand around it. "But I'm grateful to whomever, or whatever, forged the way."

As they walked along at a comfortable pace, Selena thought of Nicholas. Her brother had been merry and quick to tease, but he had also been her protector, her source of strength in time of trouble or sorrow. Though they were the same age, he had been her mentor, as well as her confidant and friend. Perhaps one reason she wanted Gabriel's friendship was because he reminded her of Nick. They were close to the same height and had much the same build, but the resemblance had more to do with their personalities than physical features. She looked up at the large oak trees shading the stream. "Nicholas will like it here."

"Tell me about him," Gabriel said gently.

"You remind me of him. He liked to tease and was easy to talk to. We were very close, probably because I was a veritable hoyden."

"Impossible. You are much too grand a lady to have ever been a tomboy."

She glanced up to see his smile. "Oh, but I was. I could climb trees and skip rocks as well as he did. I couldn't run quite as fast as he could, though, which almost caused a disaster when we decided to take a shortcut home one day. It did not occur to us that the bull would object to our presence in his domain."

"He chased you?"

"And came perilously close to trampling me. If Nick had not come to my rescue by dashing between me and the bull to distract him, I would not be here to tell the tale." She laughed, shaking her head. "He led the bull in a circle while I scrambled over the low stone wall separating the pasture from the road. A few minutes later Nick came leaping over it behind me. Thankfully, the bull was content to drive us away and did not attempt to crash through after us. I can laugh about it now, but at the time we were both shaking so badly we had to sit for half an hour to calm down."

"Nicholas sounds like a brave lad."

"He is." *More courageous than anyone will ever know.* Sudden images filled her mind: a dark, cold dungeon...wet stone walls glistening in the light of the gaoler's lantern...Nicholas lying in the filth, more dead than alive.

When she shuddered, Gabriel put his arm around her shoulders. "What is wrong?"

"I am so afraid that—that he will never come home."

Gabriel tightened his arm, as if willing her to have courage. "The war canna go on forever."

"It already has."

He stopped, gently halting her also, and turned her toward him, wrapping his arms around her. "You must have faith, lass. Wellington will defeat Napoleon. Perhaps not this month, or even this year, but we will win this cursed war."

Selena rested her forehead against his shoulder, drawing strength from his comfort. The past ten months had taken their toll, and she had the sudden urge to pour out her heart. She had only known him a short time, but some things were obvious. Gabriel Macpherson was strong and sure, with a confidence few men possessed. Intuition told her he had been tempered by hardship, his courage tested and found equal to the challenge.

After a few minutes he slowly released her, but he kept his hand lightly against her back. "Do you want to go to the house?"

"No. The exercise will make me feel better." It probably would, but in truth, it was merely an excuse. She wanted to spend more time with Gabriel, *needed* to be with him.

In his embrace, she found refuge for her tortured, weary soul.

CHAPTER Six

GABRIEL AGAIN OFFERED SELENA HIS ARM, and they continued their stroll beside the bubbling stream. Three cows lying in the shade blinked lazily as they passed. "Are you able to correspond with your brother?"

"I write to him often, and so do my parents."

"I understand the French secret police open all the mail going in and out of France, whether written by foreigners or the French themselves." Gabriel guided her around a hole in the path.

Selena nodded. "I believe the practice is widespread throughout the French empire."

While in France the last time, she had been warned not to try to send Nick any kind of coded message. Napoleon used a special intelligence section to scrutinize everything. The black chamber was made up of code breakers, technicians, linguists, and men knowledgeable about foreign habits.

"We have received two letters from him, smuggled out by visitors. Still, we are more fortunate than many détenus' families. I have been able to visit him twice." Selena glanced up, frowning when he nodded slightly, as though what she said came as no surprise to him. Her trips had not been made in secret, but how would he know of them?

"I have heard that women are sometimes allowed to visit." He looked down at her, his eyes twinkling. "Usually it is a wife, but I've also heard tales of mistresses who made the journey."

"And a few who remained there. Strange that they seemed to gain permission from both countries more easily that I did. It took five years of writing, begging, and bribing before we were allowed to go the first time."

"Did your mother go, too?"

"No. It would have been too difficult for her."

"Is she in poor health?"

"No, she's fit as a fiddle." Thinking of her mother brought a smile. "She is a sweet, lovely person but rather hen-hearted. She is thoroughly lost without my father to direct her. She dearly wanted to see Nicholas but did not have the courage to give it a try, or to trust me to see to her well being." It had not helped that her father forbade her mother to travel with her.

"So you went alone?" His brow creased in a dark frown.

"My maid, Marietta, accompanied me, of course. Since she is half-French, she was a great help. Though I suppose I could have managed with a good sensible English abigail. When I was sixteen, I made the journey home from France with only a maid to accompany me. She was even more frightened than I was. I hired Marietta shortly afterward."

He stopped abruptly, staring at her. "Sixteen? You were with your brother in France when he was arrested?"

She nodded, tugged gently on his arm, and continued walking. It would be easier to talk about it if she could avoid his intense gaze. "We were traveling with an older cousin, Owen, and his wife, Celia." She shook her head sadly. "Father was against it from the beginning. I thought he was being stuffy and overly cautious. Owen was an experienced traveler. He had already been to America, India, and China. He had been deprived of his Grand Tour and thought, since the war had ended a few years earlier, it would be safe. And he felt sharing it with Celia and us would make up for it. We were beside ourselves with excitement and pestered Papa until he finally relented." She sighed softly. "How I wish he had stood firm in his resolve and kept us home."

Traditionally, upper-class young men had not been considered finished until they took their Grand Tour, visiting Paris, Vienna, Florence, and Rome. The English aristocracy had long considered a taste of French culture a requirement for good breeding. Occasionally, wealthy noblemen who wanted their daughters to have additional refinement arranged for them to take a well-chaperoned visit to Paris.

The French Revolution of 1789, followed by the murder of Louis XVI and war between France and England, put a stop to those visits to Paris and many other Continental cities. Thus when the war ended in 1801, the British aristocracy raced to see what they had missed.

"So Nicholas was under the age limit set by Napoleon."

"Yes. He was not alone in that respect. Many young men under eighteen were held because they looked older. Men over sixty were detained, too, simply because they could not prove their age. When I visited Nicholas, I saw young boys no more than eight or ten years old who had been captured on British ships."

Gabriel shook his head, his mouth twisting in disgust. "I suppose Napoleon thinks they will one day grow old enough to fight. How long were you in France before the war resumed?"

"Almost two months. We stayed in Paris for a month, then went on to Orléans." She pressed her lips together at the memory. If only they'd remained in Paris. Perhaps then they would have realized what was afoot when the British ambassador packed up and left. "We had scarcely heard about the war before the authorities descended upon the inn."

She would never forget the confusion and the noise…the ominous sound of fists pounding on doors, thundering throughout the building…echoes of the same at other hotels down the street…the angry shouts of the French soldiers…the bewildered cries of the Britons. "The French delivered the notices to everyone at the same time. I learned later that it was the same all over the country. They didn't want to give anyone a chance to escape."

"It must have been terrible."

Quick tears sprang to Selena's eyes at the compassion in Gabriel's voice. She swallowed hard. "It was. We tried to tell the prefect that Nick was only sixteen." The scenes raced through her mind as they had a thousand times before. The hatred in the prefect's eyes...the leering soldiers guarding the door...Nick's stunned, pale face...her trembling hands as she beseeched the official. "The prefect would not listen. He demanded proof of age, but of course, we did not have any. Who carries such a thing with them?"

"No one that I know of. Most people dinna even have proof of when they were born, unless it is noted in a church record somewhere, and you canna take that with you." He covered her hand with his as it rested on his arm, a tender gesture made sweeter because it seemed unconscious. "Did he sign a parole?"

"Yes, so he would only be detained and not thrown directly into prison. Those were the only choices, both horrid. But the concept of parole makes no sense to me." She shook her head with a bewildered frown. "By signing the document, Nick acknowledged that he was a prisoner of war and gave his word of honor not to try to escape."

"It is a long-standing military tradition, one that supposedly allows officers better treatment as long as they keep their word. It does no' always work that way."

"But Nicholas wasn't in the military, and civilians have never been prisoners of war!" She smashed a dirt clod with her foot. "Detaining every one of those men was illegal, and doubly so in Nick's case because he was just a boy. He should not be expected to keep his word under those circumstances. There was *nothing* honorable in Napoleon's actions."

Gabriel looked down at her, holding her gaze. "You will find that most Britons agree with you." Again, the kindness in his expression was nearly her undoing. "I'm truly sorry, lass. Did you come back to England right away?"

"No. We women weren't officially detained, but permission to leave was not granted immediately, either. I didn't mind. We expected the French and English governments to reach some sort of agreement to release the men in a short time. Then we could all go home together. None of us dreamed it would last this long."

"I doubt anyone did. No' even Napoleon."

"When we heard the negotiations had broken off, we decided my maid and I should try to leave. We had written to my parents, telling them what happened. Since we heard nothing in return, we feared they had never received our letters. Even if they had, they would have been beside themselves with worry."

"I can well imagine my father's uproar if he'd been in that situation. Men would quake from the Highlands to London."

Selena nodded. "Father protested greatly, as did many others, but to no avail."

"They never received your letters?"

"No. According to rumor, which proved true, only requests for money or actual transfers of funds were allowed to reach their destinations. Napoleon is all too happy for Englishmen to spend their gold."

"Some speculate it is one of his main motives for keeping the détenus."

She nodded. "I would not be surprised. They have to buy everything they need, including food and lodging. Thankfully, we have plenty of money and have been able to keep Nick living in comfort." *Most of the time.* She quickly buried the thought. "Nick came into a substantial inheritance when he reached his majority. The first time I went to see him, he sent authorization for Father to begin drawing from those funds. He has been able to help others who have run out of money. Some had gone to France only intending to stay for a short holiday. Without being home to see to their business affairs, they have lost their means of livelihood. A few had little to begin with."

"You said you and your maid journeyed home alone. Why didna your cousin's wife go with you, at least to see you safely aboard a ship to England?"

"Celia refused to leave Owen. She feared that if they were

separated, she would not be allowed to rejoin him. Owen hired a coach to take us, and at the innkeeper's suggestion, he hired a guard also. The guard abandoned us the following day."

Gabriel stopped and turned to face her, slipping his arm from beneath hers, and caught her hand. "So every time you stopped, you had to deal with the innkeepers, make all the arrangements?"

Well imagining his thoughts, Selena looked away from his penetrating gaze. "Yes. My maid was useless, though I cannot blame the poor girl. She was only a few years older than I and did not speak a word of French. Thankfully, the language had been my governess's favorite subject, so I was rather proficient." She shrugged lightly. "As you might expect, the innkeepers usually turned up their noses, assuming I was not a lady at all." She grinned at him. "But I can be persistent and quickly learned how to use smiles or tears to my advantage."

"Formidable weapons." He laughed, waking up a nearby cow. The bovine bawled, protesting the intrusion on her nap, then lazily looked away. Gabe grinned at her. "How could they resist you?"

"After the initial rebuff, they usually did not." She winked and pulled her hand from his, starting down the path. He quickly fell in step beside her. "Though sometimes, the gleam of gold was more persuasive than I was. After all, I was only sixteen."

"And just beginning to realize your power as a beautiful woman."

At the gleam of masculine admiration in his eyes, her heart did a somersault. She hurried on, hoping to cover her reaction. "We reached the coast unharmed and secured passage to England, though even that was difficult. On our arrival, I sought shelter with Aunt Augusta in London and found my parents there. Father had been trying to locate us, to learn anything he could."

"He must have been overjoyed to see you."

"Yes, he was." *For a while.*

"At least Nicholas has Owen with him. That must be a comfort both to him and to your family."

Selena hesitated, the old resentment still strong, though she knew she should be happy her cousin had gained his freedom. "It was at first, though my parents were quite upset because Celia did not see us safely out of France.

"Six months after Nick and Owen were moved to Verdun, Celia smuggled her husband out of the city. She had arranged for her and her maid to visit Paris. When they left in the coach, they hid Owen on the floor between them, beneath their skirts. The coachman was in on the plan, and once out of sight of the guards, they turned toward the German border. They worked their way to the coast and caught a ship home."

"And left your brother behind." Contempt rang in Gabriel's voice.

"Yes. My parents have never forgiven them. Nor, I suppose, have I. I know I should not begrudge them their freedom and happiness. There was no way they could have taken Nicholas with them, too."

"He was still a boy. Your cousin was responsible for him. He should have waited until Nick was older." The cattle had cut across the path after a rain, leaving it roughened by their hoofprints. Gabriel again held out his arm to her, and she slipped her hand around it, grateful for his steady support.

"I agree. But Nick says others, probably better men than my cousin, offered him guidance and friendship."

"Do you think our government is right in refusing to exchange the détenus for French prisoners of war?"

"Yes and no. It would be wrong to allow Napoleon to force our country to be a part of such despicable treatment of civilians. If we do not stand against him, he will use the same tactics again and again with each new country he attacks. On the other hand, I would give anything to have my brother safely home." When she felt him tense, she glanced up at him.

He relaxed and looked down at her with a faint smile. "You said you've visited him twice. How was he?"

"Changed. Not only in the sense that he is now a grown man, but he has lost his joy. I noticed it when I first saw him three years ago. It was more pronounced on the visit last fall."

"Most men would be plagued with melancholy in such circumstances."

"I worry that it goes deeper than that. I fear he has lost hope of ever having a life beyond the walls of Verdun. He was so young when he was cut off from family, friends, and the country life he dearly loved. Even as a boy, Nicholas cherished his freedom above all things. We knew Father planned to send him away to school when he turned ten." The public schools were open at a substantial fee to the sons of the nobility and gentry, and occasionally to boys whose fathers were rich businessmen. "For over a year, Nick and I saved practically every coin we could scrape together. Before he left, I sewed them into the linings of his coats."

"I thought you could no' sew." The teasing glint was back in his eyes. It made her smile.

"I said I cannot sew well. Since my governess or Mother did not have to check my stitches, they suited our purposes perfectly. In fairness to Papa, Nick stayed at school for a month to give it a try. He hated every minute of it, so he ran away. He purchased a seat on the mail coach and secretly returned to our estate in Yorkshire. I suspected he was there but dared not go look for him in fear someone would follow me.

"He lived in a cave on the coast for several weeks, all on his own, providing for himself. He had read where Highlanders sometimes lived on gruel made of oats and water. So on his way home, he purchased a bag of oats."

Gabe laughed. "The proprietor probably thought he was buying it for his pony."

"Precisely. No good Englishman would eat oats himself." She grinned at the memory. "But Nicholas did, as well as catch fish and snare rabbits and cook them. He added some berries to his diet and did not fare too badly. He told me later it was better food than what they received at school.

"When he was ready to face Father, he left a note where he knew I would see it, telling us where he was. Papa was furious, yet at the same time, extremely thankful Nick was safe. He ordered me to stay at the house when he went to find him."

"Somehow, I dinna have the feeling you obeyed." He sent her a wry smile.

"Of course not. I fear I never was a dutiful daughter. Since the note was addressed to me, I knew my brother's location. I started off on foot while Papa explained to Mama that Nicholas had been nearby all the time. I knew she would swoon or go into hysterics for a while. I was able to warn Nick that the time of reckoning was at hand. Then I hid and watched it play out.

"Once Father quit yelling, he asked Nicholas what he had to say for himself. Nicholas explained how very much he had hated school, that being confined there made him feel as though he were suffocating. Indeed, he had been quite ill for a week shortly after his arrival at school. It had been confirmed in a letter from the headmaster. Nick stated that if, as my father had once said, the ill treatment and flogging at school was to toughen the spirit and strengthen the backbone, then he had no need of such training."

"A smart, bold lad." The approval in Gabriel's tone pleased her.

"Indeed, he was. I think Father even admired his boldness, though he dared not reveal it." The image of her father's expression—incredulity blended with a bit of pride—made her smile again.

"Nick showed father the little home he had made for himself and reminded him that he had traveled all the way alone. He had provided for his own needs almost three weeks. He had not gained his courage or abilities at school. He had learned them before he went away."

"I canna see how your father could argue with that reasoning."

"He couldn't. But he did proclaim that one could not learn to lead unless he learned to obey."

"A true enough principle." He glanced at her again. "What was your brother's response?"

"He looked Papa in the eye and suggested it was a lesson best taught at home by a father."

Gabe chuckled quietly. "I like your brother already. Surely, your father agreed?"

"Yes, but he also punished him for frightening us so." She still cringed when she remembered how he'd been confined to his room for two weeks, not allowed to talk to anyone but his tutor. Keeping him locked indoors was one of the worst punishments anyone could conceive for Nick. *At least he could look out the windows. Unlike Bitche prison.* She barely hid her shudder.

"Though Nicholas hated his time at public school, he has an excellent mind and was a good student. Under the guidance of a fine tutor, he developed a great interest in history. He looked forward to attending Oxford and visiting the historical societies in London."

"Now he feels too old to attend university," Gabriel said in understanding.

"He has repeatedly sought permission to move to Paris to study, but that opportunity also has been denied him." She released his arm, stopped, and looked around. "I suppose we should go back. If we go any farther, you might have to carry me part of the way."

Gabriel laughed quietly and kept walking in the same direction. "Then, by all means, let us keep going."

Selena laughed and rolled her eyes. "Then you'll walk by yourself." She turned and started back toward the gig.

In a few moments, Gabriel trotted up and fell in step beside her. "Coward."

"I merely do not wish to be thrown over your shoulder like a sack of grain."

"Now you've done it." He gave her a mock glare.

"Done what?"

"Insulted no' only my strength, but my manners. I do know the polite way to carry a woman."

Before she realized what he was about, he swept her up in his arms, cradling her against his chest. He kept walking as if she weighed practically nothing. Laughing, Selena looped her arms loosely around his neck.

Considering the way her heart pounded, she was not at all sure there *was* a polite way for a man to carry a woman. Most Society matrons would be scandalized if they knew she was alone with a man. Any man. If she and Gabe were seen, the whole neighborhood would soon know of it. It would only be a matter of days before the *ton* speculated about her affair with her estate manager.

After what you've done, you're worried about appearances?

Shame washed over her. She had been alone with gentlemen before, usually on a walk at a country house party or in a town house garden on the evening of a ball. She had allowed—sometimes encouraged—them to kiss her. She had never gone any further, but she despised herself just the same. None of those men had really been suitors, and seldom had she felt any true affection for them. Some she had even disliked, but they served their purpose—a purpose far less honorable than simply stealing a kiss.

If she were honest with herself, that was exactly what she wanted right now. Suddenly, Selena wanted to weep. The first time she truly wanted a man's kiss, she could not let it happen—even if he were so inclined, which he did not appear to be at the moment. She sighed softly. "Gabriel, put me down."

"No."

Selena blinked. "No?"

He angled off the path. "If I put you down now, you'll have to walk home."

"What are you—" She caught a whiff of something unpleasant and looked over his shoulder. She had been so lost in her thoughts of him that she had forgotten about the smelly present a cow had left along the way.

"I canna have you stinking up the gig." He continued on about ten feet before he stopped and lowered her to the ground.

"Goodness, no." She stepped away, putting some distance between them. He made no attempt to move closer. "Nor would I want to ruin a good pair of boots."

The man was entirely too distracting. *I must watch my step around him.* She almost giggled at her unconscious choice of words. *In more ways than one.*

CHAPTER *Seven*

IN YEARS PAST, SELENA HAD FELT God's presence in Worcester Cathedral, but the solitude and peace of the centuries-old holy place no longer comforted her. Evil had invaded her sanctuary.

Michael Ellaby stood looking up at one of the sharply pointed arches and neighboring marble columns in the Lady Chapel. A few minutes later, he slowly moved toward her. Like Selena, he pretended to casually study the carved scenes decorating the arches in the transept. If one judged the man by his appearance, they would assume he was a modestly prosperous businessman. He did not have the polished air of a gentleman, but neither did he seem the thug she knew him to be.

Ellaby frightened Selena, but at least she would recognize him if she met him on the street. She was more afraid of Bonham, the man for whom he worked, a phantom who held her life—and her brother's—in his hands.

He usually sent Ellaby with his messages, though on occasion he had spoken to her directly. Hidden by darkness, he was a chilling voice in the night, commanding her at will. His speech was cultured, knowledgeable, and arrogant. Since he only talked to her in the garden at *ton* parties, he had to be a member of the aristocracy. He knew too much about her activities not to be moving in the same circles.

Ellaby stopped beside her, tipping his head to look at the remarkable carving of the Last Judgment. It was a fitting, albeit disturbing, setting for their discussion. "Bonham is worried about you."

She glanced at him in surprise. "What have I done to cause him concern?"

"You haven't been going out. He wondered if you'd taken

sick." He looked at her. "Don't look sickly to me. So it must be the other."

"What other?"

"He thought mayhap you'd run to ground. Gone into hiding, so to speak." Ellaby's gaze lingered on her face. The odd mixture of lust and concern in his eyes sent a chill sweeping over her. "Don't cross him. You'll meet with a nasty accident if you do."

"At your gentle hands?"

He looked beyond her, toward the main entrance of the chapel where Marietta stood guard. "You'd better hope so. I wouldn't leave no scars. If he does it himself, he'll give you a reminder."

Selena's palms grew wet beneath her cloth gloves, and her heart pounded so loudly she thought it might echo from the towering, vaulted ceiling. "Then I would be of no use to him."

"He wouldn't mark your face or any place obvious. Just be careful and don't anger him. What do I tell him?"

Selena took a deep breath, hoping it would help calm her so she could think more clearly. "That I have been busy redecorating my home and starting improvements on the estate. The house was in no condition to entertain even a small number of guests, and the *ton* will expect me to do so. I am tired and in need of a rest. I'll gradually resume my social activities over the next few weeks."

"Better start right away. Major Lawrence will arrive late next week for a stay at Lord Newby's. If you suddenly start going to parties then, somebody might get suspicious."

"Very well. I'll accept some of the next invitations and also go to the assembly or theater. Do you have any word of Nicholas?"

To her amazement, Ellaby smiled. "Better than that." He reached into his coat pocket and pulled out several sheets of writing paper folded together. Her name was written across the front of a sheet. She immediately recognized Nick's bold handwriting. "Bonham said if you didn't cooperate, I wasn't sup-posed to give you these. But seein' as how you're going to do what he wants…" He held them out to her.

Selena stared at the papers, then looked at him in disbelief. "A letter from Nicholas?"

He nodded with a self-satisfied smile. "Two of them. One for you and one for your parents." His voice dropped to a whisper. "Courtesy of Napoleon himself, though I doubt your brother knows it."

She took the letters with a trembling hand and held them close to her heart.

"You'd best put 'em away to read later."

Numb, she nodded, fumbling with the strings on her reticule until it opened. She very carefully slid the precious missives inside and closed it again.

Ellaby said something, but Selena only heard his voice, not the words. Letters from Nick! They had something to hold, to read, to bring them once again into personal contact with him. She would have to concoct a story about how she got them, then have one of the footmen take the letter to her parents.

"Miss Delaroe." Ellaby's quiet but sharp tone cut through the haze.

She shook her head to clear it and focused her attention on his face. "I beg your pardon. What did you say?"

"I will send fake letters by messenger this afternoon. You can say someone smuggled them out and then sent them to you."

"Good. If there is ever any question about them, the ser-vants could verify how and when I received them."

"We have one other concern. Why did you hire Macpherson?"

She frowned. What on earth did her employee have to do with anything? "I needed an estate manager, and he is the best qualified of those who applied. He comes highly recommended by Dominic Thorne and the earl of Branderee."

"He should. He is the earl's closest friend. Gabriel Macpherson is the second son of Viscount Liath, a very wealthy man. Don't see as how he would need a job."

She knew his parents! But not well. They rarely came to England, so she had only spoken to them a few times. Peers always went by their title. If she'd ever heard that Lord Liath's family name was Macpherson, she had forgotten it.

That news, coming immediately after receiving the letters from Nicholas, took the starch right out of her legs. Selena stepped to the closest pew and sank onto the seat. Why hadn't she met Gabriel at some social event over the years? Had he merely preferred to stay in Scotland also? It seemed far too simple an explanation.

"Then why would he want to work for me?"

"A good question, but be subtle in trying to find the answer. Don't want to accidentally tip our hand. Use some of your famous charm. It's worked fine at getting secrets out of blokes in the past."

Selena winced at the reminder. Charm was a two-edged sword, one Gabriel wielded with as much expertise as she did. Perhaps more. *Why is he at Fairhaven?* She struggled to quell a sense of panic.

"Send word when you find out what Macpherson is up to." He paused, then pinned her with his gaze. "Or if we need to dispose of him."

Selena gasped. "I'm sure there will be no need for anything so dramatic. It may take time. As you said, I must be careful."

"Remember, make sure you don't give anything away in the meantime."

"Of course not. I will do nothing to jeopardize my brother's safety." Along with her resolve, some of her strength and calmness returned also. "I am well aware of how much I have to lose." Both for Nicholas and for herself.

"Good. Wait here a while after I leave."

"I will." Selena listened to his footsteps on the tile floor. The sound receded, then disappeared, and she breathed a huge sigh. She wanted to pray for guidance and wisdom, for some way out, but she didn't. God would not answer her request, no matter how desperate. She had turned her back on him, on everything she knew to be right and good.

Surely she was as abhorrent in God's eyes as in her own.

Across the chapel, Gabriel hid in the shadows of an alcove. Though Marietta guarded the main door, he'd found a smaller, less noticeable one that gave him access to the room. He had not been close enough to hear the exchange between Selena and the man she met, but he had seen most of their expressions. Whoever the man was, he frightened her. He wondered what the man had handed her. Only something very important could have evoked such a strong reaction when he gave her the papers. Though Gabriel hated admitting it, he suspected it had something to do with Nick.

She stayed in the chapel a quarter hour after the man left, then quietly departed. Gabriel followed, keeping out of sight, reaching the outer door in time to see her carriage pull away in the direction of Fairhaven. "Ah, lass," he whispered with a sigh. "What are you doin'?"

He remained in Worcester a few hours longer. First he checked on the glass for the cottage windows. Then he stopped off at the cooper's to order the large oak casks they would need in the fall to store the perry and cider. He made several other stops in various areas of the city, partly because he had business there and partly to confirm that the man Selena had met followed him. The man was subtle in his movements, but Gabriel's military years served him well. He spotted him too often during the afternoon for his presence to be coincidence.

They obviously were suspicious. When he reached Fairhaven, Gabriel braced for a confrontation with Selena. If

Cameron had successfully planted his stories, her accomplice would eventually learn of Gabriel's supposed financial difficulties, though the information would not be easily found. He only hoped Selena believed the tale and would not be too angry with him for deceiving her. The whole plan hinged upon gaining her trust.

That bit of irony left a bitter taste in his mouth.

He returned the horse to the stable, nodding a greeting to the stable boy as he dismounted. "I thought I saw Miss Delaroe's carriage in Worcester."

"She returned midafternoon. Didn't stay in town as long as usual. Looked a bit peaked. Marietta said she had the headache."

"Then I willna bother her. If anyone needs me, I'll be in my quarters." Gabriel walked across the grounds to the house that served as his living quarters and office. It was approximately fifty yards from the manor house, nestled in a pleasant flower garden and sheltered from the summer sun by several large trees.

The location could not have been better suited for an estate manager—or a government agent who wanted to keep track of the comings and goings on the estate. He had a clear view of the rear of the manor house and one side, plus a partial view of the front, including the long drive to the main road. There was no outside door on the other side of the house. From his parlor, he could see into the large windows of the manor dining room. The foliage of a huge weeping willow screened the window to Selena's second floor bedchamber in a lacy curtain.

He spent a short time in his office, listing the day's business in a large ledger. After purchasing his own estate, he'd quickly learned to make detailed notes, whether they pertained to business transactions, discussions, or merely ideas. They had proved handy on several occasions if materials did not arrive on time or instructions were questioned.

After placing the ledger in the desk drawer, he removed his coat and cravat and took them into his bedroom to put away. Under normal circumstances his valet would handle the chore, but obviously Gabriel could not bring Sanborn to Fairhaven with him. He had given the man an extended vacation with pay until he would again require his services. Gabe had done the same with his coachman, Macgregor, and rented a gig to drive himself around. The last he'd heard, the dapper manservant and the frugal Scot were seeing the sights in London, though likely not together.

Fortunately, the cleaning of his home and clothing were part of Gabriel's compensation as estate manager, as was the provision of his meals. Other necessities, such as water for his bath, however, were left up to him. He did not have a servant to carry water in from the cistern, heat it on the stove, and pour bucket after bucket into the tub. It took him a few tries before he learned the right combination of hot and cold water so it would be the correct temperature by the time he shucked his clothes and hopped into the hip bath.

Though the house had a small kitchen, Gabriel did no cooking other than make coffee in the morning and a pot of tea in the evening. His knowledge of cooking was limited to baking oat cakes on a flat griddle. Neither one was readily available. There were four more rooms upstairs, but he did not use them.

In his bedchamber, he took his valise from the back of the wardrobe and set it on the bed. He opened it and pressed a narrow piece of metal hidden in the seam across one end. This released a small catch so he could carefully lift up one corner of the false bottom. He removed a small notebook and made detailed notes, describing Selena's meeting with the man in Worcester Cathedral and how the man followed him all afternoon. He put down his thoughts as to what it all might mean, in the event something happened and he was unable to tell the tale in person. Kiernan knew where to find the notebook. If necessary, he would see that the information reached Cameron.

No summons from Selena ever came. When the footman brought Gabriel's dinner, he inquired about her.

The footman shrugged. "She stayed upstairs today after she came home from town. Asked that a tray be taken up to her instead of dining with Lady Camfield like she usually does. Suppose she was too upset after receiving the letters."

"Letters?"

The footman's eyes lit up. "You ain't heard? A messenger brought 'em this afternoon from Worcester. Marietta told Mrs. Pool they was from Miss Delaroe's brother, Nicholas, the one in France. There was a letter for her and one for her father. Some friend of his had escaped and carried them out with him."

"The friend didna deliver them in person?"

"No, sir. He sent a note. Said he was going to Wales and was too anxious to see his family to stop."

"Do you know if Miss Delaroe's brother is well?"

"When Lizbeth—she's the upstairs maid—asked after him, Marietta said he was fine. Tired of bein' in France, but fit." The young man's smile disappeared, and a frown creased his brow. "Lizbeth had a peek at the mistress when Marietta opened her door. Said she was pale and her eyes all swollen, like she had been weepin'."

"That would no' be unusual. Women cry for many reasons."

The footman nodded. "Ain't that the way of it." He left the tray and went back to the manor.

Though Gabriel's thoughts were mainly on Selena, he noted that the broiled brisket of beef was up to the cook's usual standards. Carrots, turnips, dumplings, peas, and potatoes had been cooked with the meat, giving them good flavor.

He was more certain than ever that the mysterious man at the cathedral had been the bearer of those priceless letters. Her reaction upon receiving the small packet clearly stated their value. A delivery by messenger on the same day was too much of a coincidence.

He finished the black currant pudding and took the empty dishes into the small kitchen. The footman would pick them up when he brought the breakfast tray the next day.

The light in Selena's window shone for a few hours after dark, then went out. Worried by the day's events, Gabe could not sleep. He tried reading a novel, then the Bible, but not even the Scriptures could hold his interest. So he blew out the lamp and sat in the darkness, thinking of Selena. "Lord, show me how to help her. I fear she is in grave danger, with nowhere to turn."

Restless, he put on his coat and wandered outside for a walk in the garden. He found solace in the moonlit night. Walking to the far edge of the grounds, he sat down on a stone bench. The stream that wound through Fairhaven touched this part of the estate, too. He sat for a long time, listening to the hushed music of the water as it flowed gently past. A light breeze cooled the quiet night, and he began to relax.

The faint scent of roses drifted in the air. Gabriel breathed in the fragrance then paused, frowning. The section of the garden that sported roses was a hundred yards away. He looked around, spotting Selena beyond some nearby shrubbery. When he saw how close she was to the edge of the stream, he jumped to his feet. The movement caught her attention, but she did not move away from the bank.

"Good evening," he called softly, walking toward her. "Going for a swim at this hour?"

She shook her head and looked back at the water. "I cannot swim."

Gabriel quickened his pace. The stream was deeper here, perhaps seven or eight feet. "Then you should step back."

"The water looks cool." She sounded wistful and melancholy.

"And deadly."

When she met his gaze, the hopelessness in her eyes chilled him to the bone. "Perhaps there are worse things than death."

CHAPTER  Eight

GABRIEL STARTED AT THE WHISPERED, desolate comment, then put his arms about her and lifted her off the ground, hauling her backward. When they were well away from the stream he stopped and set her down. Turning her toward him, he wrapped her in his embrace and held her close. "Lass, do no' speak such foolishness."

She sagged against him, resting her head on his shoulder, nestling her face against his throat. "Forgive me. Drowning was only a passing thought, and not an inviting one. I would never seriously consider such a thing."

"What troubles you so?"

"I received a letter from Nicholas today."

"So I heard. And one for your father, too." He smoothed his hand up and down her back, trying to soothe her. "It was no' good news? Has something happened to him?"

"I do not know. I fear he intends to try to escape again."

Gabriel stopped the movement of his hand. "Again?" When she straightened and looked up at him, he eased his hold, keeping his arms loosely around her.

"When we arrived in Verdun last year, he was not there. He had escaped four months earlier and almost made it out of France before he was captured."

"And sent to prison instead of being detained within the walls of the city."

She nodded. "Yes. When Owen fled years ago, he left his valet, Edward, behind, too. He and Nick escaped together, but weeks into their flight, the soldiers closed in on them. Nick distracted them so that Edward could slip away. Edward eventually made it back to England while Nick was taken to Bitche penal depot."

"A vile place."

"More horrid than anything I ever imagined."

Gabriel drew a sharp breath. He was not surprised she went there to see her brother, but he hated to think of her witnessing such cruel depravity.

The commandant at Verdun was extremely angry because Nicholas had eluded him. He took great delight in telling me that Bitche was the strongest fortification in France, built on the summit of an immense rock. He said there were five levels of accommodations, saying it as though he were comparing it to lodgings at an inn. He described class one as the best, two as indifferent, then each descending level as bad, very bad, and—" her voice cracked—"abhorrent."

Gabriel tightened his arms about her. If only he'd been able to protect her from ever having to see such horrors.

She went on. "Those who tried to escape France were taken in chains to the class five level, dungeons hewn out of the very rock itself. They usually stayed there for weeks or perhaps months. Over time, if their behavior was deemed acceptable to the gaoler, they might move up another level or two.

We rushed to Bitche, where I offered the commandant a generous sum to free Nicholas. He took the money, saying he would consider allowing me to see my brother, but much more would be required to free him. I called on the commandant every day, but he refused my request even to see Nicholas. In the meantime, I wrote home to my financial manager, advising him to quickly send more funds. I prayed that what I had taken with me, which should have been more than sufficient for several months' expenses, would be enough to secure his freedom from the prison. After a fortnight, the commandant said I could visit Nick in his cell."

Shock flowed through Gabriel. "He didna bring him to you?"

"No." She gently pulled away and began to walk slowly across the grounds, turning up a strawberry-bordered walk. "I suppose he wanted me to see how badly Nick fared, so I would pay what he asked without quibbling."

Gabriel's anger rose swiftly. The commandant was a monster. *If I could get my hands on him, he would be the one to pay…and no' in money.* He walked with her, not touching her, though he longed to hold her hand or put his arm around her. He wanted to shelter her from the memories, protect her from anyone and everyone who might harm her.

"The commandant, along with several guards, escorted me into the area where the men were kept. We went slowly so he might point out the differences for each class of imprisonment. The first level was the best and above ground, but few ever stayed there. Class two was also on the surface. It was small and overcrowded, but at least the windows let in the light of day. That area was reserved for the most well behaved officers and détenus who had worked their way up from the dungeons.

"Class three was the officers' souterrains, for those who had not yet qualified for the higher level. It was like a basement, damp and depressing but stone lined. A row of windows in the tall, vaulted ceiling allowed in daylight. The men were kept in large rooms and had raised bed boards and mattresses.

"We walked down fifty stone steps to level four. I know there were fifty. I counted them in an effort to control my fear. It was like a cellar, with no windows, though it was also vaulted and stone lined, and the bed boards were covered with straw instead of mattresses. There were some officers and a few détenus there, passing through on their way up. Most of the occupants were enlisted men or common merchantmen."

When she crossed her arms, Gabriel slipped off his coat and draped it over her shoulders. Keeping her hands crossed in a self-protective gesture, she grasped the lapels, then looked up at him with a tiny smile. "Thank you."

"Do you want to go inside?"

"No, I need the open air. I cannot bear to be confined right now." They strolled silently for a few minutes before she spoke again. "Nicholas told me later that the morale on that level was quite low because the nonofficers could go no higher. He said it was a rough place, with its own judicial system, basically a dictatorship of the strongest. From what he was told, and from what he saw, it never quite fell into total ruin. The officers passing through were given respect, not because they tried to wield any authority, but because most kept trying to escape, though they failed. Often numerous times. Nicholas admired them greatly, as did the other men. He said they were extraordinary—bold, tough, and men of action."

Dear God, that she should have been in such a place! Still, since Nicholas had reached that floor, she would not have seen the worst of the prison. Gabriel relaxed somewhat, until her arm brushed his as she shivered.

"Then we went down more stone steps to the last level."

Frowning, Gabriel touched her shoulder, bringing her to a halt. "I thought Nicholas was in the fourth class."

"He had already passed through there. I learned later that he had moved up to the third a week before I arrived at Bitche." She spoke in a hushed, sorrowful voice. "The commandant was a vicious and treacherous man, who violently hated the English. After my first visit to his office, he had Nick thrown back into the dungeons. If I had never gone there, he would likely have been freed in another month without having been harmed."

When she closed her eyes and hung her head, Gabriel could stand it no longer. He reached out to gently embrace her. "Say no more, Selena. This hurts you too much."

She shook her head, her hair brushing his chin in a sad caress. "I want to tell you. I need to." She inhaled on a shudder. "I've never spoken of it, not even to Marietta."

Gabriel glanced around, spotting a bench amid some nearby elm trees. "Let's sit down." Resting his hand at the small of her back, he guided her to the secluded seat, shielded almost completely from the rest of the grounds. He sat close to her and put his arm around her shoulders. When she reached for his hand, a jolt of longing and protectiveness shot through him.

She took a deep breath. "The gaoler led us to the lowest floor, hewn out of the mountain rock. Without his lantern, we would have been in total darkness. I wore a heavy woolen coat, but the cold still penetrated my bones. Water dripped from the walls, mixing with excrement in a foul, ankle-deep pool on the ground. The stench alone was enough to turn my stomach and make me fight for air. When the gaoler opened the heavy door to the large cell, the men with Nicholas huddled against the walls and hid their eyes from the light."

"And your brother?" A cold knot of dread filled Gabriel's stomach.

"There was no need for him to protect his eyes. He had been severely beaten and flogged. He lay on the rock floor in that filthy water, burning up with fever, out of his head and close to death."

"Merciful heaven." Gabriel wanted to weep.

"All because of me."

"You canna know that."

"But I do. Though beating was not uncommon, not every prisoner was abused, and few to such an extent. Nicholas had not been treated so harshly any other time during his stay at Bitche, not even upon his arrival. The commandant wanted to make certain I would pay his price."

"A high one, no doubt."

She nodded, then met his gaze in the moonlight. "At that moment, I would have sold my soul to free him."

Judging by the tortured bleakness in her eyes, he feared she had. He looked away. "So the commandant released him."

"Yes. I was able to keep enough money to move Nick to a house in the town. Over the next several weeks, Marietta and I nursed him back to health. By the time he was well enough to return to Verdun, the rest of my funds had arrived."

He felt some of the tension leave her, so he forced himself

to relax. He moved his arm from around her shoulders, resting it along the back of the bench. "Why do you think Nick may try to escape again?"

"In his letter, he said he often thought of our childhood and the amusing times we had. He asked if I remembered being chased by the bull."

"And escaping over the wall."

Selena nodded. "Though he didn't mention it, of course. He also gave a vague reference to school. No one else would realize he was talking about running away from there and hiding in the cave until it was safe to come home."

"Perhaps he gleaned something useful from the officers at Bitche who kept trying to escape."

"I hope so. Though if they really knew what they were doing, they wouldn't have been there."

Gabe chuckled, hoping to lighten her mood. "True. Perhaps he learned from their mistakes."

Selena met his gaze with an intensity that startled him. "I wish there were some way to help him! *Someone* who could see him safely back to England." The appeal in her eyes was unmistakable. For some reason—one he did not want to dwell on—she believed he could help her.

Careful. "I wish there were, too. There must be some kind of underground at work in the French empire, people who do not agree with Napoleon. Unfortunately, I dinna know how to contact them." But Cameron would. "Perhaps you could find an ally in the government."

"I've asked them before. The official word is that they are unable to do anything."

"Does your father have any influential friends who could pressure the Foreign Office?"

"He might, but it would do no good to ask. He would immediately dismiss the idea because it came from me."

Gabriel stood and gently tugged her up also. "Dinna tell me he is the kind of man who thinks women have no intelligence."

They started toward the manor house.

"He does not lump all women in that category, nor do I think he includes me. He does, however, blame me for Nick's captivity."

He stared at her. "Impossible. Keeping the détenus was Napoleon's idea."

"But I am the one who persuaded Father to let us go to France. He stood firm against Nick's pleas, but he had a soft heart for me."

"Had him wrapped around your little finger?" he asked with a smile.

"Once upon a time." Her voice caught, and tears shimmered in her eyes. "Now my father hates me. He has not spoken to me in over seven years. I do not believe he will ever forgive me."

Nor could she forgive herself, thought Gabriel. If she was helping the French, it was because of two of the most compelling forces known to man: love and guilt. Her father should be ashamed for adding to her pain, for breaking her heart.

"Only Marietta knows Nicholas was in prison and even she does not know all the details. I could not bear for my parents to learn what happened to him."

"Why did you tell me?"

"You are my friend, and I needed to talk." She shrugged. "I think I can trust you to keep my secrets."

But she couldn't. Misery filled his heart. She had known so much pain, such deep sorrow…and he would only add to it. In a way, he was glad she didn't trust him enough to tell him everything.

God help him when she did.

"I STILL THINK IT IS TOO GREAT A RISK," Marietta said the next evening. She fastened a necklace of five delicate gold chains attached to a single emerald pendant around Selena's neck and glanced in the mirror. "You should sack him."

Selena met her friend's gaze in the reflection and smiled wryly. "On what grounds do I dismiss him? Because Bonham is suspicious? And when Gabriel asks who Bonham is, what do I say? Blithely mention that he is a coconspirator, one that likely is being paid well by Napoleon?"

Marietta made a face and handed her the matching pendant earrings. "You could say Macpherson has been much too forward and overstepped his rank. His *supposed* rank, that is. I saw you with him in the garden last night." She watched in the mirror as Selena clipped the earrings into place. "Holding you close, he was. Perhaps even took advantage of your dark mood and stole a kiss or two. He's a rogue if I ever saw one. If he isn't working for the government, he's after your money."

"Were you following me?" Selena stood, turning toward her maid with a frown as she pulled on long white kid gloves.

"Of course not." Marietta sniffed and set about tidying up the dressing table. "I like to walk in the evenings, too."

"Especially if the path leads toward the coachman's quarters." Selena smiled. She could never stay irritated at Marietta for long. The maid was only six years older than Selena, and they were close friends.

"I could do far worse than a coachman." Marietta grinned at her. "And I am not at all displeased that Thomas is so handsome."

"Has he proposed?"

"Not yet, but I think he will." Marietta's expression grew

somber. "I do not encourage him too much. I cannot leave you until this is finished."

"I don't want to stand in the way of your happiness, but I own I would be lost without you."

Marietta's lips thinned. "You may be lost anyway if Macpherson stays."

Selena walked to the window, looking across the grounds at the spot near the stream where Gabriel had held her. She could still feel his strong arms around her, remember his tenderness and compassion, his fear that she might harm herself. Though he might be at Fairhaven under false pretenses—the extent of which was yet to be proven—he cared for her. She saw it in his eyes when he looked at her, felt it in his touch, heard the yearning in his voice when he called her *lass* or whispered her name. "I know I can never have a life with him, but must I be denied even these moments of joy?"

"No. But be careful, please. I am not anxious to see the inside of an English prison."

"I wish I had never involved you in this." Selena turned to her friend. "You still have the money? It should be adequate for you and Thomas to start a new life in America."

"It is more than adequate and safely hidden, but I'll not mention it to him unless we need to escape. I would rather surprise him and use it as a dowry. Then we can purchase the coaching inn he dreams of owning."

"While you are catering to the whims of elite travelers, I would fall completely out of fashion without you to advise me. And I could never find another coachman as fine as Thomas. Pray do take your time."

Marietta laughed and turned her toward the cheval mirror. "We're setting the fashion tonight. I don't know anyone else who could wear that ballgown."

Selena studied her reflection in the mirror. Made of corbeau satin, the gown, a dark green verging on black, shimmered whenever she moved. The dress was made with simplicity, having only a wide ruffle at the bottom and a narrow one around the neckline. Her shoulders were bare, save the ruffle and the puffy cap sleeves. The gold and emerald necklace nestled in the heart-shaped décolletage, which was cut low but well within the acceptable fashion.

She did indeed look quite grand. If only the one man she wished to impress would be at the assembly.

Marietta draped a gold paisley silk shawl across her shoulders. "Earlier, I noticed Macpherson working in the office. Perhaps he is still there."

Selena grinned at her. "Then the evening might not be a total waste." The countess had been delighted when Selena agreed to accompany her to the assembly that evening, though she herself had been hard pressed to show any enthusiasm. Picking up an ivory fan and a beaded black reticule, she went downstairs to wait for her aunt.

And, considering how early she was, it would make complete sense to stop in and see how Gabriel was coming with his paperwork.

As she walked down the hall, she spotted light coming from underneath the estate office door. Though Gabriel had a small office in his quarters, the majority of estate records were kept in this one. He often worked there during the day and occasionally in the evening. She knocked on the door, entering when he acknowledged her presence.

He absently glanced up from the papers spread out on the desk, his face lighting up when he saw her. His smile warmed her all the way to her toes. He stood quickly and retrieved a tobacco brown coat from the back of a chair, slipping it on. Tonight, he too was dressed in dark colors. His black-and-brown brocade waistcoat and black kerseymere trousers fit him perfectly. He was such a handsome man. How she would have enjoyed walking into the assembly by his side, gloating shamelessly as all the other women turned green with envy.

"You are breathtaking," he said softly as he walked around the desk, stopping in front of her.

"Thank you, kind sir." She smiled at him, making no attempt to hide her pleasure. "You look rather grand yourself. Why do you not come with us? You would not even have to change. The ball is at the assembly room, so no invitation is necessary."

"That would be…unwise."

Pulse racing, she boldly smoothed a corner of his lapel that had become tucked under in his haste to don the coat. "I want you by my side tonight, Gabriel. I do not know the particulars of your situation, but you are too refined not to be a gentleman. I cannot imagine you being turned away, especially since you count Branderee and Thorne as your friends." *And since your father is Viscount Liath.* But she couldn't mention that.

He stepped back and leaned against the edge of the desk, crossing his arms, his expression shuttered. "You believe an ordinary man canna act like a gentleman?"

"They can, but there is a difference in being born a gentleman and acting like one. It usually shows."

"I didna know you were so top-lofty. You surprise me, Miss Delaroe."

She frowned. "Are we back to surnames again? You know I do not mind your calling me by my Christian name."

"How magnanimous."

She glared at him, and in a very unladylike manner, reached back with her foot and kicked the door shut. Gratified at the surprise that flickered across his face, she marched toward him, tossing her fan and reticule on the desk. "Why are you baiting me?"

He stood, his legs planted wide and solid, his green eyes flashing, every inch a warrior ready to do battle.

A warrior…?

She stared at him, momentarily distracted. Had he been a military officer? That would easily explain his air of command

97

and confidence, qualities not necessarily acquired simply by being the son of a viscount. It might also explain why she had never met him in Society.

"I am no' baiting you."

"Of *course* you are." She switched tactics, softening her expression and gentling her tone. "Why, Gabriel? What have I done to upset you?"

He frowned and looked away. "I dinna wish to look the fool."

"How could anyone make you look foolish?" she murmured, stepping closer.

"I would be jealous of every man in the room," he said quietly, sliding his arms around her waist. A weakness stole over her at the longing in his eyes. "Each time you smiled at another man, I'd be hard pressed no' to plant him a facer." He pulled her closer. "If you went for a stroll in the garden with some blade, I'd be forced to throttle the blockhead."

"We would indeed cause a scene." She slid her hands around his neck. "While you were breaking noses, I'd be clawing out the eyes of awed country misses throwing themselves at your feet."

"I would be tempted to dance with you." His gaze dropped to her lips.

"I would not turn you away."

"They would say I'm after your money."

She looked into his eyes and whispered, "Are you?"

"Nay, lass. I have no need of it."

"What do you need?"

"You."

He lowered his head, touching her lips with sweet gentleness tinged with fire. Then his mustache tickled her lip, breaking the spell. When he raised his head, she automatically rubbed her mouth.

"What is wrong?" he asked with a slight frown.

She smoothed her thumb across his mustache. "It tickles."

98

His eyes widened in surprise. "I hadna considered that."

"No one else has complained?"

"You are the only one I've kissed since I grew it."

She really shouldn't have been so pleased.

"Perhaps I need to adjust the angle," he murmured, tipping his head a little more. This kiss was slow, thorough, and more beautiful than anything she had ever known.

When he slowly raised his head, she saw her wonder reflected in his eyes. "Better?" The question came out low and husky.

She could only nod.

"Your aunt will be looking for you." He did not loosen his hold.

"Yes." She brushed the soft hair at the nape of his neck.

"You'll be compromised if she finds us." Though he spoke seriously, his arms tightened minutely.

Selena nodded and closed her eyes, resting her forehead against his chin. When he brushed a tiny kiss across her skin, she sighed. She could not chain him to her in so callous a fashion, even if he seemed not to mind. She would not condemn him to a life of shame, sorrow, and pain.

She sighed. "That would not do." She smoothed his hair and caressed his cheek, then eased away from him. "You will not come with us tonight?"

"No." He walked around her and opened the door, but caught her hand when she started to leave the room. "Wait a few minutes." He leaned close to her ear. "Or within the hour, every servant on the estate will know what we've been doing."

Selena's eyes widened. "Am I rumpled?"

"No." He gently turned her toward the desk, winking when she looked up at him. "But your face has a delightful glow."

"And you are entirely too smug." But she followed him around the desk anyway, noting the map of the estate spread across it. "What are you working on?"

"An easier way to water the orchards." He moved the chair

out of the way so they could stand side by side. "See how the stream runs near each one?"

Selena leaned forward, studying the map. She pointed to the apple orchard. "This one isn't very close."

"But near enough to utilize an irrigation ditch." He put his arm lightly around her waist, resting his hand at her side, and leaned forward also.

Either the man was an expert at seduction or, like her, he found it difficult not to touch when they were so close. Selena thought she was beginning to understand what was meant by a grand passion. Or perhaps love. One did not necessarily equate the other, but she knew enough to realize both were far too dangerous for her to even consider in her situation.

She tried to focus her attention on what Gabriel was saying.

He drew a line with his index finger from a bend in the stream to the closest side of the orchard. "We can run the ditch across this corner of the pasture and down this side of the orchard. We would lose but a small part of grassland, and it would only require a short section of new fence to keep the cattle out."

Aunt Augusta stepped through the doorway, smiling as they jumped apart. "My, my, isn't this cozy? No wonder you haven't been interested in going out, dear."

"Gabriel—Mr. Macpherson—was showing me the plans for a new irrigation system to water the orchards." Heat rushed to Selena's cheeks, something that had rarely happened to her before Gabriel came along.

"I am sure it will be quite efficient." Her aunt winked at Gabriel. "It appears that Mr. Macpherson excels at most everything."

"I do try, madam."

Her aunt laughed at the grave response, and Selena hid a smile. Then she glanced up at him and laughed at his impish grin.

"You, sir, are a scamp," Lady Camfield said.

"So I've been told."

Aunt Gussie chuckled and motioned to Selena. "Come, dear. I believe you need rescuing from this young man."

"Yes, ma'am." She slanted one more glance and a smile at Gabriel as she hurried around the desk, grabbing the fan and reticule on the way by.

"Have a pleasant evening, ladies."

"Oh, we will." Aunt Augusta turned and sailed out the door with a graceful toss of her hand. "Selena is always the belle of the ball."

Selena paused near the doorway, looking back at Gabriel. His expression had grown hard. "Good night," she said quietly.

He walked toward her, his gaze dropping to the edge of her low-cut gown. Stopping in front of her, he picked up one end of the long shawl and draped it over the opposite shoulder, covering her up to the base of her throat. "You dinna want the men drooling on your pretty dress."

She shook her head, giving him a bemused smile. "They aren't puppies."

Anger glinted in his eyes. "I've seen how they act around you. Scuffling among themselves to show you their latest tricks and receive a pat on the head—"

He broke off, clamping his mouth shut and looking away. If she hadn't known better, she'd think the pink tinge that suddenly colored his face was a guilty one.

Selena turned on her heel and walked down the hall, not gracing his rude comment with a reply.

"I've seen how they act around you...."

The words taunted her all the way to Worcester. She tried to remember a party they had both attended, but came up with nothing. Still, the vague feeling she'd had the first day he came to Fairhaven—that she had seen him somewhere before—lingered. Perhaps at the opera or the theater in London, though her admirers were not usually quite as obnoxious in those settings. His description was embarrassingly accurate of the men who flocked around her at private parties.

She took little comfort in his jealousy and self-consciously pulled the shawl higher as their carriage approached the assembly room. She would instruct the seamstress to add another ruffle at the neckline or perhaps an insert of heavy lace. Blast him for making her feel ashamed of how she looked! He hadn't minded her low-cut gown when he was the only man around.

"We need to learn more of your Mr. Macpherson."

"Aunt, he's not *my* anything."

"Of course he is, dear. It is quite obvious that you are forming a *tendre* for him. I have nothing against it, for he seems to be a fine man and such a charming one. But you need to know all you can about him to decide on the appropriate action, whether he is to be your husband or your lover."

"Aunt Augusta! You know I will not take a lover."

Lady Camfield gave Selena her I-am-wiser-than-you-dear look. "It is done all the time by women of your age, both married and single if the truth be known. As long as you are discreet, there is no harm in it."

Selena stared at Augusta. She knew her aunt was far more liberal in her thinking than she, but this was a stretch even for her. She did not mention her first reason for being against such a liaison—that it was a sin in God's eyes. Augusta did not share her Christian beliefs and would merely scoff. Instead, she gave the rationale she knew her aunt would understand.

"I fear, Aunt, there could be a great deal of harm in it. If I do someday decide to marry, what gentleman of any worth would want a tarnished bride?"

"There would be no need for him to know before the wedding."

"Trap him and then let him discover the truth? Surely that would end the marriage before it even began."

"He might be angry for a while, but you are far too beautiful for him to resist for long."

"It would be folly to begin a marriage in such a way and hope that he would forgive me. Or that God would." She held up her hand to stem her aunt's response. "It could mean a lifetime of misery for both of us. If I follow your advice and take a lover now, what happens if I have a child?"

"He would be obligated to marry you, of course."

"Then why not seek him for a husband in the first place?"

"Precisely. That is why we must discover if Mr. Macpherson is suitable before you grow too fond of him."

Selena leaned back against the seat. Trying to follow her aunt's logic was not always easy, but this time she understood what Gussie wanted her to her see.

Why on earth was she encouraging Gabriel? Heart aching, she closed her eyes. *Because I need him.* The mere sight of him made her smile. He could be tender and strong and melt her heart with a look. And his kisses—if she had any sense, she would not even think of them at all.

Impossible.

She would remember his touch for a lifetime.

"It's going to be an uncomfortably warm evening." Augusta unfurled her poppy red silk fan, cooling her face. "I've been thinking that he might be related to Lord Liath. The viscount is a Macpherson, too, and they have two sons, though I cannot recall the younger one's name. Gabriel bears some resemblance to Liath, but not enough to conclude that he is his offspring."

She glanced at Selena. "Now, put a smile on your lovely face, dear. You must not disappoint your admirers, at least not until I've had a chance to delve into the secrets of your handsome young man. And quit fussing with your shawl."

CHAPTER *Ten*

SELENA DID HER BEST TO PLAY HER ROLE, though she found it difficult to be witty and gracious. *What a frivolous, useless life we live.* And to think she had once reveled in the attention and ardor of her suitors, dreading the day when another beauty would take her place.

After a few hours, she thought she would scream if she heard one more gentleman's clever remark or caught another angry or sad glance from the young women in the room. While not every man hovered about her, far too many did, leaving a goodly number of ladies without partners.

She glanced around the group surrounding her and forced a smile. "Gentlemen, your attention is indeed flattering, but you are neglecting the other ladies."

"Why should we tread among common flowers when we can gaze upon the most glorious rose in the garden?" proclaimed Joseph Stoddard, a man past his youth who should have found a bride years earlier. He had attached himself to Selena at her coming-out and remained doggedly in attendance ever since.

"Well said," agreed George Foster, a young man fresh from Oxford. Several others nodded.

For perhaps the first time in her life in such a gathering, Selena revealed a hint of irritation. "Even the most common flower is beautiful if you look at it honestly instead of through jaded eyes. But you will not find them unless you stroll through the rest of the garden."

"I do believe our lovely rose has grown thorns," muttered Oliver Hopkins. He had been a member of her court for a couple of years. Other than occasionally asking for a dance, he barely said a word to her in all that time. Yet one need only see how he looked at her to know he was enamored.

"A necessary evil to ward off a surfeit of attention. Any flower will wither if not given air and space."

"You want us to leave you alone?" Hopkins's expression was incredulous.

"Thank goodness, a man of intelligence."

He practically crumpled before her eyes. "You don't like me?"

Selena immediately regretted her careless words. She laid her hand on his arm. "I do like you, Mr. Hopkins. But you would be better served finding a wife rather than wasting your time on me."

"Don't know how to find a wife."

"Simply look for someone as kind as you and you will get along fine." She smiled and patted his arm. "Someone a little on the shy side but not too much so, or you'll never have a conversation."

He looked across the room to the wallflowers sitting in a row, then back at Selena. "Perhaps Miss Brown? She has lovely eyes."

"Yes, she does, and I'm sure she would be quite pleased you think so. She is a very pleasant young woman." She gave him a little nudge. "Go, before your lose your courage."

He grinned at her, squared his shoulders, and started around the edge of the large dance floor, working his way through the crowd to claim his prize.

Selena looked around at the other men, almost laughing at their wary expressions. "Does anyone else need a matchmaker?"

As one, they shook their heads.

"Can do my own browsing."

"Not ready to get leg-shackled."

"Some ain't bad looking."

"Won't find anyone here."

Several others murmured similar opinions.

"That little blond is pretty." The young man who'd spoken flushed and looked quickly back at Selena. "But not nearly as beautiful as you, Miss Delaroe."

"Thank you, Mr. Jones, but do not tell her that. Compliment her with sincerity and you cannot go wrong. Remember, too, gentlemen, that there are several young women here who may not be great beauties, but who bring generous dowries. Now, if you will excuse me, I need to find my aunt."

She walked away, leaving them mumbling and staring at her, but she did not care. The stilted air in the overcrowded room smelled of too much perfume and too many warm bodies. Slipping out the open French doors, she walked to the far, unlit corner of the terrace, finding comfort in the darkness and gentle breeze. She rested her hands on the wrought-iron railing, the metal cooling them through her thin gloves. No doubt her respite would be brief. Even if the gentlemen left her alone when she returned to the assembly room, they would muster their forces at the next social event. Their pride would not allow her to escape them so easily.

Trying to relax, she looked up at the heavens. The stars winked back at her, assuring her that there was order in God's universe, even if chaos sometimes reigned in hers.

Lord, Gabe is such a wonderful man. I want to fall in love and marry like everyone else, not merely enjoy his company. Though I do thank you for those moments we have together, I just wish there could be more. She sighed. Why did everything have to be so complicated? *Please take care of Nick, God. Keep him safe—*

Sensing someone behind her, Selena stiffened. Before she could turn, the man blocked her movement with his body. He gripped the railing on either side of her, trapping her in place. She gasped, her heart pounding. "Unhand me, or I shall scream."

His breath brushed her ear as he leaned closer, wedging her against the railing. "That would be very unwise, Selena." He spoke in a quiet, raspy voice.

Bonham!

Her blood turned to ice as she struggled for air. She did not know if fear or the pressure on her body kept her from breathing deeply. She forced calmness into her tone. "Stand aside."

"And risk you fleeing? I think not."

"I cannot breathe."

He shifted, easing the weight against her. "Better?"

She took a deep breath. "Yes."

He put his arms around her, catching her hands in his. For one of the few times in her life, Selena thought she might faint.

"What are you about, dismissing your admirers so callously?"

Was he one of them? Or had he simply been near enough to see what happened? Her mind raced as she tried to remember the men who had been nearby. *Think!* Though not as tall as Gabriel, neither was he short. His arms and hands, the width of his chest against her back, everything about him indicated he was of medium build. Half the men in the room fit that description. His lavender cologne held a trace of something else that subtly set it apart from the common brand worn by many men, but she could not identify it.

He tightened his arms, his strength surprising. "Answer me."

Ellaby's warning about Bonham's cruelty ran through her mind. "Sometimes I think I shall throw a tantrum if they don't talk of something other than horses, fashion, or the latest gossip."

"Poor Selena. Not a man with half a brain among them." He eased his hold.

"Do you mock me?"

"Not at all. You are a woman of many talents, not the least of which is intelligence. That is why I chose you."

"I have listened to their endless flattery and inane banter since I was eighteen. I'm sick of it and do not think I can keep up the game."

"But you do it so well. How easily you distract a man." He slowly ran the tip of his finger down the side of her neck. Nudging the edge of the shawl aside, he continued the caress across her bare shoulder to the sleeve of her gown. When she shivered, he murmured in her ear, "Do you tremble from passion or fear?"

"Fear," she whispered, fighting the overwhelming urge to struggle. She dared not risk discovery. The repercussions could be disastrous.

"Pity. I would delight in stirring your passion, but if you had said as much, it would be a lie. Stay afraid of me, *chérie*. It is what keeps you and your brother alive. As for your role, you must continue it, though perhaps a modified version. Enough not to make your attention to the officers too obvious. How soon can you entertain at Fairhaven on a grand scale?" He released her but again kept her prisoner by placing his hands on the railing on each side of her.

"I am having a breakfast in less than a fortnight. The invitations will go out in a few days." Though the party was called a breakfast, it did not begin until early afternoon and usually lasted well into the evening.

"Good. I look forward to receiving mine."

"How do you know you are on my list?"

"You are inviting everyone who is anyone, are you not?"

"Yes."

"Then I shall be there. Major Simon Lawrence will arrive at Newby's in a few days. Be certain he receives an invitation. After the party, you and I will have another rendezvous. Say, midnight in the garden? You can tell me the secrets you glean from the major and make your payment at the same time. You have not forgotten that it is soon due, have you?"

"One does not easily forget blackmail." Not only did the horrid man force her to betray her country, he demanded one hundred guineas a month to keep Nick safe.

"Is there a particular place in the garden that is well secluded yet easy to find?"

"Where the wild honeysuckle grows around an old oak. It

is in the midst of a grove of trees on the northern part of the grounds."

"Perfect. I'll simply follow my nose. Have you learned anything more about Macpherson?"

"No. Lady Camfield planned to see what she could discover tonight."

"My sources tell me he is under the hatches. Poured all his money into a Scottish estate and has it mortgaged to the hilt. Proud man. Not one to lean on family or friends for a loan, so his need of employment stands. He is a former army officer, which is mildly worrisome. But he appears to have no contact with anyone in the military or in the government. However, if he is looking for a rich wife, you are no doubt his prime candidate. Have a care, my pretty. You are in no position to take a husband."

"I have no intention of marrying."

"How unfortunate. I had such plans for us." When she stiffened, he laughed. "No need to be grumpish. You might grow to like me."

"Never."

He trailed his fingers along the side of her neck again, resting them across her throat, as if in warning. "Ah, Selena, you challenge me to prove you wrong."

The sound of voices near the doorway brought an abrupt change in his manner. He closed his hands over her upper arms, his grip just short of inflicting pain. "You will meet me after your party."

She nodded.

"Do not attempt to look at me when I leave. Do you understand?" His grip tightened minutely.

"Yes."

With a whisper of movement, he was gone.

Her heart thudding erratically, Selena stood rigidly by the railing for several minutes, clinging to it for support, hoping desperately she did not appear as terrified as she felt. When the couple at the doorway decided not to go outside after all, she sagged against the wrought iron, stifling a sob.

In the past, Bonham had always remained hidden during their meetings, even warning her to stay back when she moved too close. By his boldness, he changed his own rules. The memory of his hands on her, his body pressing against hers, made her skin crawl. Was he merely toying with her, like a cat with a mouse? Or would his demands increase until he brought her dishonor in more ways than one?

At a quarter past ten, a footman stopped by the estate office in the manor house. "Will you be needing me, Mr. Macpherson?"

Gabriel shook his head. "No, thank you, Miller. I may work for some time, but I believe I have everything I need."

"Everyone else has gone to their rooms. I'll be waiting up for the ladies."

"I have my keys. If I finish before they return, I'll let myself out and lock the back door behind me." Tugging on his watch chain, Gabriel pulled his timepiece from the pocket of his waistcoat. "They willna be home until near midnight. You might as well catch some rest."

Miller grinned. "I've learned to nap sittin' up. Good night, sir."

"Good night." As the young man left the room, Gabriel shuffled a few papers, pretending to go back to his task. Instead of working, he had spent the past hour leaning back in the chair, staring into space, thinking about Selena. He regretted his harsh words and embarrassing her. Contrary to the teaching in Ephesians, he'd let the sun set on their anger. He hoped they would not let it hang between them the rest of the night. If he was not careful, his jealousy would be his undoing.

He stood and stretched his arms in the air before walking to the window. Closing it, he rested his hands on the sill and hung his head. "I'm falling in love with her, Lord. And I'm doubting her innocence more and more." He looked up, staring outside. A movement caught his eye, and he saw Marietta hurry across the grounds. She glanced back at the house, waving when she spotted him in the window, but didn't slow down.

Straightening, he watched as the maid and Thomas met in the garden, embraced, then turned to stroll arm in arm along a pansy-bordered path. He was glad for their happiness. If only he and Selena could exchange places with them...

Good and bad were no longer black and white, but varying shades of gray, distorting honor until he no longer recognized it. He drew the drapes and sat down in a nearby green leather armchair. "Father, I have given my word and must do my duty. But I'm afraid I will lose her. Afraid she will be condemned because of me. Help me to do what is right." Shutting his eyes, he leaned his head against the back of the chair and took a deep breath, his mind a jumble. "Help me to *know* what is right."

He waited another half hour, then left the room, closing the door behind him. If anyone walked by, they would think he was still working. He turned up the collar of his brown coat, hiding the white cravat and shirt. He had purposely worn dark clothing to help avoid detection in the shadowed stairway, but first he had to get past the footman. He did not think it wise to use the servants' stairs. There was too great a chance someone might venture down to the kitchen or out to the necessary. Tiptoeing down the hall, he paused, smiling when he heard Miller's snores. The man was sprawled in a chair near the front door, his head leaning against the wall, his mouth wide open.

Good thing there are no flies buzzing about.

Gabe walked quietly up the stairs. On the second level, a step creaked loudly. He froze in midstride. Miller snorted and mumbled something before resuming snoring. Gabriel released his pent-up breath and continued to the second floor. He made a mental note to mention the squeaky board to the carpenter, but then decided against it. Selena handled the household affairs. He had no reason to be upstairs. She would certainly wonder what he was doing there.

Candles in several wall sconces softly illuminated the hallway. Because he watched the light in her room go out each night, he knew her bedchamber was in the corner. He preferred not to enter that most private domain and hoped he would find what he sought somewhere else. He opened the door next to it, scanning the room in the dim light. Bed, dresser, wardrobe—a guest chamber, not her private sitting room.

Trying the door directly across from her bedchamber, he met with success. The drapes were drawn, so he took a candle from her writing table and lit it at a sconce in the hallway. He returned to the sitting room, silently closing the door behind him. The leather-lined top of the tulipwood table was neat and tidy, with several large stacks of party invitations, ready to deliver, lined up on one side. A chair beside the table held a large box filled with more of them, over two hundred in all.

As expected, he did not find the letter from Nicholas simply lying out in the open. Nor was it in any of the three drawers. He walked slowly around the room, candle in hand, searching for a place she might put something for safekeeping. Other than tucked inside one of the scores of books on the shelves beside the fireplace, there was no suitable hiding place. He did not have the time to search through all of them.

Think like a woman. Where would she put something precious to her? With her jewelry or in some kind of keepsake box? It would be close to her, where she could easily take it out in quiet moments and reread it.

In her bedchamber.

With a grimace, he went back to the door, opening it carefully. He tipped his head, listening, but could no longer hear Miller's snores. Except for a few creaks and groans as the house settled in the evening coolness, silence reigned. He crossed the hall and entered her bedchamber. The draperies were open, so he eased the door closed, shielding the candle with his hand. Putting it on a table in the corner of the room least noticeable through the window, he quickly closed the drapes.

He paused, scanning the room. The furnishings were feminine and pretty: cheerful pinks, yellows, greens—the colors of spring. Her rosewood dressing table held surprisingly few bottles and jars. Moving the candle to the dressing table, he allowed himself a moment of whimsy as he peeked at her lotions and potions. Milk of roses for the skin; a little jar of red lip balm; and something called wash of the ladies of Denmark, made from pumpkin, melon, cucumber, and gourd seeds.

He picked up a cotton glove, one of a pair, and found that the inside had been rubbed with scented lanolin. He smiled. "So that's how you keep your hands so soft." Finally, he lifted the stopper from her crystal perfume bottle and breathed in her special rose scent.

Enough of this! Time is running out.

With a sigh, he replaced everything as it had been, took the candle, and went to check the black-and-gold lacquered jewelry box on the chest of drawers. He raised the lid and released a long, silent whistle. His lady owned a fortune in jewels—amethysts to match her eyes, emeralds, garnets, pearls, sapphires, and even diamonds. Beautiful, expensive gems to adorn her exquisite neck, fingers, ears, and arms. But no letter. He closed the lid, glad he was a wealthy man and not a thief.

He quickly opened and closed the drawers in the chest, one by one, skimming his fingers over paisley shawls, embroidered handkerchiefs, kid and cloth gloves, as well as silk stockings and cotton petticoats that would likely plague his imagination for days. The rosewood box was in the bottom drawer, beneath a lace-trimmed cotton night rail.

Straightening, he set the box on the chest of drawers and opened it. Two sheets of paper lay on top of miscellaneous keepsakes. They were folded together and addressed to Selena in a man's bold handwriting. Gabriel smiled when he noticed the unlikely collection of shiny rocks, a feather, a metal toy soldier, and a delicate pressed flower. Did the flower mark the point when the hoyden became a lady? Was it from the bouquet sent by her first admirer?

Unfolding the papers, he held them toward the light.

It was indeed a letter from Nicholas. Though her brother attempted to include cheerful things, a thread of profound sadness connected the tidbits of news and humorous incidents. Gabriel's heart ached for the boy who had become a man so far from home. He was touched by Nick's love for his family, particularly Selena. It would seem they had a special bond, one not hampered even by great distance and years of separation.

Oddly, I have been granted permission to write to you and Father. But stranger still is that I must give no illusion of this privilege to our parents. They must be led to believe the letters were secreted out. When assured they would be delivered, I asked why I had been granted such a boon. The answer that my beautiful sister found favor with Napoleon deeply troubles me.

When you returned to England, I knew something was wrong. Your sorrow on your departure was expected, dear sister, and felt equally by me. But your whispered request for forgiveness at our parting haunts me. I shudder to think what you may have sacrificed in an effort to help me.

But I do not wish to make this a missive of gloom and doom....

He continued in a lighter vein, giving tiny vignettes of life in Verdun and weaving in the remembrance of his school days in such a way no stranger would detect a hidden message. Gabriel would have taken no note of it had Selena not said she thought her brother planned to escape. But another reference gave him pause, and he read it a second time.

I wonder how you are settling in at your new country estate and am reminded of some of your youthful scrapes. Remember the episode with the bull? I heartily recommend no shortcuts across the pasture, but if you are so inclined, take extra care. This time, you might not successfully amuse the monster and lead him on a merry chase. You might be trampled.

Selena had told the story in a much different manner, with her brother drawing the dangerous bull away while she fled to safety. By making no mention of anyone climbing over the wall, he suspected Nick planned to do precisely that. He also thought her brother worried that she was trying to distract the "monster"—an occasional British epithet for Napoleon—and that she might be killed for her foolishness.

He folded the letter and put it back in the box, placing it where he found it beneath her nightgown. Blowing out the candle, he opened the drapes then the window, until the smoke from the snuffed candle dissipated. He closed the window and returned the candle and holder to Selena's sitting room. When he reached the stairway, he heard Miller moving around on the tiled entry and a carriage approaching the front of the house.

Retreating quickly but silently, Gabriel descended the servants' stairs to the main floor, praying he would not run into anyone along the way. He ducked into the kitchen and grabbed a glass of water, then strolled down the hall toward the front of the house. Selena and her aunt entered the front door as he reached the estate office. He met her startled gaze. Unable to muster a smile, he continued to the entryway to greet her. "Did you have a nice evening?"

"Not particularly." She brushed past him, her bearing aloof, and walked to a small sitting room off the main drawing room. Pausing in the doorway, she looked back at him. "Would you please join me? I have something I wish to discuss."

So did he. Unfortunately, he couldn't breathe a word of it.

CHAPTER  Eleven

GABRIEL FOLLOWED SELENA into the sitting room.

"Close the door." She sat down in a gold brocade armchair, laying her fan and reticule on the table beside it.

Gabriel followed her brisk command and sat down across from her on the green satin sofa. "I owe you an apology."

A delicate eyebrow arched. "For which transgression?"

Gabriel frowned. He was only aware of one. Unless she had discovered his deception. He studied her face, noting the anger flashing in her eyes. Had she simmered over his unkind words all evening, or had something else raised her temper to the boiling point? "For my cutting remarks and for embarrassing you. I had no right to speak to you the way I did. I can only plead jealousy."

"You said you had seen me in the midst of my admirers. Where?"

Blast his quick temper and loose tongue! "At a London ball last year. Branderee asked me to escort his sister."

"Because you have known each other for so long."

"Yes." He decided it was safer not to elaborate, for the moment at least.

She studied him with a frown. "I do not know what to think of you, Gabriel Macpherson."

"I hope you will find me a competent estate manager and a good friend."

"You want nothing more?" There was no questioning the accusation this time.

"In truth, Selena, I want a great deal more," he said softly, holding her gaze.

A light blush tinted her cheeks, even as her frown deepened.

"Aunt Augusta met a lady of your acquaintance tonight. Mrs. Norton of Warwickshire."

Double blast!

"Somehow in the conversation, Aunt Augusta mentioned that you were working for me. Imagine her surprise when Mrs. Norton said you had been a guest last year at their country estate, along with the earl of Branderee. But, of course, that makes sense, now that I know you are such close friends. Mrs. Norton did express some bemusement, however, as to why the second son of Viscount Liath, and a man reputed to be quite wealthy in his own right, had sought a position as my estate manager. I must confess to being puzzled by that myself."

Gabriel took a deep breath. He felt as if he were walking through a thick forest with a lone sniper hiding somewhere in the trees. "It is true that when I visited the Nortons, I was more than adequately well-heeled. Since then, I purchased a Highland estate and incurred heavy expenses. The property is now turning a profit, but it also requires the continued investment of that money. I stand to inherit a good portion from an uncle, but I dinna anticipate that to be for some time yet. Since I am quite fond of him, I hope he delays his demise as long as possible."

He shrugged, hoping he appeared nonchalant—but not too much so. "Simply put, I am currently short of funds. I dinna believe in living off my friends or taking a bank loan so I can live in a grand style. I have other investments that should pay off nicely within the year. I prefer to work for wages and live in a more modest fashion until I am flush in the pocket once again."

"A position I would admire if you had not deceived me about who you are. I assume *you* are John Macpherson and the estate you managed is your own?"

"Correct. Now you understand my discomfort when you were so impressed by my accomplishments. I didna like deceiving you, Selena, but I wanted the position. Would you

118

have hired me if you had known the truth about me?"

"I haven't decided."

It was his turn to raise an eyebrow.

She shook her head. "I seriously doubt I would have, though I was desperate. No one else who applied was suitable in the least." She looked at him with resignation. "Why must you be so thorough and efficient?"

"My father taught me well."

She leaned her head against the back of the chair and sighed heavily. "Or so charming?"

"Comes naturally?" he said with a cocky grin.

"I should dismiss you."

"I hope you will no'."

"Give me a good reason not to."

"I see the promise of this land and share your concern for those who work here." He lowered his voice, both in tone and volume, whispering the yearning of his heart. "And I care very much for the lady who owns Fairhaven."

She looked at him. "In what manner?"

"More than a friend."

"A suitor?"

"I would like to be, though my present circumstances prohibit it."

"Yet you court me all the same, with tender glances, honey-eyed words, and warm embraces." Frowning, she took a quick breath. "And passionate kisses."

He nodded in acquiescence. "It is difficult no' to, though if it offends you, I will make a greater effort to behave."

She turned her head, staring across the room, sadness drifting over her features. "It does not offend me," she said quietly. "But for reasons I cannot explain, I will not marry, not you nor anyone else." She met his gaze again, her eyes filled with sorrow. "Yet, selfishly, I covet your friendship, your affection."

"And I yours."

"It can go no further, Gabriel."

"I will accept that for now."

"It would take a miracle for anything more to be possible."

He stood, moving in front of her. Leaning down, he brushed his knuckles across her cheek. "I believe in the Worker of miracles, lass. Put your trust in Jesus to take care of it."

She shook her head. "I cannot."

He straightened, sensing her hurt. "Do you blame God for Nick's detainment?"

"I know God does not cause evil to befall us. But I do not understand why he has allowed it."

"Nor do I. But his ways are no' always our ways. He sees things on a different canvas than we do." He stepped back, not wanting to tower over her. "During battle, I often wondered why the man next to me fell and I was spared. Sometimes there was no sense to it. I could have just as easily been killed, yet the worst wounds I ever suffered were a few bad saber cuts and a bullet across my side."

She gasped and jumped to her feet, touching his arm. "You were shot?"

"Grazed. Nothing more than a new wrinkle." He caressed her cheek again, liking her show of concern. "I did have my nose broken. Not badly, but it left it a wee bit crooked." He grinned. "Which, I've been told by a most discerning lass, only enhances my features. I barely missed being poked by a bayonet on numerous occasions, but somehow always managed to dodge the blade. And a bagpipe helped a few times."

"You were a piper?"

"No. Kiernan was. Before he became Branderee. Most of the time I was trying to protect his hide, since he could no' carry a sword. But occasionally, he saved mine."

She smoothed her fingers up the length of his arm, pressing hard, feeling the muscles through his shirt and coat. She had never touched him in such a way before. It set his senses on edge. He held his breath until she reached the middle of his upper arm, her fingers pausing over the deep indentation there.

Gently tracing the scar, she looked up at him. "And the other wounds?"

"The sword cuts were the worst. A shallow one on my left side. It almost matches the bullet crease on the right. Two on the other arm. Some on each leg." He stopped when he noticed she looked slightly pale. "Most were minor, Selena. No' enough to keep me out of the next fight."

"What was your rank?"

He felt a swell of pride that she would think him officer material, until he remembered that she knew he was part of the aristocracy. No son of a viscount would enter the army as a common soldier. "Captain, Ninety-second Regiment."

"The Gordon Highlanders. Their valor is well known." Her voice was oddly strained.

He nodded, surprised and concerned that she knew the name of the unit. He would expect it of a Scot, but most Englishmen would not have recognized it by regimental number. "They are brave men, each and every one. The best warriors in His Majesty's service." A smile tugged at his lips. "But then, they're Highlanders."

"So they could never be poor fighters." The color drained from her face.

"Never. It's in the blood."

"Please excuse me. I'm quite tired."

He stared at her as she hurried from the room, then shook his head, muttering to himself. "Capskull! Talking to a lady about wounds and blood. 'Tis a wonder she didna faint right here."

He blew out the candles in the sitting room and stopped by the office to do the same there. As he walked to his house, he silently went over the last part of the conversation. Talking about his injuries had disturbed her, but not as badly as when she learned he had been with the Gordons. There were probably several reasons that might cause her such agitation, but one possibility greatly burdened his heart and his mind.

Gabriel sighed heavily and looked up at the heavens. "Ah, lass, has there been Highland blood shed because of you?"

That night, Selena again dreamed of war.

Heads held high, kilts swaying jauntily, Gordon Highlanders marched toward battle to the haunting strains of bagpipes. As in past dreams of other regiments, Selena ran alongside, begging them to turn back, warning them of impending danger. The faceless soldiers kept marching, her cries drowned out by the thunder of cannon in the distance.

This time, one lone officer stepped aside, saber raised. Gabriel looked at her, his expression sorrowful. Then, clenching his jaw in anger, hatred filled his eyes. He turned his back on her, swinging the sword downward, ordering his men into the fight.

Selena sat up with a muted cry, tears pouring down her cheeks. She whispered his name and doubled over in a heartbroken sob.

"God, forgive me. Please forgive me."

Pain and despair flooded her soul. *Gabriel will hate me.* She lay back on the mattress and curled up in a tight ball, weeping for what she had done, for what she had lost. Gradually the sobs eased, though the tears still flowed.

"Lord Jesus, I need a miracle. Please help me find a way to end this nightmare."

The following morning, Gabriel rode to Thornridge with the intention of sending a message to Cameron. When he arrived, he found that his former commander had arrived a few minutes before him.

"I decided I needed a visit to the country. Can only stand London a little at a time, especially in the summer. Have you learned anything?" Cameron asked as they moved into the study. Kiernan and Dominic followed them inside and shut the door.

"Yes. And I'm no' happy about any of it." Gabriel walked over to the empty fireplace, resting his hand on the mantel as the others sat down. He related much of what he had learned about her trip to France, Nick being in prison, Selena meeting the man at the cathedral and receiving the letters from her brother.

Well aware that parts of the letter added to the incriminating evidence against Selena, he had decided the previous night that Cameron's suspicions would be strengthened enough without them. He did not say that she had found favor with Napoleon. Nor did he see any need to add that Nick was worried about her, afraid she was involved with the French in some way.

He moved in front of the desk and leaned against it, watching Cameron. "If Nicholas does manage to escape Verdun, is there anything you can do to help him?"

"We can try. He might go any number of directions, but we do have contacts throughout the empire, people who have no greater love for Napoleon than we do."

"Thank you." Gabriel wished he were free to tell Selena and help ease her mind. "I'll be taking the rest of my clothes with me. Lady Camfield talked to Mrs. Norton last night at the assembly." He met Kiernan's startled gaze. "Your name came up, then mine. Since Selena now knows who I really am, I might as well wear what I want."

"I have purposely stayed home to avoid that very thing." Kiernan shook his head. "So you still have a job?"

"Yes, though Selena was angry because I deceived her." His report given, Gabriel finally sat down, taking a chair next to Cameron. "I think she dreads looking for another estate manager so much she'd rather put up with me. Cameron, I hope you spread the tale that I'm short of funds."

"I did. The information was subtly relayed to the appropriate sources. As we agreed, you are temporarily with pockets to let, due to investment in your estate. Being a proud sort, you willna borrow from friends. If Miss Delaroe or her cohorts investigate you, that is what they will learn regarding your finances."

"Well, at least it will keep the fortune hunters at bay." Kiernan grinned. "Too bad you have to lure women with your money. 'Tis goin' to be a lonely summer."

Gabe smiled lazily. "I'm doin' fine."

Cameron's brows arched. "So you and Miss Delaroe are growing close?"

Gabriel did not like his friend's tone. The major's orders to use whatever means necessary to ferret out Selena's activities still rankled. "We are friends."

"Nothing more? A woman will sooner tell a sweetheart her secrets than a friend. We need to know the name of her contact."

"I willna woo her falsely, Cameron."

The major shrugged. "I thought as much. That is why I have devised another way to learn what we need. At my request, Major Simon Lawrence is visiting the area. I suspect Miss Delaroe will make a concerted effort to befriend him. Undoubtedly he will be enchanted with the lovely lady. When she tempts him with her charms, the good major will let slip that his regiment, along with several others, will be sailing to Sweden where the British regiments and the Swedish army will join forces with Russia against Napoleon."

Gabriel bristled at the suggestion that Selena might tempt the officer with even the hint of sexual favors to gain information.

"We do believe Sweden will soon sign a pact with Russia," Cameron continued, "but we currently have no intention of sending any of our soldiers to join them. Your assignment, Gabriel, is to watch her closely and see to whom she passes the information. Do no' confront either of them. We dinna want them to know, or even suspect, that we are on to them. In fact, it will be beneficial if the information moves on up the line. Tell us who he is, and we will handle it from there."

"What will you do about Selena?"

"Nothing for now. We want to catch as many in the stream as possible. She will lead us to a larger fish. He will lead us to an even larger one and so on." Cameron stood and walked across the room. He turned back to Gabriel, his expression concerned. "It is just as well you are no' wooing her, lad. If she is indeed working for the French, though she be but a minnow, she will be punished along with the others."

Gabriel shot to his feet, clenching his fists, and took a step toward the major. "Even if she is a pawn, forced into helping them to keep her brother alive? You will use her as bait, then abandon her? There is no justice in punishing her."

Cameron shifted his weight, preparing for an attack. "What of the men she has betrayed? What if British lives have been lost because of her?"

Kiernan stood, moving between them. "You said before that you did no' believe she had passed on anything substantial, though she may have confirmed something Napoleon learned from other sources. Do you now have reason to think otherwise?"

Out of the corner of his eye, Gabriel noted that Dominic had also risen. He forced himself to uncurl his fingers. Coming to blows with his old commander would solve nothing.

"No." Cameron watched Gabriel closely. "But the Foreign Office does no' view treason lightly."

"The Foreign Office is made up of men," Kiernan said. "Hopefully reasonable ones."

Cameron inclined his head. "One can only hope. I canna

make any promises. But I must have one from you, Gabriel. I want your word that you willna give her any indication we are aware of her activities."

When Gabe hesitated, Cameron's eyes narrowed. "If I canna trust you, lad, I'll have someone else watch her. Someone much less sympathetic."

Gabriel suspected Cameron already had someone watching her. Perhaps even watching both of them. If he did not cooperate, the major was not above having him trussed up like a Christmas goose and carted off to a London tenement until they caught everyone they were after. Gabe nodded curtly. "You have my word that I willna reveal anything about your investigation."

Cameron nodded. "I'm glad to hear you have no' lost your good sense."

Gabe wanted to wrap his fingers around his friend's throat and shake him. Instead, gathering his composure like a shield, he walked to the door. "I must return to Fairhaven. We are moving a young woman and her son from the village to a cottage on the estate. Her husband was killed recently in the fighting. Selena is giving her a home, rent-free, for as long as she needs it. And she's hiring the woman as a seamstress." He tossed Cameron a challenging look. "Oddly kind for such a wicked person."

Gabriel hurried upstairs to collect the rest of his things, wondering if Cluny Macpherson's cave was still inhabitable. Could he make it comfortable enough for Selena to share it with him? Or would they be better off taking a slow boat to China?

It didn't matter to him what they did. He only wanted to keep Selena safe, and he didn't know how long he could do it in England.

CHAPTER *Twelve*

ON THE DAY OF THE BREAKFAST PARTY, the rich woodwork, furniture, and floors of Fairhaven gleamed with a soft luster. Windows, mirrors, and crystal sparkled in the afternoon light. Bouquets of roses and pinks adorned each room of the house, filling it with the sweet fragrance of summer. The grounds were weeded and trimmed to perfection. No plant dared display a dead or drooping flower.

Every comfort was considered and provided. Cushioned chairs were scattered across the grounds beneath the shade trees, and numerous footmen, some hired only for the occasion, circulated throughout the crowd offering glasses of wine and punch. The company all arrived before three. By five, they had consumed the vast quantities and array of cold foods laid out on the tables—meats, cheeses, breads, salads, fruits, puddings, and desserts.

A small orchestra played on the south side of the house where a large, blue-striped open tent provided shade for dancing on the lawn. Archery targets were set up on the far side of the grounds, with the gardener and his men assisting the participants as needed.

Under Lady Camfield's tutelage over the years, Selena had become a seasoned and confident hostess. Today, however, an unsettling anxiety plagued her. Her nemesis lurked somewhere on the grounds, laughing and talking with the other guests, eating the food, listening to the music, watching her. She tried to concentrate on her company, moving from group to group to ensure all enjoyed themselves, but thoughts of Bonham were never far from the surface.

Few of the invitations had been declined, and most of those only because the recipients were out of town. At first, many of the men in her usual entourage flocked around her, but Selena sent them off to other pursuits, pointing out her need to see to all her guests. Young Mr. Jones was there with Miss Potter, the pretty young blond he had mentioned at the assembly. Oliver Hopkins proudly escorted shy Miss Brown with the lovely eyes. The young woman appeared to be quite taken with him, which seemed to have boosted his confidence to new levels.

Pausing to skim the crowd, Selena's gaze came to rest on Gabriel. She had grown accustomed to seeing him in a kilt, since he had worn his Highland clothes most of the week. Today he wore buff trousers, the dark green coat, and a striped light green waistcoat. She admired him in the kilt; it showed off his handsome legs and gave him a bit of swagger. But the Spanish fly green coat was her favorite. He looked even more dashing than ever now that he had shaved off his mustache. She was dying to ask him why.

Her aunt commandeered him for the moment to keep her company as she watched the dancing. He said something that made her laugh and swat his arm with her fan. Seconds later, he looked over Lady Camfield's head and met Selena's gaze. The music and the conversations around her faded into a low, melodious hum, and it seemed as if they were alone in the garden. Her heartbeat quickened as he caressed her with his eyes, his expression tender and proud. She could almost hear him whisper praise on a job well done.

Then someone spoke to him, and he looked away, entering the conversation with a cordial smile. Throughout the afternoon, he had handled himself with ease and grace. The number of people, including several earls and a duke, who seemed to know him fairly well had surprised her. More important, they showed him genuine respect. How had she ever thought he might merely move on the fringes of Society?

"It is a lovely party, Miss Delaroe. My husband tells me Fairhaven has never looked so grand."

At the soft Scottish voice, Selena turned and smiled at

Dominic Thorne's pretty young wife.

"Thank you. I do not know how it looked years ago, but it has been sorely in need of repair since I inherited it." Even at forty, Thorne was an exceedingly handsome man. At one time his liaisons with women had been so numerous that most people quit remarking on them. He had long preferred to keep company with beautiful widows, so everyone had been stunned the previous summer when they learned he had married the earl of Branderee's sister, a woman half his age. Seeing them together, no one could doubt it was a love match.

"My people have been working frantically all week cleaning up the mess left from the redecorating. I've been blessed with wonderful employees, including your friend Mr. Macpherson."

"I'm surprised you still consider him a blessing." Mrs. Thorne's topaz eyes twinkled.

Selena laughed, impressed with her honesty and sense of humor. "I must admit I wanted to throttle him at one point. But he is such an exceedingly good manager, I could not bring myself to toss him out on his ear."

"I'm glad you didna. He is a wee bit dense on occasion, but he has a good heart."

Selena glanced at Gabriel. "I believe you are correct on both counts."

"I shall take great delight in telling him you think he is dense." Dominic's wife laughed, drawing Gabriel's attention in their direction.

Selena felt momentary jealousy of their closeness until she realized he wasn't looking at Jeanette Thorne, but at her. His warm smile, shaded with a hint of mischievous amusement, did strange things to her heart. She reluctantly dragged her gaze away from him. "Gabriel mentioned that your brother is his lifelong friend. So I assume you have known him forever, too?"

"Yes, though he and Kiernan were off fighting Napoleon far too long. They returned right after Father died. A short time later, Kiernan unexpectedly inherited the title. Mother is part of the gentry, but we had never really moved about in Society other than attending dinners and occasional parties at Gabe's parents' home. When we came to England, we would have been lost without his guidance."

"He does do well. It still puzzles me that I never met him before he came to Fairhaven."

"He spent twelve years with the Gordon Highlanders. Last year was the first time since joining the regiment that he had been in England during the Season. He came with us to introduce us to Society, but we all returned to Scotland early."

Selena had heard that Jeanette had been kidnapped during her first visit to England and that the family returned to Scotland soon after her rescue. "Is Gabriel's estate near yours?"

"We are on the coast, no' too far from Elgin. He lives farther inland in the mountains. The journey between our homes can be made in a long, hard day's ride on horseback, but by carriage, it takes almost two days in good weather. One does no' know how long to plan if it is raining.

"Many people consider where we live as part of the Highlands. But we were raised near Loch Laggan, so to us, the true Highlands are the mountains. Gabe's estate, Inshirra, is on the River Spey near Loch Insh. His lands run from the river up to the lower elevations of the Cairngorm Mountains. It is a beautiful setting. He has made some improvements to the main house, but no' a great many. He said he might as well wait. When he marries, his wife will want to redecorate." Mrs. Thorne laughed. "He declared that it's an inborn trait."

"I expect he is right." How little she knew about him. Had he already chosen a wife? Perhaps a pretty Highland neighbor or some elegant Edinburgh lady? *He cannot be promised to another.* Though it was the cry of her heart, she also believed he was too honorable a man to woo her if he were already tied to someone else. Still, men were so unpredictable.

Selena took a deep breath, hoping she hid her tension. She

scanned the grounds, absently noting that all seemed well. The earl of Branderee, his wife, and Dominic were returning from the archery area. When they noticed her talking to Mrs. Thorne, they changed direction, walking slowly toward them.

"Has he chosen a wife?" She was pleased that the question sounded only casually interested. Almost.

"I believe he has."

At Jeanette's serious tone, Selena's heart sank. If she could never have him—and she could not—why did it hurt so badly to lose him? "Someone he met in Scotland?"

"No. Someone he saw at a ball in London last year. Though he never spoke to the lady during that visit, he said she has lingered in his thoughts ever since."

When Selena worked up the courage to look at her, she was surprised at the gentle understanding in the other woman's expression. "Has he made his feelings known to her since he came back to England?"

"I do no' know. He is a fine, caring man, Miss Delaroe. And a lonely one. When he gives his heart, it will be with total commitment. I hope he is loved in equal measure."

"He deserves nothing less." If only it could be so simple. "Here comes your family. If your husband's smile were any brighter, we'd need to shield our eyes. He is obviously a very happily married man."

Mrs. Thorne grinned. "Who would have ever thought such a thing possible?"

Selena laughed. "Not I. But I'm glad he is. Despite his reputation in the *ton*, I always found him to be a perfect gentleman. After I inherited Fairhaven, I learned what a kind and generous man he is. Everyone in the area thinks very highly of him. And I know Gabriel appreciates his advice."

"Did I hear my name mentioned?" Gabriel surprised her by leaning over her shoulder.

When she jumped, he chuckled and stepped beside her. How long had he been standing there?

131

"Perhaps I should have joined you sooner." He grinned at Dominic's wife. "What have you two been talking about?"

Selena held her breath.

"What a wonderful person my husband is. And how I helped make him that way." Mrs. Thorne smiled at Selena. "Though we did talk about you, which, of course, is what you are wondering. Miss Delaroe agrees that you are a bit dense on occasion."

Gabriel laughed. "I dinna know whether to be glad or sad."

"Why would you be glad about such a thing?" asked Selena.

"You dinna think I'm a total dunce. Only part of the time." His smile faded as he looked into her eyes. "For that, I am grateful."

Selena wanted to wrap her arms around him and tell him what she really thought of him. "I also agreed that you have a good heart."

"That is comforting."

Mrs. Thorne eased away to meet her husband, leaving them alone for a minute or two.

"Why did you shave off your mustache?" Selena asked softly.

"I canna have my lady rubbing off my kisses, now, can I?"

His lady. How she wished that could be true. "She would never wipe away your kisses. They are far too wonderful. But the tickle was distracting."

"Precisely why the mustache had to go." He leaned slightly closer. "When I next kiss you, nothing will interfere."

Selena unfurled her floral silk fan, fanning them both.

Gabriel chuckled quietly, then greeted the others as they joined them. "Who won?"

Branderee and Dominic glanced at each other and grinned.

"Mariah," the earl said. "It was close. I almost tied her."

"But I thought—" Selena caught herself. Some women did not like to speak of pregnancy in mixed company.

"You're right. I am in the family way." Lady Mariah smiled at Selena, instantly putting her at ease. "Up until a week ago, I was dreadfully ill. But now I feel perfectly well."

"I was so excited about her improved health, I didna pay enough attention to my own shots." Branderee smiled at his wife, love quite evident in his tender expression.

"Well, I have no such excuse." Dominic smiled lazily. "I've never had the knack for archery. I only went along so the other one who lost would not feel so bad."

"And I suspect you both graciously let me win." Lady Mariah looked around the grounds. "Your party is quite the hit, Miss Delaroe. I hope you feel justifiably pleased."

"Reasonably so. With any social function, there is a great deal of relief mixed in. It did not rain. No one complained about the food. The musicians are more than competent, and no one has fallen into the pond."

Branderee slanted Gabriel a glance. "So far. If things grow dull, let me know. I'll throw Gabe in."

"You and who else?" Gabriel's eyes twinkled merrily.

"Behave, you two," chided Lady Mariah with a smile. "Pay them no mind, Miss Delaroe. They are grown men. Most of the time they act like it."

Selena laughed, though a bittersweet ache touched her heart. She envied them their close friendship, the depth of affection they all seemed to share with one another. She had been so caught up with her place in society, and even more so with trying to find a way to gain Nick's freedom, that she had never developed any such relationships, other than with Marietta. Her maid was her one true friend of long standing. It seemed a sad commentary on her life.

"Well, you have to admit we are no' boring," Gabriel said.

"You could never be boring, Gabriel." Selena responded automatically, speaking the words of her heart. When she caught the look that passed between him and Branderee, she realized what she'd said. Her cheeks grew hot.

"Now you've done it." Lady Mariah laughed. "He will have such a big head, there will be no living with him."

I'd like to try. Selena looked at Branderee. "Perhaps you'll have to throw him in the pond after all."

The earl shook his head, his eyes dancing. "He'd drown. Sink head first."

"I think it's time to find the punch bowl before we put Miss Delaroe to the blush again." Dominic held out an arm to his wife. "Perhaps you can come to dinner next week, Miss Delaroe, when you've recovered from the party. We'll keep it small, though we might invite Gabriel if you two are still speaking by then."

"I would enjoy it." She glanced up at Gabriel. "And I believe I could tolerate his company for the evening."

"We shall look forward to it," Mrs. Thorne said.

The earl and his lady smiled and quietly agreed, then walked away with the other couple.

"I wish we were alone right now," Gabriel said, casually looking around at the crowd as if they were talking about the weather. "I'd like to check out my theory."

"Theory?" Selena smiled and nodded politely to a couple of elderly ladies looking their way.

"That you are rather fond of me."

She met his gaze and saw her longing mirrored in his eyes. "I am. Though I'm not sure *fond* is the appropriate word."

His expression subtly changed, growing more intense. "What is the right word, sweetheart?"

She treasured the endearment, hiding it forever in her heart. She should look away. But she couldn't. "Adore." *Love. Cherish.*

For a heartbeat, even two, she thought he might kiss her right then and there. "And if you don't walk away right now, everyone will know it," she whispered.

"Would that be so bad?"

With Bonham watching, it could prove life threatening. "Yes."

His expression hardened and he could not hide the hurt in

134

his eyes. With a curt nod he turned on his heel, walking briskly toward his house.

It took all her willpower not to run after him.

CHAPTER *Thirteen*

EARLIER IN THE DAY, SELENA HAD TALKED briefly to Major Lawrence but put off attempting to spend time alone with him. In less than an hour evening would be upon them, but most of her guests remained. She was certain Bonham was among them. Knowing he watched her every move, she could avoid Lawrence no longer.

The major was a handsome man, tall and athletically built, with dark hair and eyes. Talking with a handful of gentlemen, he stood near her aunt and some of her cronies. Selena joined her aunt and her friends, exchanging pleasantries. He glanced her way, but she pretended to give her full attention to one of the elderly ladies. When he looked at her again a few minutes later, she met his gaze and smiled. It was all the encouragement he needed, though he waited a few minutes to break away from his conversation.

"Good afternoon, ladies." Lawrence nodded to Selena and bowed to the older women. He chatted with them a few minutes, paying her aunt and each of her friends compliments. Then he turned to Selena with a smile. "Might I spirit you away for a walk, Miss Delaroe?"

"Of course." She took his arm and excused herself from the other ladies.

He adroitly guided her away from most of the guests. They strolled down a path edged with multicolored carnations on one side and pinks on the other. Their sweet fragrance filled the air. "You have an excellent garden."

"Thank you. I must give most of the credit to my gardener, though I did suggest the carnations and pinks. I love their scent and bright colors."

"But they cannot compete with you. You would be pretty in a grain sack, but in that color, you are quite striking."

Selena knew the purplish blue silk dress was one of her most flattering. The short sleeves and square neckline showed enough skin to be alluring while staying quite modest. She wanted to attract the major, but not too much so. "Thank you, though I hope I never have to test your statement and wear a grain sack."

He laughed softly. "If you had one made into a ball gown, you would start a new fad."

Selena shook her head. "Even I cannot accomplish such a feat. I apologize for being unable to spend more time with you today."

"I am flattered that you would want to."

"I have a great respect and admiration for our military men. Without your heroic efforts, we might now be citizens of the French empire instead of free Britons."

"There is no need for worry, Miss Delaroe. We will never allow Napoleon to defeat us." He covered her hand with his as they walked toward the archery range. "Shall we give the bow and arrows a go? At one time I did fairly well at the game."

"I am no good at it, sir, but I would enjoy watching you shoot."

The major laughed quietly. "You may not be impressed."

Selena stood to one side as he took the equipment from the gardener. He carefully fit the arrow into the bow, pulled the string taut, and let it fly. It struck the target a fraction of an inch inside the outer edge. When the major groaned and made a face, she laughed. "At least you hit the target. I'm certain you will do better on the next one."

He flashed her a devastating smile. "With such encouragement, how can I do poorly?" His next shot hit the target several inches from the edge. Each successive arrow moved closer toward the center, until on the last one he hit the bull's eye.

"Wonderful, sir." Selena clapped her hands in approval. "You are quite proficient."

"I usually am." He smiled and leaned closer, murmuring, "At many things."

Humble, too, she thought. She did not look forward to being alone with him, though it was necessary.

"Now, my dear, it is your turn."

Selena smiled and shook her head. "I think not."

"I will assist you. I expect all you need is a little guidance in lining up the arrow within the bow."

She knew his offer was mainly a ploy to stand close and put his arms around her. With luck she might actually improve her aim, but she doubted he would be overly concerned with that minor detail. A few months earlier she might not have turned down such a handsome man's assistance. Now she only wanted Gabe's arms around her, whether it be to shoot an arrow or in a warm embrace.

"I think I shall pass." She made her tone and smile as gracious as she could. She nodded to another couple walking across the grass. "I'll leave archery to others. I'm far better at feeding the ducks." She turned to one of the assistants. "Do you have any bread left?"

"Yes, miss." He removed a small loaf of bread from a box on a nearby table and handed it to her. "'Tis the last one."

"I hope they're still hungry." She started slowly down the path toward the pond.

"No worry there." The servant nodded in a shallow bow.

The major handed the bow to the man and quickly joined her.

"What part of England do you call home, Major Lawrence?"

"Kent. I spent some time with my family before coming here. Though it was good to see them, I tend to grow restless when I am confined to one place too long."

"Ready for a new adventure?" She smiled up at him.

"Always. What do you have in mind?"

She tore off a large chunk of bread and sent him a lightly flirtatious look. "Why, fending off wild animals, of course."

He laughed and held out his hand for the bread. "I daresay I've wrestled with more dangerous creatures."

138

"Have you been in many battles?"

"All over the world, it seems. But I'm a career soldier, so that is to be expected. It has enabled me to visit many places I otherwise would never have ventured. Egypt, Malta, Spain, Portugal, and many other countries."

"Must you return to the fighting soon?" They reached the pond, and the ducks immediately swam across it to meet them.

He chuckled at the rapidly advancing, quacking armada. "Perhaps in about two seconds."

"They won't attack us, though they occasionally get quite rough among themselves. I'm afraid we spoil them dreadfully. I enjoy their antics, and my gardener has made pets of them all." She tore off small pieces of bread and tossed them into the water. The major followed suit.

They laughed at the squabbles and skirmishes that broke out. He moved to one side, distracting most of the birds while Selena made certain one little crippled fellow received his share. After the food disappeared, the ducks waited a few minutes then swam away.

"Fickle creatures." Selena smiled as she brushed bread crumbs from her hands.

"Well, they do know which side their bread is buttered on." The major laughed when she rolled her eyes, then settled his hand at the small of her back, gently urging her to walk to the other end of the pond. It would take them to the edge of the forest.

Now came the part Selena most dreaded, trying to learn the information needed to betray him. Her heartbeat quickened with apprehension, even as she fervently hoped he would not reveal anything important. "Do you think the war will last much longer?"

"I do not see how it can end quickly. Napoleon's forces are still too strong. He holds too much power in the empire." He offered her his arm when the ground became mildly uneven.

"I heard a snippet of conversation earlier as I passed some

of the gentlemen. Something about Sweden possibly joining forces with Russia?"

"Many believe they will soon form an alliance, unless something arises to thwart it."

"Is it likely that the alliance would fall apart so quickly?"

"No, but given the unpredictable nature of kings and politicians, one can never be certain the agreements will hold even after the papers are signed." They reached the edge of the woods. Major Lawrence guided her down another path through the elms until they were sheltered from view. "I leave Worcester tomorrow."

"So soon? Must you return to your unit right away?" She turned toward him, studying his face, alert to subtle changes in his expression.

"Within the week." He caught her hand, lightly caressing the back of it through her glove. "We sail in a fortnight."

"Back to the fighting?" She did not need to pretend, for her concern was real. She hated to see anyone go off to battle.

"Yes." He tugged her toward him and put his arm around her.

Caught by surprise, Selena placed her hand on his chest, pressing firmly to keep him from thinking she would easily do his bidding. "Where do you go?"

"I cannot tell you."

Her eyes widened. "It is a secret mission?"

He smoothed her cheek with the back of his knuckles in much the same way Gabriel had the night of the assembly. Though his touch was not unpleasant, it did not evoke excitement or yearning in her heart as Gabriel's had.

"Do I detect a note of worry?"

"Of course."

He smiled into her eyes. "You are so lovely. I deeply regret having only met you today. It is my hope that when I return we might see each other again."

"You are welcome to call at Fairhaven any time."

"Said with the politeness of a gently bred lady. But I shall remember your invitation. May I also have a kiss to take with me?"

It was a simple thing, a gift to give a man who might soon lose his life. She had easily enough complied with such requests before. This time, with the memory of Gabriel's touch burning in her mind and heart, she found it exceedingly difficult. "I hardly know you."

"True, but is it such a huge thing to ask for a memory to keep me warm on cold, dark nights very far from home?"

What gammon! She was tempted to tell him he was doing it up a bit strong. Still, she had to try to find out where he was going. *It is just a kiss. It means nothing.* Then why did self-loathing flood her soul as she slid her hand around his neck and tilted up her face?

Triumph flickered through his eyes as he lowered his head, kissing her with great expertise.

The knowledge that she probably meant little to him did not ease her despair. Selena pressed her eyelids tightly closed to hold back tears of remorse. When the major lifted his head and she opened her eyes, a tear slid down her cheek.

"What is this?" he asked with a frown, gently brushing away the moisture. "You weep for me?"

"Yes." For him. And all the others. For Gabriel and a love that could never be shared.

"I do not wish to remember your beautiful face filled with sorrow."

"But such a mission must be dangerous."

"Quite so. But I do not go alone."

"Thank goodness you will have a few others with you." She watched her fingers as she toyed with the gold cord on his uniform coat.

He smoothed his hand up and down her arm. "Not a few. The whole regiment. Several regiments, in fact."

She frowned, looking up at him. "How can you keep it

secret if so many are going? They will be hard to miss."

He chuckled softly. "True. In due time, the enemy will work it out. But we don't want to let them in on our plans too soon." He leaned closer. "Now, one more to send me off to Sweden."

Her mind racing, Selena responded absently to his kiss. Why would Britain send forces to Sweden now? Britain was not officially allied with Sweden or her potential partner, Russia. Unless the treaties had been reached in secret.

When he raised his head, she forced herself to slowly open her eyes instead of staring at him in amazement. "Sweden?"

He touched her lips with his fingertip. "We will be joining with the Swedish and Russian forces in an attack against the French. Remember, it is not common knowledge. I only tell you so that when you think of me—and I hope you do—you will know where I am. The War Office believes a combined force can defeat Napoleon on that front. It will not end the war right away, but it could make a significant difference."

"Then I wish you Godspeed, sir. And pray that the Lord will have his hand upon you and keep you safe."

Seething, Gabriel watched Selena and the major from the shelter of the woods. He was close enough to hear their quiet discussion. *Take your hands off her!* He wanted to beat Lawrence to a pulp. The major had no right to kiss her. He was only there to pass on information, to set a trap in which to snare her.

Rage, frustration, and sorrow almost overwhelmed Gabe. Listening to the conversation confirmed the suspicions surrounding Selena. She was with the officer to learn his secrets so she might betray her country.

He understood her reason for working for the French. He did not approve, but he knew how much she loved her brother. If she had used another way to pry the information from Lawrence, Gabe might even have found some means to help save her pretty neck. But this he could not tolerate.

How could she dismiss his love so callously, mocking him

by kissing another man? Not once, but twice!

And she said she adored him. *Balderdash!*

The woman was a consummate actress. Professing her affection for him one moment, then a few hours later kissing another man, even shedding a tear on his behalf. It was one big performance to her, a part she played to perfection. And she had called the ducks fickle. She had it down to an art. The woman didn't have an ounce of integrity. She seduced a man with her siren's song until he did not know right from wrong.

Unwilling to see what other tokens of gratitude she gave the major for so heroically saving England, Gabriel turned away. Moving with a stealth he'd learned tracking game in the Highland forests and perfected while spying on French encampments, he faded into the woods.

He kept walking, well out of anyone's sight or hearing. Picking up a stick, he snapped the tiny branch into a dozen pieces. What had happened to him? He was normally easygoing, quick to laugh and slow to anger. Yet since Cameron first mentioned Selena, he had wanted to break more jaws and smash more noses than he had in the whole time since returning home from the war. Right that second, he wouldn't mind throttling a raven-haired beauty, either. He glanced around and spotted another stick. It met the same fate as the first one while he trudged farther into the forest.

If this was love, he wanted no part of it.

CHAPTER *Fourteen*

A FEW MINUTES BEFORE MIDNIGHT, Gabriel stepped outside to take a look around before retiring. Checking the area was a habit left over from his military days, and one he seldom disregarded. He did not expect to see anything unusual. The manor and all the outer houses were dark, the occupants most likely in bed, exhausted from the extra work involved with the party.

Therefore, he was greatly surprised to see Selena walking briskly toward the northern portion of the grounds. The full moon and cloudless sky illuminated the yard with soft, clear light, so there was no mistaking her identity. For a brief instant, he was tempted to call out to her but decided against it.

She was not taking a leisurely stroll. She had a definite purpose in mind.

Of course, he had no reason to care what she was doing. He had washed his hands of her. Still…He frowned. He did have an obligation to Cameron to keep an eye on her.

Grumbling silently about once again slinking along in the shadows like some beast of prey, Gabriel followed Selena on a parallel course. He bent low, keeping behind a long, curving line of shrubs and bushes. When he saw her destination, a large grove of oak trees on the northern perimeter of the gardens, concern swept him. He'd expected her to make contact with the French agent within a few days, but surely the man wouldn't dare meet her here?

He pressed his lips together as another thought crossed his mind. Perhaps she had agreed to a moonlight rendezvous with the major, eager for more of his amorous attention.

The first option worried him. The second made him furious. Clenching his jaw, he silently moved closer. He kept to the edge of the trees, walking at an angle to where she entered the woods. With only moonlight to guide him, he could not go through the undergrowth without snapping twigs or sending rabbits and mice scurrying noisily for safety.

Selena made her way a short distance into the grove, stopping near an old oak embraced for decades by honeysuckle. The vine circled the trunk and entwined the branches, perfuming the air with its sweet fragrance. Gabe knew the spot well. On more than one occasion he had paused there during a walk. He carefully eased past a few trees until he was hidden in the shadows and had a clear view of Selena.

If she was meeting someone, he would be close enough to hear their conversation.

She stood still for a moment, peering into the darkened recesses of the woods in front of her and on each side. Then she slowly turned, scanning the area behind her. She shifted a small bag from her left hand to the right. When it jingled with the movement, she quickly clenched her hand tightly around it.

Coins? Why would she bring money to someone in the middle of the night? Gabriel sensed her fear. He prayed that whomever she was meeting would not detect it also.

Suddenly an oddly shaped creature moved from behind the vine-covered tree trunk. Gabe almost called out a warning before he realized it was a man wearing a black cloak and a large, brimmed hat with a feather, reminiscent of the style a century or two earlier.

"You are quite punctual, my dear."

Selena jumped and spun around at the soft, raspy voice. The man stood only a few yards away from her. Gabe shifted for a better view, but the man's face was hidden in the darkness.

"I did not want you to think I was not coming." Gabe noted with approval that Selena's voice was steady.

"Good. I don't like to be kept waiting." The man stepped into the moonlight, the shiny black cloak swirling around him. He wore a black mask over his eyes. Gabriel frowned. He was a few inches shorter and much thinner than the man she met at the cathedral. "Lovely party."

"Would you have preferred a masquerade, Bonham?"

He laughed quietly. "Do you like my disguise? I thought it appropriate for such a bright night."

His voice no longer held its raspy tone, but it did not sound familiar to Gabriel. Nor did the name hold any significance.

Selena tensed and stared at the man, as if she were taken by surprise at the change in his voice. Could it be that she didn't know his identity? Perhaps, yet she had obviously expected to meet him here. Had he worn the disguise to keep others from recognizing him in case he was seen, or was it to keep Selena guessing? If that was the case, then why would he speak in what seemed to be his natural voice?

"I am impressed with Fairhaven," the pretend cavalier said. "You have done wonders with it." He laughed again and walked around her, lifting the front edge of the cloak and trailing it down her arm.

Gabriel's heart began to pound. He prayed she had planned some means of escape. Why had she met the scoundrel in such a secluded place?

"You look puzzled, my dear. Ah, yes, the voice. Familiar, is it?"

"Yes…but I cannot put a face with it."

Bonham dramatically swept his hand through the air and placed it on his heart. A gold ring on his little finger glimmered faintly in the soft light. "I am crushed that you do not recognize me."

"If we were in a more normal situation, I expect I could."

Gabriel detected a slight quiver in her voice.

"Perhaps. Though I doubt it." The man languidly trailed one finger down her arm.

Gabriel clenched his fists. Had he only imagined her shudder?

"You see, my dear, I am two people. One the *ton* sees. The

other, my true self, I only reveal to a select few. It is a game I have played since childhood. It has been infinitely amusing, and at times, greatly beneficial."

"Then you are not offended that I do not know you?"

That's it, sweetheart. Be gentle. Dinna provoke him.

Bonham tipped his head to one side, pondering her question. "I should be. I thought I meant something to you."

"I expect you do, only as you said, you are a different person in my everyday world."

Good answer, lass.

"True. Then I shall take no offense. What did you learn from the major?"

"Very little. He said he was leaving Worcester tomorrow and would join his unit within the week. They sail in a fortnight, but he would not tell me where they were bound. He said it was a secret."

Gabriel frowned. Why did she withhold the information about the regiments going to Sweden? She played a dangerous game, but he was proud of her. Cameron had ill-judged her.

"You disappoint me, Selena. Have you suddenly forgotten how to persuade a man to confide in you?"

"I tried. I even shed a few tears and let him kiss me, though it was most distasteful."

Gabriel started at this. She certainly had not seemed to mind Lawrence's kiss, but there was no reason for her to lie about it.

"Did you show your distaste?"

"Of course not. That would have been unkind."

Gabe looked forward to seeing Lawrence's face when he told him that she had kissed him out of duty to her mission and pretended to enjoy it out of kindness. That would take the popinjay down a peg or two.

"And it would have ended all chance of learning anything else. He has been in the army a long time. He is too well trained."

"And you are not trained well enough!" A bird near Gabriel took flight at Bonham's raised voice. Bonham quickly looked around, then gripped Selena's arm, propelling her away from Gabriel's hiding place. "Walk in that direction, my dear. We do not want anyone to see our little tryst."

Blast! Gabriel could not follow without revealing his presence. By carefully moving a few steps he could still see them, but he could only hear part of their conversation.

Bonham said something, and Selena shook her head.

"…dare you?" he demanded.

"…safer if I don't know who you are."

He removed his hat and tossed it aside. Selena edged away, but he grabbed her arm and roughly hauled her against him.

"No!" Selena swung the bag of coins, hitting him in the side of the head. Swearing, he released her, taking a step back.

Gabriel could take no more. "Selena, *run!*"

She threw the bag at Bonham's face. As he blocked it with his hands, she lifted her skirt and petticoat above her ankles and darted into the woods. Judging by her direction, Gabe knew she would intersect a trail, one with which they both were familiar. Though it was somewhat winding, it would take her toward the house. He hoped she wasn't too terrified to miss the path. Gabriel raced around the periphery of the trees. Though he had farther to go, the smoother ground allowed him to move faster than if he went through the grove.

He could hear Bonham running after her, crashing through the undergrowth. Selena burst into the clearing well ahead of her pursuer, but he quickly closed the distance between them. Gabriel ran as hard as he could, trying to intercept the other man, but he couldn't make it. Bonham grabbed Selena by the shoulders and shoved her to the side, throwing her to the ground directly in front of Gabriel. Her startled cry broke off at the hard impact.

Gabriel leaped over her, skidding to a halt, and spun around to look at her as Bonham ran toward the manor house.

She didn't move.

Terrified, he dropped to his knees beside her, checking her neck. There was no indication that it was broken. Turning her gently, he saw a small cut on her forehead. Blood trickled across her temple. The cut did not appear to be deep, but she wasn't breathing. He rolled her onto her back, praying she'd only had the wind knocked out of her. "Selena, breathe. Come on, love, take a breath." Holding her head, he slid his other arm beneath her and lifted her torso, arching her back.

Seconds later, she gasped.

"That's it, sweetheart, take another one." As she drew in air, he looked up to see a man on horseback leading another horse come around the side of the manor house, toward Bonham. He jumped onto the second steed, and they sped down the lane toward the main road. It would be useless to try to follow them. Gabriel turned his attention back to Selena, relieved to see her breathing deeply. "Are you injured?"

She groaned. "Everything hurts."

"You took a hard fall. Does any place hurt particularly bad?"

"My head." With a struggle she sat up, leaning against his chest. She touched her forehead with her fingertips. "I'm bleeding."

"I dinna think it is serious." He braced one foot on the ground, scooped her up in his arms, and stood. "But we'll go take a look." She rested her head against his shoulder as he carried her to his house. It was closer—and private. He did not want anyone to see her like this. Nor did he want anyone to interrupt the questions he intended to ask.

Still holding her, he unfastened the door, kicking it open. He laid her on the blue-striped sofa, tucking a pillow beneath her head as she leaned against the padded, curved arm. After shutting the door, he lit a candle and set it on the table near her head and examined the wound. "It is barely more than a scratch. Has already stopped bleeding, but I'll clean it." He ran his gaze over her. "Are you bleeding anywhere else?"

"Nothing else feels like a scrape or cut. I'll probably be one giant bruise tomorrow." She plucked a leaf from her sleeve and a twig from her skirt. "I'm a sight."

"Yes, you are." He was torn between wanting to hold and soothe her and wanting to yell at her for putting herself in such a dangerous situation. Bending down, he brushed another leaf from her hair. "But at least he dinna hurt you as he could have."

"I'm an idiot for meeting him there."

"I'll no' disagree with that." He walked into his bedchamber to the washstand. Pouring water from the pitcher into the basin, he brought it, a washcloth, and a towel out to the parlor. He set them on the table, dipped the cloth in the water, and wrung it out. "You cast yourself into the briars in more ways than one."

She avoided his gaze by closing her eyes.

He washed the small cut, then pressed the cloth into her hand. "You might feel better if you wash your face. It's covered with dirt."

She wiped her face and her arms with the cloth, scrubbing harder than she needed to, as if she were trying to wash off the feeling of the other man's touch.

"Easy, lass." He took the washcloth from her and tossed it into the basin. After handing her the towel, he sat in a nearby chair where he could see her face clearly. "Who is he, Selena?"

"I don't know." She caught her lower lip between her teeth and searched his face. Frowning, she sighed heavily. "He calls himself Bonham. He has been blackmailing me since I returned from France last year."

"How much?"

"One hundred guineas a month." The equivalent of one hundred and five pounds, more money than many people earned in a year. "He has accomplices in France who will hurt Nick if I do not pay him regularly."

"You are certain of that?"

"He knew all about Nick being in Bitche, including how ill I found him. He described Nick's house in Verdun, right down to the furniture. He named his friends and his typical routine. I did not tell Bonham any of it. How else would he know if he does not have people there?"

"Perhaps he was also a détenu."

"If he was, he came home near the same time I returned to England. He contacted me a week after I arrived here at Fairhaven."

"How?"

Fear flashed through her eyes before she looked away. "By letter. He instructed me to meet a hooligan named Ellaby at Worcester Cathedral and give him my first payment. Later, when I went to London for the Season, the meeting place changed to Westminster. Until tonight, Ellaby was always the one who picked up the money.

"Occasionally during the Season, Bonham would arrange for me to talk to him personally at garden parties where he could hide in the darkness. I never had a glimpse of him. He always disguised his voice, speaking in a whispery, raspy way. Tonight was the first time I heard his normal voice." Her frown deepened, and she shook her head. "It sounds familiar, but I cannot put a face with it."

"Then he is a member of the *ton*."

"Yes." She sat up, wincing as she swung her feet down to the floor. "He says I know him, but I cannot determine who he is. There are dozens of men in Society who are the same height and build and have brown hair cut in a similar style."

"He wears a gold ring on the little finger of his right hand."

She nodded. "I noticed that, too, though I could not see it well enough to discover any details."

"Could you tell the color of his eyes?"

"Only that they are light. They could be blue, green, gray, or something in between. The mask hid his features very effectively in the darkness. He said that he is two people. One the *ton* sees; the other he only reveals to a few. I take that to mean he presents a completely different demeanor in Society than what he showed tonight." She looked at him questioningly. "But perhaps you already know what he said."

Gabe was tempted to tell her he heard their conversation about the major and demand that she tell him the whole of it. But he had promised not to reveal anything about Cameron's investigation. If he pressed too hard she might guess what was afoot, and they might never catch Bonham or his superiors. Selena would be the scapegoat, forced to pay for the crimes of others.

He wished with all his heart she would turn to him, trust him to be wise and strong enough to help her. But she did not. It was his turn to lie. "I only spotted you when the bird flew, and the two of you moved. I could no' hear anything that was said except when you cried out. What did you hit him with?"

A tiny smile touched her face. "The blackmail money. I had the coins in a small bag. It made a rather effective weapon."

He grimaced. "It slowed him down, 'tis all." A shiver raced over him and his throat tightened. Gabriel glanced at her, then looked away. Too upset to sit still, he rose and paced the room. "When I think what he could have done to you…" He leaned his hands against the mantel and stared at the small fire glowing in the grate. "Why did you put yourself in such danger?"

"I did not have a choice."

He heard the sofa creak as she stood. Tipping his head, he watched her cross the room to his side. She moved stiffly, without her normal grace. He hated to think how sore she would be in the morning.

When she rubbed her arms, Gabriel quickly laid another log on the fire, then gently drew her into his embrace. "Tell me about it."

She put her arms around his waist, resting her cheek against his chest. "During the assembly a few weeks ago, I stepped onto the terrace for a breath of air."

"Alone?"

"Yes. I did not think twice about it. There were over a hundred other people within calling distance. I had not wanted to go in the first place and found the whole gathering annoying."

"That was the night I spoke so harshly to you."

"Yes. Unfortunately, what you said was true. I kept thinking about how ridiculous the men behaved. I spoke unkindly to them, then marched outside like a grand duchess."

"You would make a lovely duchess, as long as you didna have to marry a duke to become one. Was Bonham there?"

"Yes." She eased away, walking slowly about the room, straightening a picture here, rearranging a vase there. "Though I did not realize it, of course. When I went outside, I walked over to the far corner of the terrace to be away from the noise and light. It was dark enough there to see the stars. Looking at the heavens usually calms me when I'm upset. I had only been there a few minutes when I sensed someone behind me. Before I could turn to see who it was, he put his hands on the railing on each side of me, pressing me against the wrought iron." A tiny shiver rippled through her. "I was trapped."

"Bonham." Rage swept through him at the thought of the man being so close to her, holding her at his mercy.

She nodded. "I was terrified. He had never been close enough before to touch me."

Gabriel caught his breath. "Did he touch you any other way?"

"He put his arms around me and held me so I could not look at him. Thankfully, he did nothing indecent. He slid a fingertip down my neck and across my shoulder."

Her bare shoulder. Gabe silently swore he'd see the man in chains.

"He did not have to do anything more to make me quake. Before, he had been a voice in the darkness, frightening because I could not see him. Suddenly he was flesh and blood, but I still could not see him. I could feel his strength, his breath on my cheek, his raspy voice directly in my ear instead of separated by the night." She stopped behind a chair, clenching the edge of the back until her knuckles turned white.

"He could have done anything to me at that moment, and I would not have cried out. I could not risk what might happen to Nick if anyone found us. Bonham would extract revenge if I spoiled his place in Society, but even more so if I discovered his identity. I think he knew the power he had over me, but thankfully he did not take further advantage of the situation. Knowing how he frightened me seemed enough for him."

"Then. He thought differently tonight."

"Yes, he did." Another shudder shook her, and Gabriel put his arm around her. She took a deep breath, slowly regaining her composure, and moved away, pacing around the room once more. "At the assembly, he ordered me to meet him tonight in a secluded place in the garden. I was too scared to refuse. Later, after I could think more clearly, I realized I'd made a grave error, but there was nothing I could do about it."

"You could have confided in me. I would have caught him if I had been better prepared." And not hampered by more secrets, lies, and his word. "I am no' without influence. We could have him arrested for blackmailing you."

"The people he works with might hurt Nicholas. I cannot take that chance. The only thing to do is keep paying until my brother is safely home."

Bonham and the French coerced far more than money from her, and Gabriel was powerless to say or do anything that might dissuade her. Bound by his honor, he could not help her. Yet that very honor, the obligation of a man to protect the woman he loved, decreed that he must.

Anger and frustration threatened to explode. He pounded the side of his fist against the wall above the mantel, feeling only the teeniest remorse when she jumped. *Tell me the truth! Let me help you!* But how? He hated being so powerless. With sudden clarity, he realized how she must feel. Powerless. Totally alone.

Bending in front of the fireplace, he stirred the fire with the poker, whispering, "Father, what can I do?"

Forgive her. For her lack of trust. For being with Lawrence.

He wasn't sure he could. Even though she might not have enjoyed the other man's touch, it still hurt that she had allowed it. When he thought he heard God sigh, he promised the Lord he would work on it.

Give her to me. Tell her to trust me. I love her and her brother.

Gabe took a deep breath, releasing it slowly. *Lord, letting go isna easy, but I place her in your loving hands. Protect her and love her, and open her heart to your love. I will encourage her to trust you and tell her of your love. Guide me.*

He straightened and moved in front of her. Gabriel tipped her chin up until she met his gaze. "I apologize for startling you. 'Tis frustrating to see you in such trouble and no' be able to help. Will you promise me something?"

She eyed him warily. "Perhaps."

"Promise me that you willna meet Bonham again."

"What if he demands—"

He gripped her shoulders, firmly but gently. Fear and weariness seemed to be overcoming her good sense. "Selena, you must draw the line. After tonight, he will expect you to do so. Even if you do everything he demands, you canna guarantee it will keep Nick free from harm. You must put your brother in God's hands. He is the only one who can truly keep Nick safe."

"I want to, but…" Her voice trailed off, and she hung her head.

"But what, sweetheart?"

"I don't think God hears my prayers."

"Why?"

"I—I cannot tell you."

Sensing her rising panic, Gabe smoothed his hands along

her upper arms. "You dinna need to. But I have a message to you from God."

She raised her head, then looked away, whispering brokenly, "Do not tease me, Gabriel."

He put his arms around her, holding her close, wanting desperately to comfort her and mend her tortured heart. "I am no' teasing, sweetheart. God and I talk often. I discovered it sitting on a Scottish mountain peak and being within touching distance of heaven. But I've learned that he does no' only speak to us on mountaintops but in the darkest valleys, too. All you have to do is start the conversation."

She swallowed visibly, then looked up at him with big, frightened eyes. "What did he say?"

"For you to trust him. And that he loves you and Nicholas."

She shook her head, looking down again. "He cannot love me."

"Yes, he does. Trust him to watch over Nicholas because he loves him." He took a deep breath, understanding how hard it would be for her to let her brother go, even to rest in God's hands. He fought the same battle where she was concerned. "Trust him to take care of you, too. Faith and trust dinna come easily. We have to work at them. But I know that if you seek God, you will find him. He gave us that promise in the Scriptures. The Bible also says nothing can separate us from the love of Jesus." He cupped her face in his hand. "Nothing. No matter what we do, he is always there for us. So quit worrying about complying with Bonham's whims and let God do his work.

"Now, I'll walk you back to the house and see you safely inside before Marietta goes into hysterics."

He escorted her to the manor, wondering if he'd said too much or too little. When they reached the back door, he leaned down and kissed her gently. "Lock the door behind you."

She nodded then paused, her eyes filling with tears. "Thank God for his message."

"You thank him. Set to rights whatever has come between you, lass."

She gave him a quick, hard hug. "Thank you for rescuing me."

Trying to cheer her, he grinned. "'Tis a specialty of mine."

"I suspect it is. I won't see Bonham again, at least not intentionally."

"No evening walks, even here."

"Not alone." She smiled up at him. "But I think I'd be safe walking in the company of a certain gentleman."

"Safe from Bonham, at least." Giving in at last to his heart, Gabriel drew her to him, kissing her deeply, wishing he never had to let her go. He was greatly reassured when she was in no hurry to leave, either. And she certainly had not responded to Lawrence the way she did to him. Reluctantly, he reached behind her and opened the door. "Dream of me."

"I always do." With those sweet, tormenting words, she hurried inside and shut the door.

CHAPTER

When Gabriel arrived at Dominic's the next morning, Kiernan met him near the front door. "Lawrence is in the study."

"Has he given Cameron his report?"

"He's doing it now."

"And you think I should wait out here until he's finished."

"No' necessarily. But if I were in your shoes, he would no' be one of my favorite people."

"That's putting it mildly, but I think I can control myself. Unless he brags about how she let him kiss her."

Kiernan raised an eyebrow. "Which you watched, I suppose."

Scowling, Gabriel nodded. "Before I trudged off into the woods."

"I wondered where you disappeared to." Kiernan gave his shoulder a friendly squeeze as they walked down the hall. "I'm sure her heart wasna in it."

"I know." Gabe managed a tiny smile. "I have it on good authority that she didna enjoy it."

"She told you?"

"No, I overheard her tell someone else." He sighed quietly. "I'm ready to end this whole charade. Sneaking around behind trees, watching her, eavesdropping on her conversations. 'Tis going to make me old before my time."

Kiernan made a great show of inspecting his hair. "Aye, I see some gray up there."

"I would no' be surprised."

When they reached the door to the study, Kiernan stopped him before they went inside. "I watched her yesterday, too, especially when she looked at you. If she's no' already in love, she's falling fast."

"I hope so, because I'd hate to be in this alone." He took a deep breath and squared his shoulders. "Dinna let me punch him."

Kiernan grinned. "Which him?"

Gabriel smiled back, thankful his friend was there to keep him steady. "Both of them." When he opened the door, Lawrence was speaking.

"...delectable little morsel."

Cameron shot Lawrence a warning glance as he rose. "Gabriel, good to see you. Lawrence was just telling me that he passed on our information to Miss Delaroe."

"I know he did." Gabriel looked directly at Lawrence, gleaning some satisfaction in making the man squirm. Then he turned his attention to Cameron, coolly dismissing the presence of the other man. "And she passed on part of it to her contact."

"Part of it?"

"She said nothing about Lawrence or the regiments going to Sweden. She only said he was leaving with the regiment soon, but that he hadna told her where he was going."

"Interesting," Cameron said thoughtfully.

"I believe she is trying to give them only enough information to keep her brother from harm, but no' relay anything that might compromise our forces."

"Possibly. Any thoughts on this, Lawrence?" Cameron shifted his gaze to the officer.

"I told her that a combined attack of Swedish, Russian, and English troops might defeat Napoleon on that front and hasten the end of the war. If she is working with them only to protect her brother, then she would want the war to end as quickly as possible. That might explain why she withheld information in this instance."

"You dinna know that she has done any differently other times," Gabriel pointed out.

"True," Lawrence said. "Though she is very good at making

159

a man say things he should not. She did ask me straight out where I was bound."

"But she didna press you to tell her." Another subtle reminder to Lawrence that he had watched him take advantage of her situation, and that the major had not acted like a true gentleman. A tiny flash of apprehension in the man's eyes indicated Lawrence understood his message.

"I do not think she was satisfied with merely knowing I was soon leaving along with several regiments. But no, she did not make any further effort to learn our destination. I do believe she expressed true sorrow, though I cannot say for a fact that it was due to my going off to fight." Lawrence met Gabriel's gaze. "It may have been caused by something else entirely."

Cameron glanced at Gabriel. "When did she speak to her contact?"

"Late last night. He met her on the edge of the manor grounds in a large area of woods. Unfortunately, he wore a domino and mask so I canna identify him or give you much of a description. He's medium height and build. Has short brown hair and wears a gold ring on his little finger. He goes by the name of Bonham, but that's no' his real name."

Lawrence frowned. "How do you know?"

"Selena told me."

"You talked to her about this?" Cameron's eyes narrowed and his jaw tensed.

"No' about the investigation. The man is also blackmailing her. And last night he tried to force himself on her." He paused at Kiernan's sharply drawn breath, glancing at his worried frown. "Investigation or no', I could no' let that happen."

Cameron sat down, slumping in the chair. "So you rescued her."

His annoyed tone raised Gabe's ire a notch. "I tried. She fought him off. Hit him in the head with the bag of coins she brought to pay him. I was on the edge of the trees and could no' get any closer without them hearing me. When she hit him,

I yelled at her to run. It was enough of a distraction to give her a head start. I tried to cut him off, but he caught her before I could get to them. Threw her down right in front of me. I barely managed no' to step on her."

"Was she hurt?" Kiernan asked.

"A small cut on her head. Knocked the wind out of her. This morning she is stiff and sore, has some bruises on her arms and legs, but she isna seriously injured." Gabriel had talked to her briefly before he rode to Thornridge. He also returned her bag of money, which he had retrieved along with Bonham's hat from the woods shortly after daylight.

"And while you were checking on her, the man managed his escape." Cameron's irritation was evident.

"I didna pursue him. You told me no' to confront him, remember?"

"But you did."

"Only because he tried to hurt Selena."

"Would have done the same thing myself," Lawrence muttered. When Cameron looked at him, he straightened minutely. "A man can't stand by and do nothing when a woman is attacked, even if she is a foreign agent." He glanced at Gabriel. "A kiss when she seems willing is one thing. Force is something else entirely."

"They do no' know I was following her or overheard the whole conversation. I always check the grounds before I retire. Selena assumed that's why I was out last night." She had mentioned it that morning when he stopped to see how she was. He did not correct the misconception. "I told her I didna know they were there until I heard her struggling with him."

He explained all he knew about Bonham and Ellaby.

"So he's a member of the *ton*." Cameron digested this bit of news thoughtfully. "He might be a détenu, though none have returned to England since last summer. A couple escaped then. I'll have a man check on anyone who returned in the last few years, see if any match the description. He could have known

Delaroe in Verdun, then been given the information about Bitche. We have a list of everyone held in France, so it isna possible for someone to come home and circulate in Society without our knowing it."

Kiernan nodded. "It would be common knowledge if someone were freed or escaped. Something like that would feed the gossip mills for months. Selena would know the person."

"True. That basically rules out a détenu, but we'll look into it anyway."

They talked about the situation a while longer, not arriving at any concrete decisions.

"I may have another officer come to Worcester," Cameron said. "Someone who has done some work for me in the field. We might have him meet up with Miss Delaroe along the way, if I can think of some false information of substance. Otherwise her associates might become suspicious. Easier to do this sort of thing in London during the Season. No' unusual for officers to be on the scene there."

Gabriel sincerely hoped Cameron would give up on the idea. "In the meantime we'll look for leads on Bonham. Did you have any luck finding Ellaby?"

"He had been at the Silver Goblet Inn, but he had already moved. My men checked all the other inns but did not find anyone using that name or fitting his description. I'd wager he's still around. Even a city the size of Worcester has a criminal element, and they know all about hiding someone who doesna want to be found."

Deciding they had no further business, Gabriel took his leave.

As the groom brought him his horse, Lawrence called to him from the front door. The major trotted down the steps, making general conversation until the groom left them alone. "I owe you an apology, Macpherson. Until moments before you arrived this morning, I was unaware of your strong affections for Miss Delaroe. If I had been apprised more fully of the situation, I would never have taken such liberties with her."

Gabriel glared at him. "Even though she is a delectable little morsel?"

Lawrence looked sheepish and scratched the back of his neck. "I know that sounded bad. Actually, I was complementing you on your good taste in women. She is extremely lovely."

"Aye, she is that." Gabriel's opinion of the major improved somewhat. Not every man would have tried to make things right. He held out his hand. "Thank you. Both for the apology and appreciating my good taste."

Lawrence laughed and firmly shook his hand. "I'm considered something of an expert with women, but I could tell the lady was not impressed." He smiled ruefully. "I suppose that's why I made a second attempt, but she was even less amenable that time."

Gabriel smiled. After the man's honesty, he did not have the heart to tell him that Selena found his kisses distasteful. "That's encouraging."

Lawrence's expression sobered. "She seems like a good woman caught up in some nasty business. I hope they are lenient with her."

"I hope so, too."

He had never uttered a more fervent prayer.

That morning, Fairhaven buzzed with talk about the party and speculation on the mysterious horsemen who had galloped by the manor shortly after midnight. Though several of the indoor servants heard the noise, no one saw them.

There was concern, too, over Miss Delaroe. According to Marietta, the mistress had decided to check all the downstairs windows sometime after the riders disturbed their sleep. On the way down the stairs, she tripped and took a tumble. Though not hurt seriously, she was quite sore and decided not to receive callers that afternoon.

Midmorning, Marietta stopped by Selena's private sitting

163

room to see if she needed anything. Selena lay on the yellow velvet chaise longue, trying to rest. She decided every bone in her body must have been jarred loose, and all the muscles hurt in sympathy.

"Do you believe Macpherson was inspecting the grounds before he went to bed like he said?" Marietta looked pensive. "He does every night, but he's usually earlier."

"I don't know what to think. I want to believe him, but it seems too much of a coincidence for him to be that close when I needed him."

"So you think he followed you?"

"Quite possibly. And if he did, he probably overheard most of our conversation, if not all of it." She shifted, trying to find a more comfortable position.

"Do you think he will report you to the authorities?"

Selena threw up her hand, wincing when the movement hurt her arm. "I don't know. He was a soldier for a long time. I'm sure his loyalty to our country runs deep. He was angry last night, perhaps because I did not completely confide in him." She thought of how he held her and comforted her, the way he kissed her at the door. "But he was also very tender and loving. If he did hear it all, then I have put him in a very difficult position."

"Are you going to talk to him about it?"

"I suppose I'll wait and see if he brings it up. If he did not hear us and I mention it, I'll cook my own goose."

"And if he did hear you and you say nothing, he might throw you in the kettle." With that not-so-comforting thought, Marietta left to see if she could remove the grass stains from the dress Selena had worn the night before.

A few minutes later, Augusta breezed into the sitting room, shutting the door behind her. "Now, young lady, I would like an explanation." She sat down across from Selena and held up her hand when Selena took a breath to speak. "Do not bother with the balderdash about falling down the stairs. I know you did not. According to the talk flying about the house this morning, the worst damage is bruises. Is that correct?"

"Basically. I'm very stiff and sore."

"You should be. You are fortunate you were not hurt much worse—" she fixed her with a firm look—"either when you were alone in the woods with that man or when he threw you down."

Selena gasped softly. "How do you know about it?"

"I heard you leave your room last night shortly after we'd retired. I took the liberty of watching through the hall window to see where you went." She sniffed at Selena's wide-eyed expression. "Really, my dear, I may be too old for intrigues, but I still remember the excitement of a rendezvous with a hand-some gentleman. When you went into the woods instead of going to Gabriel's, I was quite put out with you. Then I was more curious than ever, so I kept watching.

"The next thing I knew, you were running across the lawn with a man in a cape chasing you. I would have raised the alarm had Gabriel not been there. I knew he could handle the problem far better than anyone else." She gave her niece a speaking look. "Besides, it certainly was not the kind of thing we want the servants gossiping about. It would have been nice if Gabriel could have caught the villain, but I suppose he had to see if you were still alive." She sniffed again, obviously annoyed that the scene had not played out as she'd wanted.

"Yes, ma'am." Selena half expected her aunt to tell her she was confined to her room for a week, or at the least that she would be sent to bed without her supper for a fortnight.

"I also decided that if you were hurt seriously, he would have brought you here and sought my assistance instead of taking you to his house. I trust he tended your wounds adequately?"

"He washed the scratch on my forehead." Selena brushed aside her hair to show her aunt the small cut. "He gave me a scold—" she couldn't restrain a smile—"then held me quite nicely."

"Good. You needed both. Now, tell me whom you were so foolish to tryst with in the woods. Was it Major Lawrence? He's certainly dashing and seemed gentlemanly enough, but I caught a distinctly lecherous light in his eyes when you went off with him yesterday afternoon. I should not need to remind you that the son of a viscount, even if he is temporarily with pockets to let, is a much better match than a major. Not likely to get his head blown off, for one thing."

Selena flinched at her aunt's choice of words. "No, it was not the major. He was nice enough, though he pushed the limits of propriety. Nothing greatly troubling." Unless one's heart belonged to another. "He behaved no worse than many officers leaving for the war. I think they all feel a sense of urgency about enjoying life while they can."

She paused, deliberating on how much to tell her aunt. Though she was ashamed to admit her part in the espionage, she wondered if she put her aunt in danger by keeping it from her. She decided to say nothing at the moment about working for France. "I am being blackmailed to keep Nick safe. I do not know the identity of the man behind it, the one who was here last night. He wore a mask, so I could not recognize him." She went on to explain about Ellaby and Bonham's accomplices in France and how, until the previous night, she had never seen Bonham—only occasionally spoken to him.

"So he moves about freely in Society." Aunt Gussie pursed her lips thoughtfully. "And you have no idea who he is?"

"None." Selena briefly described him. "Though his voice sounds vaguely familiar. He implied I knew him well, but that the image he presents to the *ton* is different from the one I saw last night."

Aunt Gussie grinned. "I should expect so. I can't think of anyone who runs around wearing a cape and a mask all the time."

Selena laughed, thankful for her aunt's sense of humor. "Nor can I. You missed the cavalier's hat." She wondered if

Gabriel had picked it up when he retrieved the money. "So will you be a dear and receive our guests for the next few days? I cannot move without groaning. And I would prefer not to spend all afternoon explaining over and over again why I am in pain."

Her aunt shrugged. "Though it's a clanker, tumbling down the stairs is a common enough occurrence. It is certainly more believable than being chased and thrown to the ground by a masked blackmailer."

Selena laughed and shook her head. "It is ridiculous, isn't it." Her smile faded. "But sadly too true. Did Gabriel follow me last night?"

"The first time I noticed him was when he came running around the edge of the trees. If he did follow you, then he's in the wrong profession. Should be in espionage instead of estates."

Selena's heart did a somersault. Was that why he came to Fairhaven? Was he there to spy on her? A wave of dizziness washed over her.

"Selena, dear, what is wrong? You look sick."

She was. Sick at heart. "I fear it has all caught up with me, Aunt Gussie. I feel a trifle faint. I need to rest."

"Of course, dear." Lady Camfield stood. "I'll tell Marietta that you're going to nap. And don't worry about the hordes of callers. I'll see to them. It will be tiresome anyway, everyone gushing about how grand the breakfast was. Of course it was grand. You gave it." She winked at her niece. "Seeing as I was your teacher, it could not be otherwise. I've always thought guests calling on the hostess right after a party to rave about it was a stupid tradition. One knows if her guests had a good time or not. Even if they didn't most will say they did so they'll be invited again. I've half a mind to have Hardwick tell them I'm under the weather, too."

"Then they'll think the food was bad and dozens will suddenly become ill. You must see them, Auntie. Bonham might come, in his *ton* persona, to find out what is being said about last night. And perhaps to see if I was hurt."

"The stair bit will have to do. And I should mention the disturbance that caused you to go downstairs in the first place." Augusta pursed her lips thoughtfully. "I suspect a couple of blades stayed too long at the inn. Being castaway, they took the wrong road and did not realize it until they discovered the stables weren't where they were supposed to be. Afraid of being shot for trespassing, they scrambled past the house in a mad dash, rousing everyone."

Selena chuckled. "Aunt Gussie, you should be a novelist. We would become rich."

"We already are rich, dear. Now, have a good rest. The only visitor I'll allow up to see you is Gabriel."

Selena wasn't at all sure she wanted to see him, but it wouldn't do to mention it. Her aunt would want an explanation. "Thank you."

After her aunt left, Selena did try to rest. She was exhausted and ached more as the day progressed. But for more than an hour sleep eluded her. Her thoughts dwelled on Gabriel, darting from moment to moment, examining the time they had spent together. It seemed as if his every word, expression, and gesture were written indelibly in her mind. Each touch. Each embrace. Each tender and passionate kiss. He would forever dwell in her heart, mind, and soul.

It was not impossible that all was exactly as he said. And yet…his serving as a government agent made more sense than his needing money and working for common wages. Still, if he'd come to Fairhaven only to catch a traitor, why did he stay? Surely he knew enough to convict her.

A whisper of hope went through her. Perhaps he was trying to think of a way to help her.

Or perhaps he wanted her accomplices, too, she thought with a heavy sigh, and he didn't know who they were.

Gabriel stood in the doorway, watching Selena sleep. He probably shouldn't be there, even though she was in her sitting room and not across the hall in her bedchamber. But he'd had to come. Had to see how she was doing.

In the grips of a dream, her hand twitched, her brow knitted in a frown. He tiptoed into the room, kneeling beside the chaise longue.

The opening at the neckline of her dressing gown had slipped, revealing a dark bruise on her shoulder where Bonham had grabbed her. Rage rose swiftly, and Gabriel silently cursed the man who had hurt her. The man, he guessed, who even now tormented her.

When she whimpered, tenderness filled him just as rapidly. He leaned closer, whispering in Gaelic, uttering words of comfort and love. She grew calm at the sound of his voice, and he gently clasped her hand in his.

Smoothing her hair with his other hand, he spoke again, this time in his own particular combination of English and Scots. "Shhh, sweetheart, dinna be afraid. I'm here. I'll no' let anyone harm you." He bent down, brushing a kiss on her cheek, and tasted the salt of her tears. "Ah, lass, you carry such a heavy burden. Let me help you, my love. Trust me. God will help us find a way."

He held her hand and smoothed her hair for several minutes until she slept peacefully. Laying her hand on her stomach, he released it and gently kissed her temple. "I love you."

With a silent prayer for God to watch over her, he carefully pushed to his feet and left the room.

Her head tipped to the side, Selena watched through the veil of her lashes as Gabriel went out the door and disappeared down the hall. A lone tear slid across her cheek, anointing the place his lips had touched with such gentleness and care.

"I love you, too," she whispered, her heart aching. "May God grant us mercy."

CHAPTER *Sixteen*

Verdun, France

NICHOLAS BUCKLED THE SECOND STRAP holding his valise firmly against his back. By equally distributing the weight, he could carry it for some distance without growing too weary. That would leave his hands and arms free if he had to bury himself in a thicket, scramble up a tree, or attempt any other evasive maneuvers. It was a lesson he'd learned from the British officers confined at Bitche penal depot.

"You have everything?" his friend Joseph Gains whispered, glancing around nervously. It was almost impossible to see beyond a few feet in the cloud-darkened night, but others kept watch a block away, ready to alert them at the first sign of a guard or a citizen. With any luck, everyone else in that section of Verdun slept peacefully, unaware of the escape attempt happening right under their noses.

"I believe so. One nicely forged Swiss passport, thanks to our French friend." Nick patted the money in his pocket and the rest carefully sewn into the lining of his waistcoat. "A good supply of gold *louis* to fill open palms and hopefully pave the way to success. Map, compass, and another pair of boots in case it doesn't. A change of clothes. Enough food to last a few days. A cask of water, easily replenished. And a few other odds and ends."

Since he was traveling under the guise of a historian and occasional tutor studying in France, those odds and ends included notebooks and two heavy French history books. Nick held out his hand to his friend. "Bid adieu to Johann Ochs."

Gains gripped it firmly. "I'd rather say Godspeed to an old friend."

"I'll take all the help I can find." Nick released his hand, giving him a bear hug. "Take care of yourself."

"No need to worry about me. You know I never do anything to raise the commandant's hackles."

"Other than what you're doing right now."

Nick turned to their other companion, Robert Brown, who had come to France as Gains's coachman. The big man had been invited to join others in escape attempts from Verdun, but he refused to leave his employer. He was quite willing and able, however, to lower a man over the wall. "Robert, be careful."

"Always am. You're the one who needs to have a care. No one should be on the road this time of night, but cut across country until you're well away from the city."

"I will. Can't have the guards spotting me too easily." Nick shook hands with each of them, then slipped on a pair of supple leather gloves. Gains handed him the looped end of the rope. The rest lay on the ground in a neat coil. Several lengths of rope were tied together to lower him down the seventy-five-foot rampart.

Brown boosted him up to the top of the wide, medieval-city fortification. Nick lay flat, peering over the edge, but could see no one. That was one disadvantage to picking such a dark night for his escape. Still, it would be just as hard for him to be seen, so it was worth the risk. He listened for footsteps below—as well as he could over his thundering heart. Nothing. He could only hope that the guards kept to their regular routine, which he had studied meticulously over several months. He shifted to the other side, speaking to his companions. "Ready?"

"Ready." That meant Brown had the rope firmly in each hand, bracing it across his back as he uncoiled it.

Nick slipped his foot securely into the loop and grabbed hold of the rope with one hand, easing himself over the outer edge. He tried not to think about the long drop. In that respect, it was good he couldn't see the ground. When the rope grew taut, he released the top of the wall and gripped the rope with both hands. Seconds later, Brown began to ease the length of it over the wall, slowly lowering him.

Halfway down, his descent suddenly halted. Nick held his breath, brushing his fingertips against the stones to stop his movement as he swayed back and forth. Heart in his throat, he waited for the shout of discovery and the clamor as more guards came to challenge his friends. But no shout came. No stomping boots and angry accusations. Thankfully, the rope again began to move downward again, and Nick drew in a huge breath.

Seemingly hours later, though in reality it was only a few minutes, his foot touched the ground. He quickly wiggled his other foot from the loop and tugged on the rope. It whisked upward past his head, vanishing into the black night.

Bending low, Nick moved directly across a stretch of open ground. Instinct urged him to run, but he walked cautiously over the unfamiliar terrain. He would get nowhere if he sprained an ankle or twisted a knee. Staying in the weeds to better hide his footprints, he skirted around the woods, methodically increasing the distance between himself and captivity. Clearing the first large stand of trees, he cut across to the road. He would never have dared move to it so quickly on a clear night. He kept to a fast walk, not wanting to risk the remote chance that the sound of running might travel back to the guards pacing the perimeter of the city.

Unless it rained, he should be able to reach the next town before daylight. He kept up a brisk, steady pace, anxiously listening all the while for pounding horses' hooves and furious gendarmes bent on capturing him. When the clouds parted and the half moon shone in the sky, he didn't know how far he had walked. But he thought he had been on the road long enough to be safely out of sight. He paused and turned around. In the distance, he could just make out the walls of Verdun.

A strange mixture of elation and sadness swept over him.

Other than the months spent in his previous escape attempt and at Bitche, he had lived a third of his life behind those walls. Short excursions out of the city into the nearby countryside had sometimes been allowed, but for no longer than four hours at a time. For a moment he hesitated, thinking of the friends he left behind, the rented room that still contained most of his possessions, and the books at the library, especially the ones on history, that he had read over and over. In an odd way he felt a sense of loss. He knew Verdun, all its streets and houses, many of its citizens.

He'd arrived there a boy, afraid and alone. Even when Owen was detained at Verdun, he seemed to forget about his young cousin. His only concern had been escaping at the first opportunity. The other détenus had taken Nick under their collective wing and looked after him, some nurturing him, others teaching him things perhaps best left unlearned.

Selena said his parents had aged beyond their years but retained an active life. Had his father remained stern but loving? His mother flighty but sweet? His precious sister had grown into a beautiful and kind woman, but what had she done for him? How dear a price had she paid to keep him safe? Could he ever make things right for her?

Closing his eyes, he pictured Yorkshire and the family estate. What would he do at home? How would he do? He had tried to make good use of his time, studying French, Latin, and geography, and reading the classics. Several of the captive noblemen welcomed his interest in the business of running an estate and spent many hours discussing all aspects of it with him. But most of all he indulged in his love of history, reading everything he could find, regardless of whether it was written in English or French.

He'd also spent time, over the past several months, with a Swiss clockmaker who set up shop in Verdun. Not that Nick had an interest in repairing or making timepieces, but he needed to know as much as possible about Switzerland.

His parents would probably throw a huge party to celebrate his return. Would he be welcomed in their neighborhood or treated as an oddity?

He had attended some social functions among the British elite in Verdun, but the daughters were few and the bachelors many, most more accomplished than he was. Would he embarrass his family because he had no university education, no social polish? Would he seem ignorant and crude? Nick felt ill prepared to take his place in the world to which he had been born. He left Verdun a man, alone, and in many ways, still afraid.

But there were worse things than being rough-hewn. Taking a deep breath, Nick squared his shoulders and turned his back on the city. His life there had not been without joy, but sorrow had been a far more persistent companion. He would never be a captive again. This time he would reach his beloved England. He would live in freedom.

Or die trying.

As he had hoped, he arrived near the small town about an hour before daylight. He left the road, hiding in a thick wood. Unfastening the valise from his back, he stored the straps inside it, then dozed until the sunlight shining on his face woke him. He ate, washed his face in a nearby stream, and brushed off the leaves and twigs clinging to his clothes. After replenishing the water in his cask, he stored everything away in the bag, put on his hat, and sat a while longer, waiting for the town to come to life.

Though painfully shy with aristocratic English ladies, he felt slightly more relaxed with French women, probably because those he knew were mostly shopkeepers' wives and daughters, maids and laundresses, and a few of less sterling character. They all thought his shyness sweet and invariably made a fuss about how handsome he was. He remembered one woman going on about him being tall and strong, saying his black hair was like the night, his dark blue eyes like the deepest ocean.

Though he dismissed the exaggerations, he supposed there was some validity to their assessment since he greatly resembled his twin sister, though thankfully in a more masculine way.

The one thing for which he could take personal credit was his physique. After the failed escape attempt the year before—and the horror of Bitche—he had worked hard to build up his strength and stamina. He hoped to ride in a carriage all the way to the French coast, but if that plan failed, he was prepared to walk several hundred miles.

He had acquired great proficiency in French during his stay, conversing in the language as easily as if it were his native tongue. That talent should go far in aiding his cause.

Hearing laughter and the creak of wheels, he crept around the trees until he had a good view of those passing by. Two families walked along together, laughing and talking. One man led an ancient horse pulling a two-wheeled cart piled high with fresh vegetables. The members of the other family each carried baskets of fresh eggs.

Market day! Grinning, Nick watched them pass. The town would be much busier than normal. He checked his watch. Eight o'clock. If he waited another hour it would be more crowded, lessening the chances of anyone taking particular note of a gentleman traveler. Unfortunately, the longer he waited the greater the potential of gendarmes from Verdun coming after him.

During the earlier part of the war, all the military prisoners and détenus at Verdun had to gather for the *appel,* or muster, between eight and ten, then again in the afternoon between two and four. This remained the requirement for midshipmen, who were not commissioned officers, but over time, the rules were relaxed for others. Officers only reported from once every five days to once a month depending on their rank. Détenus were often exempted completely through expedient bribes.

For several months after Nick returned to Verdun from Bitche, he was required to attend the *appel* twice a day.

Gradually the time between his mandatory attendance was extended to once a week. He'd done his duty the day before, which should give him a cushion of time before they discovered his disappearance. However, the city was rife with the commandant's spies. If anyone suspected he was missing, it would not take them long to become certain of it. Mounted guards would fan out across the countryside looking for him. Though he had walked steadily for a good six hours, men on horseback could cover the distance far more quickly.

Nick waited until several more farmers passed with their wares, then cautiously moved to the road, strolling along as if he had every right to be there. He was relieved to see the town bustling with even more activity than he had expected. A traveling troupe of jugglers occupied part of the small square, along with a puppet booth. Another time and place, he would have enjoyed seeing the whole show. He watched them both for a few minutes, mainly because everyone else did. It might be too obvious if he did not.

He slowly made his way through the crowd, pausing now and then to admire the local produce and handiwork. He bought some cheese and a small basket of fresh strawberries. By then he had determined there was only one inn, which would be the most likely place to rent a carriage. As he started back to the inn, he spotted eight mounted gendarmes arriving from the direction of Verdun.

He quickly turned around, putting his back to the street and pulling his wide-brimmed black hat down a little farther. The fine cloth and tailoring readily available in Verdun were what normally comprised his attire. But now his dark blue coat, gray-striped waistcoat, and buff pantaloons, as well as the clothes in his valise, fell several levels beneath those high standards. His clothing was better suited to a historian and tutor than a wealthy British gentleman.

Ducking his head, he concentrated on inspecting the pies and pastries set out on a table in front of the bakery. Bending to sniff a strawberry tart, he set his valise on the ground and slid it under the table with his foot. Though the gendarmes rode past slowly, enough people were between him and the guards to adequately block their view.

Nick leaned over the table, appearing to try to decide on the treats while surreptitiously watching the soldiers go down the street.

A pretty young woman came out of the bakery, giving him a flirtatious smile. Hips swaying provocatively, she walked around the table and stopped beside Nick. She glanced at the gendarmes, who were still moving away from them. "Too many choices, monsieur?" she asked in French.

Heart pounding, he nodded—and silently prayed that she would not inadvertently draw attention to him. "They all look very good, but I was hoping for peach." His answer also was in French.

A boy about twelve carried out a metal tray of bread and dumped the loaves into an almost empty basket on the table. He bent down and picked up Nick's valise, shielding it from view with the tray as he carried it inside the bakery.

The young woman slipped her arm around his. "I believe we might have some inside the store."

Nick glanced down the street as they walked through the doorway. The guards were turning around.

Since they had a variety of baked goods on display outside, the store was empty at that moment. A man, perhaps close to Nick's age, sat on a high stool behind the counter, a pair of crutches within arm's reach. He nodded at Nick as the woman ushered him into the kitchen. She shoved him into a small supply room, thrusting his bag at him when the boy handed it to her. "I must go back outside. Stay here. We will help you."

He desperately wanted to believe her, but Frenchmen who aided escapees were severely punished. On the other hand, they were paid quite well for helping capture them. "Why?"

She playfully flicked her finger beneath his chin. "Because

you are so handsome." She flashed him a mischievous smile. It faded as she touched her heart. "And because we have a special regard for English gentlemen. I will explain later. Do you go east or west?" There was no guile in her dark eyes.

Nick was well aware that, with Verdun in eastern France, most escapees went toward the Rhine, trying to reach either Austria or Russia, depending on which country was friendly with England at the moment. He had planned to go west through France to the coast and somehow find a way across the English Channel, straight to England. He reasoned the plan was no more daring than trying to go through several other countries allied with France. Especially since he couldn't speak one word of German or Russian.

Hoping he was not buying a ticket to Bitche, he took a deep breath. "West."

"Then I saw you riding east." With a wink, she shut the door in his face.

Nick stood, his ear near the door, alert to any sound of alarm. There was no room in the small pantry for him to sit. From his quick glimpse out the open back door of the kitchen, he noticed an older man near a large brick oven. There appeared to be several houses nearby, then open country. Even if he made it past the houses, the gendarmes would spot him easily in the fields. He might be able to work his way around the stores and back to the main street, taking his chances at hiding in the crowd.

He shook his head. Or he could remain where he was. It seemed as good an option as the others.

If these people truly did mean to help him, it was the best one.

The young woman returned an excruciating half hour later, opening the door wide so he could see she was alone. "They were looking for a small man with blond hair. A midshipman. So I truthfully told them I had not seen him and gave them each a pastry for their breakfast. They questioned others, then gave up and kept going. East," she added with a smile when he stepped out of the cramped storeroom.

She led him into the dwelling part of the building, motioning for him to sit down next to her on a red brocade settee. "How can we help you?"

"Why would you?"

"I have lost three brothers in the war. The Russians captured the fourth, Anton, whom you saw in the bakery. He was greatly mistreated by them, but a British officer serving under the Russian commander saved him. He even managed to have him released and sent home to us." Her eyes misted with tears. "For that, we help any British gentleman that we can."

"I am not an officer, but a détenu."

"That does not matter."

"How did you know I was English? Am I so obvious?"

She shook her head with a smile. "No, monsieur. You speak like a Frenchman. But you were wary of the gendarmes, though even that was not too obvious. I only noticed because I was already watching you." Her gaze lingered on his face as she sighed wistfully. "I do not often see such a beautiful man."

Nick couldn't stop the flush heating his face. He only hoped he didn't turn beet red.

She laughed in delight and brushed her fingertips across his cheek. "Are you not used to such praise?"

He shook his head.

"Then the Englishwomen in Verdun are stupid."

"They have many men from whom to choose."

"They are still idiots."

Nick decided he had better change the subject. He shifted away from her. "Even a thief would be wary of the gendarmes."

She shrugged and leaned against the arm of the sofa, as if understanding his subtle message. "They only send such a large number of guards if someone escapes. A thief, he is only worth two or three."

"What if it is a female thief?" he asked with a teasing smile.

He couldn't believe he was actually flirting. He *never* flirted. But his relief at not being found out, and the woman's kind and warm manner, left him feeling a bit giddy.

"Ah, it depends. If she is ugly, maybe one or two. Pretty, then a whole company."

Nick laughed. "For you, half the garrison."

She grinned. "Perhaps you should stay here for a while."

"I wish I could. But the sooner I leave the safer it will be for all of us. I'd like to rent a carriage to go to Chalons. I can drive a gig if necessary and leave it there to be picked up."

"You are bold." Admiration glowed softly in her eyes.

"I tried it once on foot. Almost made it, but it was a long and difficult journey. Unless you travel only at night, it is easy to be noticed that way."

"A carriage is not a common means of escape. That is an advantage. Do you have a passport?"

"Yes. Swiss."

She glanced at the stopped clock on a shelf nearby. "A clockmaker, by chance?"

"No. I was afraid someone might ask me to repair one."

"Too bad. Stay here until I come for you. I will see if Jacques will drive you. His father owns the inn. They have a few carriages for hire." She hopped up and was out the door before he thought to ask if she needed to see the money beforehand.

Nick leaned back against the comfortable cushion, though he did not relax. He would not be at ease until he reached England.

She returned a few minutes later. "Jacques will take you. Come buy some bread for the journey."

Nick followed her out of the living quarters into the store. Her older brother had already placed a loaf of bread and several tarts in a small basket that sat on the counter. He leaned on his crutches, watching Nick and his sister. The younger boy lounged by the door.

Nick handed Anton several gold *louis*, much more than the

cost of the food. When he shook his head, Nick did not withdraw the money. "Please, take it. It is far less than the value of what you have done for me." When the Frenchman still did not reach for it, Nick nodded and counted out an estimated amount for the food, leaving it on the counter. He put the other coins back in his pocket and glanced out the front window. If anything, the cheerful crowd had increased. No one seemed to even notice the three people inside the bakery.

He held out his hand to Anton. This time, the man smiled and shook it firmly. "I cannot thank you enough," said Nick. He looked at the young woman, knowing he would never forget her. "All of you."

"We merely pass on the gift God gave me. My little brother will take you to the inn." Anton looked at his sister, nodding toward the door. "We have a customer, Suzette."

She met Nick's gaze. "Adieu, monsieur. Go with God."

Nick's throat tightened. As a child, he had believed in a loving, heavenly Father and in Jesus the Savior. During his long years of captivity, he decided that neither one of them cared much about him, if they even existed. Now it seemed perhaps heaven had taken note of him after all. "Thank you."

When Suzette moved out the door to wait on a customer, Anton motioned for Nick to lean closer. "Go to Caen, to 15 Rue de Charles. The lady there, Adrienne Le Clare, will help you. Tell her William Mahieu sent you."

Nick nodded, smiling at the name. *William* meant "protector," and *Mahieu* meant "gift of God."

"I will. Thank you."

"Jacques is my sister's betrothed." Anton winked at him. "It would not be wise to kiss her farewell."

Nick had thought about it, even though he knew he wouldn't do it. "Thanks for the warning."

Grinning, the younger boy picked up Nick's valise and headed out the door. Nick took the basket of bread and pastries and followed him, glancing once more in Suzette's direction. She ignored him, probably to keep from drawing the customer's attention to him.

May your Jacques treat you well and make you happy.

They wove their way through the throng of people clustered around the market stalls. To Nick's immense relief, no one gave him a second glance. When they arrived at the courtyard of the inn, a large, muscular man stood waiting beside a closed carriage. He grinned when he saw them. Nick decided Jacques could probably keep Suzette interested.

He greeted the Frenchman with a handshake, then asked him how much it would be to hire the coach. Jacques named a reasonable price, and Nick paid it. He thanked the boy for carrying his valise and generously tipped him. The lad took the money with a grin and scampered off down the street.

Nick climbed in the carriage, and Jacques shut the door. The carriage swayed as the big man climbed into the driver's seat. Nick set his valise on the floor, the basket of bread beside it.

The whip cracked and the coach lurched forward. Since the inn was near the edge of town, it only took a few minutes before they were on the open road. The carriage was not luxurious, but it was fairly comfortable. It beat walking a hundredfold. Every turn of the wheels put him farther from Verdun and closer to freedom.

A sudden swell of emotion rushed through him, clogging his throat and misting his eyes. "Dear God, am I really going home?"

He heard the gentle, loving reply in his mind and heart, clearly and distinctly. It made him shiver and sent joy flooding through his soul.

Yes.

CHAPTER *Seventeen*

SELENA WAS RECOVERED WITHIN A FEW days, but Gabriel had been so attentive she was tempted to pretend to be unwell a little longer. At Lady Camfield's suggestion, Gabe dined with Selena in her sitting room the first evening after the encounter with Bonham. He told her tales of Scotland, both personal ones and legends, moving her both to tears and laughter. The next evening, he joined her for dinner at her request. Afterward he challenged her to a game of chess and proceeded to soundly trounce her because he kept her laughing too much to concentrate. She could not remember ever having such enjoyable evenings.

Mr. O'Conner and his four strong boys, along with young Mr. Altby, were digging the ditches for the irrigation system. Gabriel had borrowed her coachman, Thomas, to help him survey the area and mark the route with stakes. She suspected he asked for Thomas's help mainly because he liked the congenial coachman.

It was a lovely afternoon, so Selena ordered her gig brought around. She planned to drive out to watch the work and gladden her heart by spending a little time in her beloved's company.

Neither of them had spoken openly of their love. He did not know she had heard his whispered declaration. Nor, she was sure, had he heard her response. Sadly, it needed to remain so. No matter how desperately she wanted to spend her life with Gabriel, Selena could see no way for it. But she would take every precious moment they had together and treasure them forever.

Tying the ribbons on her bonnet as she started down the stairs, she heard the front door open. Selena could not make out Hardwick's words, but his tone caused her concern. Occasionally there were times when the butler's overbearing, haughty manner came in handy. She decided, however, that it was his true nature and not merely an attitude to be used when needed.

She'd spoken to him more than once regarding his high-handed treatment of the other servants, but saw no change. He and Mrs. Pool had been at Fairhaven when she inherited it. Since moving there, she kept a watchful eye on them both, not particularly pleased with either of them. Unless there was a very good reason for his current behavior, the butler's time was up.

As she rounded the landing and started down the last flight of stairs, she caught sight of a man standing in her open door-way. He was rumpled, dirty, and looked weary to the bone. Though several inches shorter than Hardwick, when the visitor took a step toward him, her butler moved back.

"Dinna order me 'round to the back door, ye stuffed-up popinjay. I came to see the laird's son and I willna be put off by the likes of ye."

"How *dare* you!" Hardwick bristled and snapped his finger to the footmen standing nearby, obviously intending for them to throw the man out on his ear.

"Miller, Barnes, stay where you are." Selena raised her voice and sharpened her tone as she hurried down the steps. She frowned at the butler as she approached. "I shall handle this, Hardwick."

He glanced at the Scot and sniffed, but stepped aside.

Selena admitted the middle-aged man could use a bath, but she suspected he had ridden night and day from Liath Hill.

When he saw her he quickly doffed his cap, nodding respectfully.

"I'm Selena Delaroe, mistress of Fairhaven. I assume you are looking for Mr. Macpherson?"

"Yes, ma'am. I need to see him right away. 'Tis most urgent that I speak with him."

"I am driving out to where he is working. If you like, you can ride with me."

He glanced down at his dirty clothes and frowned. "I'm no' exactly fit to ride with a lady."

Hardwick made a sound in his throat, rudely agreeing with his assessment. Selena glared at him, then looked back at the other man. "You are also exhausted."

The man nodded. "Aye, that I am."

"Then you shall ride with me." She turned to the butler. "See that the blue room is prepared for our guest. When Mr…" She paused and looked questioningly at the Scot.

"Mackenzie."

"When Mr. Mackenzie and I return, I want everything readied for him, including a hot meal."

The butler sniffed again, then nodded reluctantly. "As you wish, madam."

"Precisely, Hardwick. Things are done here as I wish." She smiled at Mackenzie. "If you would kindly wait for me outside, I will be right out."

He nodded, glared at the butler, and turned on his heel, donning his cap as he went out the door.

Selena turned to Miller. "Tell Cook I want the heartiest meal he can prepare on such short notice. See that our guest has a hot bath and anything else he needs. I leave his welfare in your capable hands, Miller."

"Yes, ma'am. I'll take care of it." He nodded, his expression serious.

"I know you will. If you have any problem, come directly to me." She liked his response and attitude. Good thing, too, since in essence, she had just stripped the butler of his authority over the footman—and both men knew it.

Selena hurried out the door, fearful that only a crisis would prompt the kind of urgency Mackenzie had displayed. He was busy brushing the dust off his clothes. Another footman held the reins of his horse, waiting for instructions. "Please see that Mr. Mackenzie's horse is properly taken care of."

"Yes, ma'am."

Miller followed Selena out and helped her into the gig. "I'll take your bag up to your room, sir."

"Thank ye, lad." Mackenzie climbed into the gig beside Selena, keeping a respectful space between them.

The groom who had brought around the carriage handed Selena the reins. She was an experienced driver, and they were quickly on their way, reaching a brisk trot on the winding road around the manor. "Mr. Macpherson isn't far. He is supervising the digging of some new irrigation ditches."

Mackenzie smiled. "Would no' surprise me to see a shovel in his hands. He's no' afraid of hard work."

"No, he isn't."

Since he did not offer any information regarding what brought him to England, she did not pry. Whatever his news, he obviously wanted to tell Gabriel first. The road straightened, and Selena encouraged the horse to go at a fast clip. As they approached the work area, she slowed the horse and carriage. Gabriel and Thomas were at the other end of the orchard, pounding stakes into the ground. Selena turned down the narrow lane and drove as close to them as she could.

Gabriel gave a stake one last whack, then straightened and turned to her with a warm smile. It faded when he saw Mackenzie. Handing the heavy hammer to Thomas, he jogged over to meet them. "Angus, it's good to see you." Gabriel held out his hand.

Mackenzie shook it firmly. "Good to see you, too, sir. I wish I wasna the bearer of bad news."

Frowning, Gabriel glanced at Selena, worry in his eyes. "What has happened?"

"Your father took a nasty spill from his horse and hit his head. He'd been unconscious for two days when your mother decided I should come for you. He may be awake and doin' fine by now, but the doctor wasna encouraging. He feared he might no' live."

Gabriel gripped the side of the carriage and met Selena's

gaze. Her heart ached at his anguish. She wanted desperately to hold him, but because he was on the other side of the gig, she couldn't even take his hand.

"I'll leave right away." Gabe ran his fingers through his hair and glanced around. "Thomas and O'Conner can finish up here. They know what to do. The workmen have one more window to put in a cottage. They dropped the last one. I ordered another."

"Don't worry about any of it," Selena said. When Gabriel did not seem to hear her, she touched Mackenzie on the arm and handed him the reins. Hopping out of the gig, she hurried around to Gabriel.

"I have interviews set up for tomorrow. Need to find more men to work on the estate."

"I'll talk to them, Gabriel. Then you can interview them more thoroughly when you return. Things won't fall apart before then." When Selena touched his arm, he looked at her in a daze.

"My father…"

She put her arms around his waist and held him close. He embraced her desperately, holding her so tightly she could barely breathe, but she didn't utter a word of complaint. She felt him take a deep, shuddering breath, and leaned back to meet Gabe's eyes. "Your father's a strong man, isn't he?"

"Yes."

"Then he will fight to live."

"Yes." He took another deep breath, steadier this time. "Yes, he will." He eased his tight hold, looking down at her with a worried frown. "They say the longer a person is unconscious, the harder it is to come out of it."

"Perhaps he already has. We won't give up on him." She caressed his cheek, not caring that Thomas and Mackenzie were probably watching them.

The tenderness in his eyes told her how much she comforted

him. "No, we will no' do that." He released her. "I need to tell Kiernan."

"I'll go to Thornridge after I leave Mr. Mackenzie at the house. The poor man needs to eat and sleep. Do you want to borrow my coach?"

He shook his head. "I have a coach at Dominic's." He paused, glancing thoughtfully across the orchard. "My coachman is in London, but it would be faster to use post horses and postillions, anyway. I willna have to stop and let the animals and driver rest."

"Nor will you rest yourself."

"I can sleep sitting up."

Selena had never traveled by post, but many aristocrats did, especially using their own chaises. The postillions, or post boys, rode the lead horse, guiding the team and coach. The horses and post boys were changed every fifteen to twenty miles at inns along the way. "Promise me that you'll stop and rest at an inn if you become too tired."

"I promise. Ask Dominic to have someone bring my carriage to Fairhaven. Then his man can take my horses back to Thornridge after I make the arrangements for posting in Worcester."

"I will."

"Thank you." Gabriel brushed her cheek with his knuckle, then turned back to Mackenzie. "How did it happen?"

"Willie Todd went down tae one of the burnies a'fishin'. He had that big dog o' his with him, like he always does. Ye know how ol' Geezer is when he spots a rabbit. Your father was giving one of his young horses a good run. The rabbit and dog ran right across in front of them. Willie said the filly dug ruts in the heather with her front feet, trying to stop. Threw his lordship right over her head. He hit the back of his head on a rock when he landed."

"But he showed no signs of regaining consciousness?"

"No. But restin' peaceful, he is. To my thinking, rest and time be what he needs to heal. He could still swallow, so your mother has been spoon-feeding him water and broth. He had a big lump and bruise on his head, and the doctor bled it. He wanted to bleed him again, but your mother would no' let him. She said he would be draining the very life from him."

Gabriel nodded. "Good. Leviticus says the blood is the life of all flesh. I've never understood the reasoning behind blood-letting. In battle, those who lost much blood were more likely to die than those who didna, even though the wounds might be similar."

He nodded to Mackenzie. "Thank you again for coming to tell me. Give yourself time to recover from the journey. I'm certain Miss Delaroe willna mind." He glanced at Selena.

"He is welcome to stay as long as he wishes." She turned Gabriel toward the horse he used around Fairhaven and gave him a gentle nudge. "Now, go gather your things. I'll have Cook prepare something to take with you since you'll want to travel as far as possible without stopping."

"Thank you. I'll come to the house before I leave."

"You'd better."

He looked back at her over his shoulder and smiled. "Yes, ma'am." Then he turned and cupped her elbow, guiding her around the carriage. "I can take time to help you into the gig."

"The step isn't very high. I can manage it by myself." She smiled up at him. "Though I appreciate the courtesy."

Once she was settled in the vehicle, he rested his hand against her upper back. "Take a groom with you to Thornridge."

"Of course." She smiled at him. "It might cause a scandal if I drove so far alone."

"I'm more worried about your safety. Make sure he has a pistol."

She abandoned her attempt to make him smile. "I will. I promise to be very careful while you're gone."

"You'd better." This time, neither of them smiled.

Selena drove quickly back to the manor. She showed Mackenzie into the house and sent a footman to the stable for a groom. She asked the cook to prepare some food for Gabriel and paused a few minutes to apprise her aunt of the situation.

Then she and a groom named Morley left for Thornridge. The county road was well maintained so she drove at a fast pace, slowing only when she noticed Morley's white-knuckled grip on the side of the gig.

When they reached the Thorne manse, she left the carriage with Morley and scurried up the steps to the house. The footman who opened the door showed her directly into the withdrawing room. She was relieved to see that all four of Gabriel's dear friends were home. They had a guest—a Scot, who appeared to be a few years older than Gabriel. She merely nodded to him as he rose when she entered the room, then focused her attention on Dominic as he came to meet her.

"Good afternoon, Selena. How nice to see you." Dominic's friendly smile quickly turned to a frown. "You look a bit harried. Is something amiss?"

"Gabriel's father was thrown from a horse and hit his head on a rock." She shifted her gaze to Kiernan. "Mr. Mackenzie, the man who came to tell him, said Lord Liath had been unconscious for two days before Gabriel's mother sent for him. The doctor was greatly concerned about the injury and feared Lord Liath might not live."

Kiernan's face was deeply lined with concern. "How is Gabriel?"

"Upset, but packing his things to leave." She looked back at Dominic. "Could you have someone take his carriage to Fairhaven? He intends to rent post horses, but will need the man to bring his horses back here."

"Of course. I'll take care of it immediately."

"I should go with him," Kiernan said, turning to his wife with a troubled frown.

Mariah's response was instant. "Of course you should. I want to go, too, but you need to move faster than I'm able."

When Dominic looked at his wife, she nodded. He turned to Kiernan. "Jeanie and I will bring Mariah. We'll leave in the morning and travel at a rate comfortable to her. I'll take very good care of her."

"I know you will. Thank you. If you'll excuse me, I'll go pack a bag." On his way out of the room, Kiernan stopped next to Selena. "Thank you for bringing us the news."

"It was the best way I could think of to help. I was with him when Mr. Mackenzie told him. Gabriel took it hard. I'm so glad you are going with him. If his father's condition worsens…" Her voice faltered. She paused and cleared her throat, blinking back unexpected tears. "Gabriel will need you by his side. Take care of him, Kiernan. Please."

"I will, lass." He patted her arm and left the room. Mariah quickly excused herself. Giving Selena a sympathetic and understanding smile, she hurried after him.

"Would you like to rest a few minutes? Have a cup of tea?" Jeanette asked.

"No, thank you. I must hurry back. There might be something more I can do for Gabriel." Selena looked at the man she did not know. "Please excuse my rudeness, sir."

"You are no' at all rude, miss." The Scot walked over to her. "I am Major William Cameron, retired, Gabriel's former commanding officer. Please tell him both he and his father will be in my thoughts and prayers. If there is anything I can do, he only need send word."

"Thank you, sir. I know he will be most grateful. Please excuse me. I really must go back to Gabriel."

As she headed toward the door, Jeanette fell in step beside her. "I'll walk you out." When they were in the hallway, she added, "You are welcome to go to Scotland with us."

Selena looked at her in surprise. "I cannot impose."

"I am certain it would be no imposition. Gabriel would be

greatly comforted by your presence, no matter what happens."

How would Bonham react if she suddenly left Fairhaven? Especially without paying him his money? It would not take him long to learn where she went and with whom. She dared not risk subjecting these good people or Gabriel's family to Bonham's anger. "I cannot go. I—I have obligations here I must attend to."

"I understand."

Though the words were spoken with kindness, Selena thought she detected a note of disappointment. "You will see that he does not drive himself too hard? That he eats properly and has enough rest?"

Dominic's wife laughed softly as they stepped onto the wide porch. She motioned for the footman to shut the door, giving them some privacy. "You sound like a woman in love."

Selena caught her breath, then sighed. "I am rather obvious, aren't I?"

"Delightfully so. Which is just as well, since I think he is head over heels for you."

"I desperately wish I could be there for him." How could she explain?

"But other things hold you here," Jeanette said quietly. "I understand more than you might imagine." She paused, then slipped her arm around Selena's shoulders in a friendly, comforting manner. "Gabriel is a mighty warrior, both by nature and by training. He will protect the woman he loves with his life."

"I could not bear for anything to happen to him, especially because of me."

"Selena, God's hand is upon you and Gabriel. And on your brother, too."

Selena glanced at her, then quickly looked away. Jeanette's eyes held an amazing gentleness and depth of knowledge. Selena felt as though she had glimpsed the love of Jesus in those eyes—and with it, forgiveness and redemption.

Dare she hope?

"Put your faith in Jesus and the one he has sent to help you. Dinna be afraid to trust Gabriel or to go to him in your time of need."

Selena did not know what to say, so she merely nodded and walked down the steps to her carriage. "Please drive, Morley."

The groom nodded and scooted over to the left side of the seat. Dominic's footman assisted Selena into the gig, and she looked back up at Jeanette. "Have a safe journey."

Jeanette nodded. "I will write to you straight away and advise you how Gabriel's father is." She smiled. "Though I expect Gabe will send you a letter even before we arrive. Just remember that it takes the post longer to travel between here and the Highlands than it does a messenger."

"Thank you."

As they pulled away, Selena glanced up at the house. Major Cameron stood at the closed drawing room window, watching her with a troubled frown. Obviously he was worried about Gabriel and his father...but Selena had the strong impression something else concerned him.

Something to do with her.

CHAPTER *Eighteen*

FROM THE MOMENT GABRIEL started back to the house, he began to pray. He asked God to spare his father's life and to restore him to good health. He prayed for his mother, that she might have strength, wisdom, and courage, and requested help in those areas for himself, too.

As he laid out his clothes on the bed, his thoughts turned to Selena. How could he leave her unprotected, not only from Bonham but from Cameron and the government, as well? Dominic would watch over her if he could, but knowing Jeanie, Gabe suspected they would join him in Scotland as soon as possible. He had no doubt that Kiernan and Mariah would make the journey, though they could not travel as quickly as he intended to. Kiernan and Jeanie were like family, not only close to him, but to his parents also.

It would do no good to turn to Cameron for assistance. The major was even more diligent in this work than he had been in the army. The uncompromising determination Gabriel had admired in battle now worked against him. In the major's mind, there was only guilt or innocence. Selena had betrayed her country. She must pay.

He needed to warn her of the danger, but there was no time for a detailed explanation. Gabriel sighed, resting his hand on the top of the wardrobe. How could he ever explain what he had done and why? And what of his promise to Cameron? He had given his word not to reveal anything about the investigation. *Father, is my honor more important than her life?*

Suddenly, he knew what he had to do. He might bring disgrace upon his family, his friends might turn against him and his country condemn him, but that did not matter. As for Selena, when she learned his role in the government's plan, she would most likely hate him. But nothing was more important than trying to protect her, to save her. Not his honor or his life. Not even his love.

Gabriel pulled the valise from the wardrobe and opened the secret compartment in the bottom, removing the small notebook in which he kept his notes.

Everything about Selena's activities was written there, and much of his own actions as well. Included were bits of Gabriel's private conversations with Selena and his thoughts on why she cooperated with the French. He shared thoughts about her character, her good and gentle heart, and how he believed working for the French tormented her.

Though he described the episode with Lawrence, there was no indication that the man was anything other than a military officer soon to leave on duty. He had been careful to write nothing that would give any hint of anyone's involvement with the government investigation.

There were other things he had not put in the little notebook—the secrets of his heart. His love for her. How much he hated spying on her. His self-contempt for deceiving her. And the reason he had become involved with the investigation in the first place.

Gabe set the notebook on his dressing table and quickly folded a few changes of clothes, stuffing them into the brown leather valise. After he arrived at Liath Hill, he would send to Inshirra for more things to wear. He threw in various toilet articles and other things he might need on the journey. Taking the notebook, he went to his desk to write her a letter.

The impossibility of pouring out his heart in a few moments stymied him. Finally he scribbled a couple of pages, hoping she could read between the lines and understand all he longed to say. He also drew a simple map, showing the way to Inshirra and his father's house in case she needed to get in touch with him quickly.

He skimmed through the notebook, refreshing his memory

on a few points. When he came to the page describing how he had read Nick's letter, he stared at it, almost physically ill. It seemed to be the most despicable of his offenses, one he could not bring himself to tell her in person. She would hate him, not only for reading the letter but also for searching her bedchamber and rifling through her most personal belongings.

Sighing heavily, he closed the notebook and folded the letter and map around it. Wrapping them in another layer of heavier paper, which served as a cover when he sent something by mail, he tucked them into his coat pocket.

He put a brace of pistols in the valise and slipped a knife into his boot. After a quick glance around the house to make sure he was not leaving anything important, he picked up the bag and went to the manor.

Leaving the door to the estate office slightly ajar, Gabriel placed the letter and notebook in the top drawer of the desk. He made a few notes for her about estate business and looked quickly through the other papers on the desk, trying to think of anything else that needed to be taken care of soon.

There was no need to send word to Cameron, no way he could without the possibility of Selena finding out. Unless the major's plans had changed, he was still at Dominic's. If he had left, Dominic knew how to reach him and would advise him of the situation.

A few minutes later, Selena stuck her head around the open door. "May I come in?"

"Of course." He jumped up from the desk and went to meet her, shutting the door behind her. Catching her hand, he drew her over to the desk. "The ledger is up to date." He pointed to various papers on the desk. "I made a few notes on the irrigation system, things I dinna think I told Thomas and O'Conner. Here are some questions to ask the laborers tomorrow. We could use a couple more men now, so if any of them impress you, go ahead and put them to work. O'Conner will know where they are needed."

She smiled and smoothed his frown with a gentle touch. "You trust me to hire them?"

"You hired me." He smiled back.

"Then I must be brilliant."

He sat down on the edge of the desk and pulled her into his embrace. "I'm going to miss you, lass."

"I'm going to miss you, too." She met his gaze, her expression soft with tenderness. Sadness—and another emotion he wanted to name but dared not—lingered in her eyes. "Hurry back as soon as you can."

"You know I will." He kissed her with all his love, hoping that when she knew the truth about him, the memory of his touch would soothe her broken heart. Ending the kiss, he held her close, resting his cheek against her soft black hair. "I love you, Selena."

"I love you, too," she whispered, her voice catching.

He briefly closed his eyes at the joy and pain sweeping through him. *Father, why does this have to be so hard? How can I leave her?* "Come to Scotland with me. I can keep you safe there."

She shook her head. "You need to reach your father as quickly as possible. I would only slow you down."

"Then come tomorrow."

"I dare not. Bonham will want his money. I cannot risk his anger if I do not pay him. He could have something done to Nicholas or even exact his revenge on someone here."

Gabriel leaned back so he could see her. "Promise me you willna see him."

"I promise." She brushed a kiss across his lips, resting her hands on his shoulders. "Kiernan intends to go with you. Dominic, Jeanette, and Mariah will follow tomorrow."

Gabe breathed a sigh of relief. "I'm glad he's coming with me. I'll need his steady hand if…" He couldn't bring himself to speak of the possibility of death.

"We must have faith that he will survive."

"I do, part of the time. Then the fear takes over."

"That is only natural."

"Is Mariah able to make the journey?"

"They all seemed to think so. No one even questioned it. They plan to take their time, stopping whenever she needs to."

"Good." He caressed her back, gazing at her beautiful face, memorizing every curve and line.

"A friend of yours, a Major Cameron, was at Thornridge."

Gabriel tensed, watching her face carefully. "He was our commander for the last several years we were in the Gordons."

"So I understand. He said to tell you that you and your father will be in his thoughts and prayers. And if there is anything he can do, you only need to send word. He seems very nice."

"He's a good man, loyal and dependable." He paused, listening to noises coming from the front of the house. "Sounds as though Kiernan has arrived." He cupped her face in his hands, searching her eyes, a near desperation filling him. *Father, please…I canna lose her.*

"Remember that I love you with all my heart."

"And I love you the same." Her eyes pooled with tears as she touched his face. "No matter what happens, cling to that truth."

He held her tightly. "There is so much I need to tell you. So much I need to explain. But I do no' have the time." He released her, catching her hands, kissing the palms. "I left a letter for you here in the desk. In the top drawer. And a map to Inshirra and Liath Hill. The post will eventually arrive there, but if I need to know something quickly, you'd best send it directly by messenger."

"I will."

Gabriel eased away from the desk, guiding her toward the doorway. He put on his hat and picked up the valise. "Time to go."

"I'll see you out. And keep you in my prayers."

He nodded, opening the door. "And you'll be in mine." He stopped and cupped her chin in his hand, nudging her face gently upward. "Stay safe, my love. Dinna do anything to bring harm to yourself."

"I'll do my best."

As they walked down the hall, Lady Camfield and Kiernan came out of the drawing room to meet them. "Haring off already, dear boy?" Her face was lined with concern.

"Yes, ma'am."

"Well, do not push yourself to exhaustion. Regardless of what you find on your arrival, your mother will need you to be of sound mind, not rummy with fatigue."

"A good point."

"Of course it is." She looked at Kiernan. "I'll expect you to see that he follows my advice, Branderee. Don't go dashing off in a stew."

"I'll do my best, madam, but he can be contrary."

Lady Camfield's eyes twinkled. "That I do not doubt. You simply must be all the more so." She stepped up to Gabriel. "Bend down here, my boy." When he complied, she kissed him on the cheek. "I expect you to come back, Gabriel Macpherson. Finish what you started, both on the estate and with my niece."

Gabe glanced at Selena, then directed his gaze back to the countess. "I intend to, Aunt Augusta."

She winked at him. "I like the sound of that. Give my best to your parents. Tell that handsome father of yours that I shall expect a dance the next time he is in London. And your mother shall come over for an afternoon coze so I can tell her what delightful mischief you've been up to."

"That might be dangerous."

"One never knows what conclusions we might come to." She patted him on the cheek. He noted the sheen of tears in her eyes. "Now, forgive me if I don't see you off. I detest sad farewells." Lady Camfield glided back into the drawing room, ordering the footman to close the door behind her.

Kiernan gripped Gabriel's shoulder. "How be ye, lad?"

"Over the initial shock. A bit numb, I think." He attempted a smile. "Mayhap that's good. Then my backside willna get so sore."

Kiernan winked at Selena. "He'll complain every mile."

Selena smiled, though she looked as if she, too, was holding back tears.

Gabe took a deep breath. "Shall we be off?" He couldn't quite keep his voice steady.

"I'm already halfway there." Kiernan smiled at him then looked at Selena, his expression sobering. "Take care of yourself."

"I will. Have a safe journey."

Kiernan nodded. "Now, walk my friend to the coach and kiss him good-bye."

Selena hooked her arm through Gabriel's, walking outside with him. "When you reach Liath Hill, don't try to do everything yourself. Let Kiernan help you."

"I will." Gabe watched him saunter down the front steps. "He's a good man."

"So are you."

"I'm glad you think so." Unhappily, in a few minutes, she very likely would not have the same opinion of him. When they reached the carriage, he handed Kiernan his bag to stow in the boot and turned to Selena. "Come here."

She stepped into his open arms, kissing him with pure sweetness.

Gabriel held her for a few minutes more and leaned down, whispering in her ear. "Please forgive me." When she started to pull away, he tightened his hold. "Watch your back, love. There are others to fear besides Bonham. Men who may be even more of a threat."

When he released her and met her gaze, he saw understanding mingled with the sadness in her eyes. His worry that she had suspected him of working for the government was confirmed. Would she hate him when she realized the extent of his involvement? Or was her loving heart generous enough to forgive him for his failings? He trailed his fingers along her jaw, willing her to believe how desperately he loved her.

She grabbed his hand and turned her head, touching her lips against his palm. When she released his hand and looked at him, tears shimmered in her beautiful violet eyes. "Go with God."

Gabriel nodded. "May he keep you safe." He turned quickly and climbed into the coach after Kiernan.

The footman shut the carriage door.

Gabe looked at her through the open window. "You'd like Inshirra."

"I'm sure I would."

"It could be your sanctuary."

She shook her head. "There is no refuge for me."

Fierce resolve ignited within him. He defied anyone to try to take her from him. "Yes, there is. With me. Never doubt that."

He tapped the roof of the coach, giving the order to leave. The driver cracked his whip and called to the horses. Seconds later the carriage began to move down the lane. Gabe watched her out the window until she disappeared from view.

"Did you tell her?" Kiernan studied him from the opposite seat.

Gabriel hesitated, unsure of what Kiernan would think of him. They had always been honest with each other. He would not start lying to him now. "I told her to watch her back. That there were others to fear besides Bonham."

Kiernan frowned thoughtfully but said nothing.

"I left her a letter and my notebook."

Kiernan's frown deepened and he turned his face toward the window.

Uneasiness rippled through Gabriel. *Please, God, dinna let me lose his friendship.* "The letter explains why I came to Fairhaven and that I've been working for the government. There is nothing in the letter or notebook that could implicate Cameron or anyone else. No' even Lawrence. But it will tell her everything I learned or suspected about her association with the French. I love her, Kiernan. I want to spend my life with her. There wasna time to talk to her, to explain it all. It was the only way I could think of to protect her." He shook his head. "I had to do it, but I dinna know if it was right or wrong."

"Neither do I." Kiernan looked at him, his expression grim. "Though if I were you, I probably would have done the same. But now ye be in a muckle mess for sure."

CHAPTER *Nineteen*

SELENA RETREATED TO HER BEDCHAMBER and curled up in the overstuffed yellow-and-green print chair by the window. She did not need to read Gabriel's letter to know he worked for the government. His whispered warning was enough to confirm it. Judging by the way he tensed when she mentioned Major Cameron's name, she suspected Gabe reported to him. It would also account for her feeling that she somehow troubled the gentleman.

Who better for the major to enlist in his cause than someone formerly under his command, a man who could be charming, sweet, and so persuasive? How good Gabriel was at using tenderness to ferret out one's secrets. A gentle touch, a kind word, or a concerned expression, always at the right moment and with perfect finesse to disarm even one who thought herself a master of such techniques.

Selena shook her head. How ironic that she had been duped so easily by her own methods. Bitter, yet fitting. "I never made anyone fall in love with me," she said angrily. At least no one she knew of. She had not received any letters declaring undying devotion. But then, most of the information she needed had been gathered fairly quickly, gleaned after a drive or two in the park, a few strolls in the garden, and occasionally a kiss or two.

What Gabriel sought required a slow unveiling, layer by layer, until he knew all her secrets. Sadly, for him, he had failed. He did not quite learn them all, since she had been unable to identify Bonham. Would she have revealed her contact if she had known? Perhaps.

It hurt to think he'd come to Fairhaven only to catch a spy, but she would never believe his tenderness and concern were only an act. Those traits were inherent in his nature, as much a part of him as breathing. Some of the charm came naturally, too, although he must have cultivated much of that particular talent.

Given his faith, he obviously held strong views about right and wrong. Deceiving her could not have come easily to him, though serving and protecting his country and its soldiers validated his actions. Surely the lies and knowing he betrayed her tormented him, just as her treachery against her countrymen, and her lies to him, tortured her.

Was his love a sham? "Never!" she whispered fervently. He would not have warned her of the danger if he did not love her deeply. Even though forced from her side, he did not leave her completely vulnerable.

As loneliness enveloped her, Selena leaned her head against the chair and closed her eyes. "Please take care of him, Lord. Please do not let his father die, but return him to good health." She could no longer hold back the tears. "I love him so much, Father. But I'll only bring him pain and sorrow."

More than a quarter hour passed before she felt composed enough to read his letter. When she unfolded the sheets of paper, a small notebook fell out onto her lap. Having a good idea what it contained, she stared at it in dismay. "Gabriel, what have you done?"

With trembling fingers, she tilted the letter toward the light shining through the window.

My beloved, concern for my father forces me to write far too hastily. My mind is a jumble, and I fear I cannot begin to adequately explain. Would that I did not have to write at all, but could talk to you face to face! Please try to look beyond the hurt and anger and know this one thing—I have come to love you more than life itself.

You likely have questioned my true purpose for being at Fairhaven, as my story of needing work and money was flimsy at best. It was a lie. I am a very wealthy man. Though we never spoke last year, you have lived in my thoughts and dreams since the Altbury ball. A friend said you stayed on my mind because God chose you for me. I questioned such wisdom but now believe it to be true. One of the reasons I returned to England was to seek you out, to see if you were the woman of my dreams.

When I was told the government suspected you of espionage, I did not believe it. As illogical as it sounds, I came to Fairhaven to try to prove your innocence. But I also promised that if circumstances proved otherwise, I would honor my duty to my country and pass on any relevant information. I never imagined the choice would be so difficult.

I have longed to discuss this with you, to tell you that I understand your reasons and to find some way to solve the dilemma. But I gave my word, upon my honor, that I would not speak of it. It was difficult to do, but not impossible, as long as I could be here to protect you. Now honor seems far less important than your safety. I cannot leave you and keep silent. Nor can I go without telling you of my duplicity, though it shames me.

I have spied on you. Eavesdropped. Relayed information shared in confidence and during time of great stress and need. But I only passed on things important to the investigation. What I learned of you and your activities, all I have done to discover those things, and many of my thoughts are in this notebook, recorded in case something happened to prevent me from giving the report to my superior in person.

Selena shuddered at the thought of something so dire happening to him.

You will find that I followed you and Lawrence when you walked to the pond and woods. Though I included your conversation, I saw no reason to mention certain other aspects of your walk. I do not know what happened after the second kiss anyway. I could not bear to stay.

Selena paused, sickened by what he had witnessed. The very fact that he loved her in spite of such behavior showed the goodness of his heart.

My superior is aware that you do not know Bonham's identity. That may keep you safe for a while, but I fear he will eventually arrest you. For now, he is more interested in finding Bonham and others involved. You will be watched! Government agents searched for Ellaby in Worcester but did not find him. They will expect you to meet him at the cathedral, then try to follow him to Bonham. Stay away from them both! Avoid military officers. It might be a trap.

I beg you to come to Inshirra. Or to Liath Hill if I must remain there. You will be safe with me until we can sort this out. I love you, Selena, and want to grow old with you. I cannot believe God brought you into my life and heart only to allow you to be taken from me. With his mercy and help, we will find a way to end this so we can be together.

She released her breath in a whoosh, hoping they would not end side by side on a hangman's gallows. If anyone found the letter, it would condemn him along with her.

He signed with his love, than added a postscript.

My superior promised to see what could be done to help Nicholas escape. He gave no guarantees, but I know he will do what he can. Now, be a good lass and burn this letter and the notebook immediately after reading it. Then flee, my love. Come to me.

"Oh, Gabriel, if only I could."

With deep sorrow and regret, she began reading the notebook

filled with neatly written, thoughtfully chosen words that branded her a traitor yet defended her again and again. He gave his observations honestly, yet endeavored to point out the reasons for her actions, primarily that her brother's life might rest in her hands. Gabriel called her a pawn, someone forced to comply with the wishes of the enemy against her will and at much personal sacrifice.

She read how he followed her to the cathedral and saw Ellaby give her the letters from Nick. He knew all along that the story about them being smuggled out of France and delivered to the house was a lie. Yet he had tried to comfort her and ease her torment. Tenderness filled her as she remembered the way he held her that evening, strong and unwavering, gentle and loving. Yes, loving, even then.

Gabriel included much of what they talked about: Nick escaping, being captured, and sent to Bitche…how, after her arrival, he was thrown back into the dungeon and beaten and flogged…her agony and desperation at seeing her beloved brother near death. He asked, *"In the same circumstances, how many of us could have turned away and left him there to die? Would we no' promise anything to save a brother's life?"*

He even mentioned that her father blamed her for Nick's detention and that he had not forgiven her for persuading him to let them go to France. Nor could she forgive herself.

Selena laid the notebook in her lap. Gabriel knew her well. Was he always so insightful, or did love intensify his perception? She decided the bond they shared greatly increased the understanding between them. They had much to learn, but their keen awareness of each other should only make them more sensitive to the other's feelings. She also knew that, given human nature, sometimes sensitivity would fly out the window, leading to disagreements and arguments. But she longed to share even those times with him.

His superior had promised to try to help Nick escape. How did she know that night in the garden to seek Gabe's help? Was it merely intuition, or was she prompted by the Holy Spirit to follow a plan God had already set in motion? A shiver swept over her, not of apprehension, but an unexpected sense that God did indeed have his hand upon them. How she hoped it was true.

She read on, weeping at Gabe's description of reading Nick's letter, not so much because he took away something private and precious, but because it seemed to hurt him so much to do it. She also noted that he did not include any hint of Nick's veiled concern over her possible involvement with the French. Nor did he mention that she had found favor with Napoleon. Any other man would have considered those items important evidence.

When he described her walk with Major Lawrence, his writing style changed. The sentences became short and concise, the penmanship more a hasty scrawl instead of his usual neat lettering. Every word shouted his anger and hurt. After her treatment of him earlier that day—bluntly telling him she did not want anyone to know how she felt about him—it was a wonder he merely stated the facts in a forthright manner. She dearly hoped she would have the opportunity to explain why she had turned him away.

As she suspected, he had followed her across the grounds when she met Bonham. He heard practically every word and emphasized that she did not say where Lawrence was bound, though the major had let it slip to her. There was nothing new in the rest of what he related about that night.

Selena closed the notebook and laid it and the letter on the table beside the chair. She supposed she should be angry with him, but she wasn't. He had done the job required of him but with a care for her far beyond what she deserved.

She tried to assess the situation objectively and calmly. If she avoided Bonham and Ellaby, then Major Cameron—if he was Gabriel's superior—might grow impatient and arrest her anyway. The thought of Newgate prison and the gallows filled her with terror, though she once had accepted them as the penalty for her crimes. But now, having found the love of a lifetime, she could no longer simply resign herself to that fate.

She could not lead the major to Bonham and Ellaby and risk the French retaliating against Nicholas. Even if she turned to Cameron for help, she greatly doubted he would show her leniency. Why should he? And what if she had jumped to the wrong conclusion? What if he wasn't Gabriel's superior at all? He would turn her over to the proper authorities in a flea's leap.

Jeanette's words echoed in her mind: *"Put your faith in Jesus and the one he has sent to help you. Dinna be afraid to trust Gabriel or to go to him in your time of need."*

Had God sent Gabriel to help her? He and Jeanette both thought so, and their faith was strong. "Heavenly Father, I do believe you have sent him, perhaps all of them, to help me. I don't know why. I don't deserve it. But I know you are a loving and forgiving God. I cannot handle this on my own. I never should have tried to."

Guilt and despair brought her to her knees in front of the chair. "Please, God, forgive me for all the wrong I have done. Please protect those I put in danger; keep them safe. Forgive me for not trusting you from the beginning to help me work through this. Lord Jesus, I give this whole situation to you and ask you to help me resolve it. Please be with Nick and keep him safe. Please help him to escape and bring him home to us soon! I put him into your hands, Father. Nothing I do can completely assure his safety. Only you can."

Selena had given her heart to the Lord long ago. She had trusted Jesus as the Savior of her soul. For a while she'd turned away from that trust, certain she had gone beyond Christ's love and reach. Now her heart opened, and she fell on that trust once more, hoping with all her being that Gabriel was right, that God would not give the two of them this love and then separate them. She wanted to be his wife, to have his children, and to grow old with him.

She took an unsteady breath, reaching deep within to do what was right. "Father, if I must pay for my crimes, then I accept that fate. I do not ask to become Gabriel's wife yet, for it would be wrong to bind him to me now. But please give us some time together, even a few weeks free from the secrets that have kept us apart. And if I can make recompense without going to prison or hanging, then please show us the way.

"My heart and mind cry out for me to go to Gabriel. Guide me, Jesus, in all that I do. Set my feet on the right path and show me every step to take. Draw me close to you, Lord God. Help me hear your voice as Gabriel does."

Selena sat quietly for a long time, resting in God's presence and love. His forgiveness cleansed her—reminding her that through Jesus, even sins as great as hers were washed white as snow. He did not speak to her audibly, nor did she hear words whispered in her mind. But as the shadows lengthened in the garden, she felt the peace of Jesus and his healing touch in her heart, mind, and soul.

She knew with a certainty beyond her understanding that she needed to go to Gabriel. He was crucial not only for her safety but for her redemption as well. Warrior and peacemaker, Gabriel was to be her champion, her guardian angel.

"Give me wisdom, Lord. Tell me how to do this in the right way."

Selena rose and walked across the room to the bell pull, ringing for Marietta. Her maid joined her a few minutes later.

"Well, you certainly look happier than I thought you would." Marietta frowned. "Though you do look like you've been crying." Suddenly a twinkle lit her eyes. "Tell me, miss, are we by chance leaving for Scotland in the next half hour?"

Selena laughed, feeling freer than she had in months. "Not quite that soon. I have made my peace with God, something I should have done long ago. I believe it is his will that we go to Gabriel. But we must proceed carefully. I do not think I want Bonham and the English agents to instantly know where we are bound."

Marietta swallowed hard. "English agents?"

Selena's smile faded. "We were right about Gabriel. He has been working for the government all along."

The maid's eyes grew round. "He told you?"

"He whispered a warning." She picked up the letter and notebook. "And he left me these to explain what he did and what they know about me. Which is everything."

"Why didn't they arrest you?"

"Because none of us knows who Bonham is. They are hoping I'll inadvertently lead them to him."

"So you are being watched."

"Yes, by someone unknown now that Gabriel is gone." She wagged the letter and notebook. "I require my fire laid a bit earlier this evening. We need to destroy these immediately."

Marietta quickly crossed to the fireplace and began the task of starting a fire, laying several pieces of wood on the grate. She placed a bit of kindling on the wood, then reached for the letter. "It should serve to start it."

Selena sighed wistfully and reluctantly relinquished the sheets of paper. "I know I must destroy it, but I hate to."

"There will be other love letters from him," Marietta said with a gentle smile. After adding the paper to the kindling, she took the tinderbox and matches from the mantel, striking a flame. The maid paused before she touched the match to the letter. "You're sure?"

"Yes. If someone found these, Gabriel could be tried for treason, too."

"Mustn't have that." Marietta lit the paper. The kindling quickly ignited, and within minutes they had a nice fire. "Tear out the pages from the notebook."

Selena ripped out a few at a time and tossed them onto the

blaze, adding the leather cover when all the pages had burned. It, too, quickly succumbed to the flames.

"When do we leave?"

"Perhaps in three or four days. I'm supposed to interview laborers tomorrow anyway. Tell Thomas what is afoot, but no one else. I need to think about how to proceed."

"What about Bonham?"

"I'll send a letter and his money to Ellaby, but I dare not meet him." Per Ellaby's instructions, whenever she needed to contact him, she sent a letter directed to R. A. Michael at a specific address in Worcester. Since it was in an undesirable part of town, she had never driven by it. Thomas always made the deliveries. He said it was a house of ill repute.

"And your aunt?"

Selena pondered for a minute. "It would not be safe for her here. I doubt agents on either side would have any qualms about terrorizing an elderly lady when they want information."

"What are you going to tell her?"

"Everything."

Selena had never before seen her aunt at a loss for words. Augusta stared at her as if she had grown horns and breathed fire, destroying everyone and everything in her path. Finally she turned away, sadly shaking her head.

Though her aunt's reaction hurt, Selena had expected nothing less. Despite her carefree ways, Augusta loved England with a passion and held military men in the highest regard. Her youngest son, Winston, had served for a time with the cavalry before he was wounded and sent home from the fighting. Thankfully, the injury had no lasting effects.

"You have sent men to their deaths?" Her aunt's voice was strained with sorrow and disbelief.

"I pray not, but I do not know. I had no way to be certain what information might be most harmful. A few things seemed quite unusual, so I kept them to myself."

Augusta drew a deep, shaky breath. She straightened her spine and looked directly at Selena, her expression grim. "I cannot approve or condone what you have done. Yet I can see how you felt you had no choice but to obey their demands. You and your young man are both in a dangerous situation. I suppose it jeopardizes me as well."

"Yes, ma'am. I think it would be wise if you were to spend the rest of the summer visiting your sons."

"They will be thrilled when I arrive without warning."

"You know they will delight in your visit."

"Not if I am fretting over you." Augusta held out her hand. When Selena clasped it, her aunt drew her down on the settee beside her. "Do you go to Scotland?"

"Yes. I need Gabriel to help me sort this out and decide what to do. I know I have done a terrible wrong, but perhaps there is some way I can compensate, other than hanging or spending my life in prison."

"Much better to spend it with him. How will you elude the men watching you?"

"Hope I catch them napping?" When her aunt frowned, Selena shrugged. "I don't have that worked out yet. I am done with lies, except to Bonham. I dare not be completely truthful to him."

"Why not take me to see Winston? You could then proceed to Scotland, since his estate is practically on the way. I can always send for my carriage later. No one here need know you are not going to stay with me. If some crisis occurs here while you are gone, they will try to contact you at Winston's. Unless something quite out of the ordinary happens, he and I should be able to handle it. Otherwise I will send a message to you."

Her aunt would be in capable hands. Winston would not allow anyone to harm Augusta or the rest of his family. Nor would he betray Selena if he learned what she had done. He and Nick were very close. As children, they had seen the world in much the same light.

214

Was it a lie not to tell anyone she intended to go to Scotland, and by that omission, lead any who sought her to believe she would be staying at her cousin's? She didn't know, but she saw no other way to handle it. If she informed any of the staff of her plans, they could pass the information on to Bonham or an English agent without even realizing it. She might never reach Scotland or the safety of Gabriel's arms.

"So when do we leave, my dear?" Augusta watched her thoughtfully.

"Three days should give me enough time to put things in order. I have men to hire." Selena suddenly remembered that she needed to deal with Hardwick. "And one to fire."

"Who?"

"Hardwick."

"It's about time."

"I'm going to make Miller the butler."

Her aunt considered the matter. "I think he will do well. He is a smart young man, and the other servants seem to respect him. Are you going to send Mrs. Pool on her way, too?"

"Not yet. I have to leave someone here who knows how to keep the place running. Hopefully Hardwick's dismissal will make her realize she must change or she, too, will be out the door."

"I should hope so." Lady Camfield sniffed. "Someone needs to remind her that she is not the queen."

Selena smiled, thankful for her aunt's restored good humor. "I'll see what I can do."

And then set my mind on more important things.

"There he is again." Marietta tipped her head toward a man coming into the inn.

Selena surreptitiously watched as the gentleman waited to speak to the innkeeper. It was the third night in a row that he had stayed at the same inn as they did—even when there were other hotels nearby. He had been traveling their same route since they left Augusta at her son's. He rode behind them, though seldom close enough to actually be seen, and always entered the inn a short time after their arrival.

This was the first night she and Marietta had been forced to eat in the common taproom instead of a private dining room. Since they drew an uncomfortable amount of attention from the other occupants, the experience was not to her liking. However, it provided the first opportunity for a close inspection of the man they believed to be following them.

Selena listened carefully as he requested a room for the night. His voice held a note of authority and his speech was refined. He was small and wiry but carried himself with a certain air, confident but not arrogant. In that sense, he reminded her of Gabriel. "I'd wager he was—or perhaps is—a military officer." She spoke softly, so only her maid could hear, as the man signed the guest register.

Marietta nodded. "He has that look. Watch the way the others size him up. There's not a one in here who wants to test him."

Selena glanced around the room. Marietta's assessment appeared correct. Though the other men eyed the newcomer with the curiosity afforded any stranger, there were none of the challenging comments sometimes thrown out by men deep in their cups.

"What do you think?" Marietta whispered. "Bonham's man or the government's?"

"Government. Bonham prefers thugs." Selena looked down at her plate as the gentleman turned away from the desk. She glanced up as he walked past them, toward another table. He met her gaze and nodded politely, not breaking his stride. Still, she had the impression that those dark brown eyes and quick mind missed nothing—especially that she was on to him. She took some comfort in the fact that if he meant to arrest her, he would have done it long ago.

"The guest register is still open, and the innkeeper stepped away." Marietta scooted back her chair. "I think I need to make an inquiry."

"About what?"

"I'll think of something." She walked up to the desk, waiting patiently as the owner conversed with another guest. Selena saw Marietta glance down at the registry and wondered how adept she was at reading upside down. The innkeeper returned to his post, greeting the attractive maid with a friendly grin. She asked her question so quietly Selena couldn't hear it, then thanked the man politely.

Seconds later, Marietta slid back into her chair, mischief in her eyes. "His name is John Brown."

"Why am I not surprised at such a common name?" Selena smiled ruefully. "At least it gives us something to call him. What did you ask about?"

"Breakfast. They begin serving at six."

"We knew that."

"True." Marietta grinned. "But then, I'm the forgetful type."

Selena barely stifled her giggle. Marietta could recite what her mistress had worn to every social event during the Season, describe the paintings on the wall two inns back, and probably correctly state the number of chickens scratching around the inn yard when they'd arrived.

Noting that a drunken gentleman in the corner kept staring at them, Selena and Marietta quickly finished their meal. As they stood to leave the taproom, the jug-bitten man stumbled to his feet and came staggering in their direction.

Seconds before he reached Mr. Brown's table, the government agent looked up, meeting Selena's gaze. A tiny smile hovered about his mouth, and a twinkle lit his eyes. Calm as you please, he stretched his leg out into the aisle. The drunk tripped over his foot and sprawled across the floor.

"Beg your pardon." Mr. Brown hopped up, then leaned over

the dazed man. "I didn't notice you walking by. Have to straighten my creaky knee every now and then. I do hope I didn't hurt you."

Struggling, the man pushed himself up on his elbows, and Brown slapped him heartily on the back. He fell flat with a muffled "Oomph!"

Mr. Brown straightened, glancing at Selena.

"Thank you for your assistance, sir." She smiled, hoping he would blame the slight tension in her voice on the excitement of the moment.

He nodded politely. "Happy to be of service, ma'am."

"It seems we are traveling in the same direction."

"Indeed it does." His smile held a trace of caution. "I'm bound for Inverness, but traveling at a leisurely pace." His admiring gaze swept over her. "Allows me more time to enjoy the scenery." The man at his feet began to stir, and Brown motioned for her and Marietta to make their exit.

Selena glanced over her shoulder as they went up the stairs.

Brown had hauled the drunk to his feet. "Now, my good man, let me buy you some dinner to amend for my clumsiness." He shoved him down in a chair, drawing his attention away from them with genial conversation.

Smiling to herself, Selena continued up the stairs. *Lord, you certainly do move in mysterious ways. Thank you for watching over us.*

CHAPTER  *Twenty*

AT CHALONS, NICHOLAS LEFT JACQUES and boarded a diligence to Paris. The other passengers on the stagecoach were a tailor and a wine merchant with their wives. They were all congenial people who, to Nick's relief, had never been to Switzerland. They were eager to hear about the country, however, so he told them many of the tales the clockmaker had shared with him. In turn, he asked questions about France and their businesses, carefully avoiding any mention of the war or Napoleon.

Though the trip passed pleasantly, the hours seemed to drag by. The worry of making a mistake and being discovered hovered constantly in the back of his mind. Twice, mounted soldiers overtook the carriage, causing his heart to pound until they passed by without stopping them. He shared his bread, cheese, and strawberries with the other passengers. They in turn gave him a couple of boiled eggs and a delicate pastry.

In Chalons, and even more so in Paris, Nicholas noted that the streets were crowded with people trying to sell their possessions or begging for bread. Since his fellow travelers seemed familiar with this situation, he did not remark upon it. It was obviously something widespread throughout the country—except in Verdun where Englishmen's ready gold kept the inhabitants prosperous.

The other gentlemen discussed the matter enough between themselves for him to discover that France was in the depths of a severe depression.

As the coach moved through the Paris streets, the wine merchant's wife stared out the window at the dejected faces of the beggars. "Those poor people. A year ago everyone was prosperous. I do not understand how things could have changed so quickly."

"It's all due to the failure of the French textile industry." The tailor threw up his hands. "Half the time I cannot purchase the fabric I need to make my clothes. There isn't enough cotton, and what there is costs too much."

"It is the fault of the British. Who do they think they are to interfere with our maritime trade and capture French colonies?" The wine merchant tapped his fingers on the seat cushion, emphasizing his words.

"The British are not totally to blame. We should have known this was coming when Napoleon closed our ports to British goods." The tailor crossed his arms with a frown. "Without enough raw material, the textile manufacturers cannot operate. They lay people off. And the banks charge too much for loans, so more businesses have to close."

The merchant nodded. "Which means more people without jobs, less money, and fewer loans, so the banks close, too. It affects us all. Even my business has slowed."

They passed a crowd congregated around a man speaking from the bed of a wagon. Nick didn't catch his words, but the people around him shouted angrily and waved their fists in the air.

"Every day we hear of market disruptions, strikes, poverty, and riots. Even the threat of starvation for many." The tailor shook his head, his expression grim. "I fear the chaos of the revolution has returned."

"No, no, your worry is unjustified." The wine merchant waved his hand. "The emperor will find a way to solve the problem and feed the masses. He has not yet failed us."

The whole exchange was eye-opening to Nick. Selena had told him that Britain suffered from the continental blockade because it dramatically cut into the country's exports. Prices had greatly escalated in England, even for food. Now, it seemed, France was suffering in much the same manner.

When they arrived in Paris, Nicholas decided to rent a room for the night lest exhaustion cause a blunder. He did not stay at the coaching inn but walked to another respectable hotel nearby. Though he slept lightly, he awoke refreshed, his mind clear and alert. He ate a hearty, expensive breakfast since it might conceivably be his last full meal for a while.

On his way back to the coaching inn, his thoughts dwelled on his journey thus far, particularly the moments when he left the town near Verdun. He knew without a doubt that God had spoken to him, promising that he was indeed going home. Nick discovered that he had not lost his faith. He had only mislaid it for a while. The biblical teachings of his childhood came back to him with a clarity that amazed him. Yet he felt a hunger in his heart and mind to know more about God and Jesus, to study the Scriptures from a man's perspective and experiences, both good and bad.

One verse kept running through his mind. Oddly, though remembering references had always been a weakness for him, he even knew where it was found in Scripture: Proverbs 3:5–6. It was a command given to all believers, but Nick felt as though God was personally speaking to him again, a loving father giving him guidance. "Trust in the LORD with all thine heart; and lean not unto thine own understanding. In all thy ways acknowledge him, and he shall direct thy paths."

God had certainly directed his path on this journey, in ways Nick never dreamed of. *Heavenly father, I do trust you and I trust Jesus. Please continue to direct my path. Not just until I get home, but always. Strengthen my faith and guide my understanding. And forgive me for my sins, Lord, for I know they are many.*

When he came across a bookstore, he decided to stop for a few minutes. He immediately found a Bible written in French. He also found several new copies of a guidebook to the French empire, the perfect companion for a journey across the country and out of it—in any direction. Nick almost bought one until he spotted a used copy of a similar travel guide gathering dust on the bottom shelf. When he picked it up, the proprietor shook his head.

"You do not want that one, monsieur. It is out of date. The emperor has added three countries to the empire since it was printed."

Countries in which Nick had no interest. He thumbed through the book. "Since I am only visiting France itself, this one will do nicely." He pointed to some notes scribbled on a page. "It will be enjoyable to see if my opinions agree with the previous owner's." Plus, the well-used book would subtly reinforce his story of having traveled around the country.

The shopkeeper shrugged and named his price. In moments, Nicholas continued on to the other inn to catch the diligence to Caen.

While waiting, he scanned the book to check the handwritten notes. Depending on the man's greed, the bookshop owner might have sold it despite derogatory comments written in the margins, which could prove risky if it fell into a proud Frenchman's hands. He spotted nothing to cause concern, so he read about several places he would have visited if he'd had the time. Then he turned to the section on Caen and the area around it, reading until the call came to board the coach.

Nick tucked the guidebook into his pocket and took his seat inside, the first passenger to do so. When five highly decorated French army officers climbed into the carriage with him, he almost went out the window. Another officer stood outside, waiting to sit beside the driver. Nick offered to take his place so he could be with his friends, but the man declined with a smile.

Praying that his fear was not noticeable, Nick introduced himself as Johann Ochs from Switzerland.

The officers introduced themselves, and the captain sitting next to him pulled out a pocket watch. He tapped the face of the timepiece and frowned. "Are you by any chance a clockmaker?"

Nicholas almost laughed out loud. He should have learned a bit of the trade when he had the opportunity and earned money during his escape. He smiled at the gentleman and shook his head. "Unfortunately, no. I am a historian and tutor." He pulled the travel book from his pocket. "I am having a wonderful holiday visiting your country."

"Is this your first time here?" asked the captain.

"Yes. I have read about Caen, both here and in history books, but I am anxious to see it." He felt his face light up and hoped they would take him merely for a history enthusiast and not a man whose main interest in the city was its proximity to the English Channel. "I have read where the spire of the church of St. Pierre is the finest in all Normandy. And, of course, I must see the abbey of St. Etienne, where William the Conqueror was buried. And the university, library, and the castle." He stopped and grinned sheepishly. "Forgive my excitement, gentlemen. This is a trip I have dreamed about for many years." Eight to be exact.

"And what do you think of Paris?" another officer asked.

"I only saw a little passing through." He did not think it wise to mention places he had seen when he first came to France. Under Napoleon's reign, things had a way of being changed at whim. "I am visiting the outlying cities first, so I may spend all my remaining time in your beautiful capital."

"How long do you stay?" asked the captain, frowning once more at his watch before he tucked it away.

Nicholas shrugged. "Perhaps a long time if I find employment." Or if he didn't turn the conversation over to the officers. Talking too much could prove his downfall. "Are you on holiday, too?"

"We have been. Now we are returning to our post at Caen." The captain glanced at his friends with a grimace. "Until we go to Russia."

Nicholas quickly surveyed the faces of the men across from him. None made an effort to silence their friend. If their expressions were true indications of their feelings, they also believed they were destined to fight in that distant, great unknown. And meet their deaths. To his surprise, he felt sympathy for these friendly French soldiers. "Surely you will not leave anytime soon. You would be caught in the Russian winter."

One of the other officers answered. "We will not go before next year at the earliest. There is much to prepare in order to fight fifteen hundred miles from our frontier."

"Perhaps Napoleon and the czar will reach a compromise and avoid such a terrible war."

"Perhaps. Last month our ambassador returned from Russia bearing many gifts from Czar Alexander, along with his assurances that he does not want war. But that goes against other information the emperor has received, that Alexander has tried to woo Polish nobles and Austria to attack our forces in Poland." The officer shook his head. "No, I fear war with Russia is inevitable. Both Napoleon and the czar want to rule Europe. Someday you will teach all this to your pupils, or perhaps write a great book of history of the empire."

"The dream of every historian."

A young lieutenant piped up. "If given a choice, I would rather go back to Spain."

"It would be warmer." Nick smiled at the man. "The women wouldn't have frostbitten noses."

The soldiers laughed.

"How do the women stay so pretty in your country?" asked the captain.

Nick thought of his sister and other fair English maidens. "They are born beautiful." He almost added that the generally mild English climate helped, then remembered he was supposed to be from Switzerland. "The pure mountain air." He smiled again. "And they learn early how to wrap up and stay warm."

"In the arms of a Frenchman," one of the men said with a hearty laugh. The others joined him, then launched into a lively discussion about the merits of women from different countries.

Nicholas listened enough to laugh when appropriate or toss

in a comment now and then, but his thoughts were far away. If he ever sought a wife, he would look no farther than England.

CHAPTER *Twenty-One*

ON HIS ARRIVAL AT LIATH HILL, Gabriel stepped into his father's bedchamber, easing the door shut. Pale moonlight shone through the window and a lamp turned low illuminated the room with a soft light. He walked quietly across the thick rug, stopping at the foot of the elaborately carved, oak four-poster bed. Though frighteningly pale, his father appeared to be resting comfortably.

Which was more than Gabe could say for his mother. She sat next to the bed in a blue wing chair, her feet propped up on a padded footstool. Though asleep, her head lolled to the side. The housekeeper told him that, though she was exhausted, it had been hard to convince her to let anyone else stay with her husband.

Gabriel moved next to her and knelt beside the chair, lightly touching her hand. When her eyes fluttered open, he smiled. "Mother, you're going to have a sore neck."

"Thank God you've come!" She threw her arms around him.

Gabe held her gently. "Did you doubt I would?"

Smiling, his mother straightened and looked at him. "No. But since you implied in your letters that you were at Fairhaven because of a beautiful woman, I wondered a wee bit if you could tear yourself away."

"I might no' have for something of lesser importance." Smiling, he rested his hand on the arm of the chair and glanced at his father. "How is he?"

"Better than when I sent for you, at least in some ways. He drifts in and out of consciousness, so he has been able to eat and drink."

"That should help him regain his strength. Angus said you

were able to give him water and broth, even at first."

"Yes, but so little at a time that I wondered if it did any good at all. I tried spoon-feeding him, then finally resorted to using a quill."

Gabriel frowned. "How?"

"Dinna you remember playing with quills and reeds as a boy? Cut off both ends and put it in a glass of water."

He nodded. "The water goes up inside it to the level in the glass. If you put your finger tightly over the end of the quill, you can keep the liquid in it until you lift your finger."

"It was easier to slide into his mouth than the spoon. Thankfully, now he rouses enough to take real nourishment. But he's very weak and dizzy if he tries to sit up. His head still hurts much of the time." She paused and took a deep breath. "Gabe, he canna see."

Gabriel stared at her for a heartbeat, then looked at his father. He felt as if someone had punched him in the belly. "He is blind?"

"Yes." She covered his hand with hers. "But I have hope that it willna last. He regained consciousness the day Angus left to go for you. For several days he had trouble with his hearing, too. Could no' hear us at all at first."

"How awful. No' to be able to see or hear." Gabriel could not imagine Patrick Macpherson in such a predicament. He had always been strong and healthy, with a robust enthusiasm for life.

"It was very difficult for him."

"And you."

"Aye, it was. I didna know how to pray. I desperately wanted him to live, but no' if he would be trapped in a dark, silent world."

"But he has regained his hearing?"

"Yes. Even down to understanding a whisper, so I have faith that in time God will restore his sight, too."

"God has already answered my prayers by keeping him alive, so we will trust the Lord for complete healing. If I talk to Father, will he know I'm here?"

"Possibly. Sometimes he rouses when I try to wake him. Other times he does no'."

Gabriel stood and leaned over the bed, taking his father's hand in his. He spoke to him for several minutes but got no response. Releasing his hand, he straightened sadly. "I'll come back in a while, Father." He turned to his mother. "Will you let someone else stay with him while we both rest? You look worn out, and I know I am. After I sleep a few hours, I can come take care of him."

She shook her head. "You wait until tomorrow for that. Send up Cadha. She is good with him. Did you come alone?"

"Kiernan came, too. He's waiting downstairs to see you."

"Then I'll be down soon."

"Dominic is bringing Jeanie and Mariah, though they willna arrive for a few days at the earliest." Gabriel stretched his back. They had traveled every day from dawn until dark, occasionally longer, stopping only when the horses needed rest. He had not been so exhausted since leaving the Gordons.

"Mariah is feeling better? I had a letter from Kiernan's mother telling me she was going to be a grandmother again. She canna wait to spoil his baby as she does Jeanie's."

"I saw Mariah a few days ago, and she said she felt wonderful. When we heard about Father, Selena drove over to Thornridge to tell them. She said they didna seem to think Mariah would have any problem with the trip if they took their time."

"Selena?" His mother's eyes lit with curiosity as she stood and joined him.

Gabe draped his arm across her shoulders as they crossed the room. "The sweetest, most beautiful woman God ever created."

Elizabeth stopped and studied his face. "You love her."

"Aye, Mother, with all my heart."

"Does she love you?"

"Yes." And yet they might never have a life together. He sighed softly.

"But?"

"There are complications."

"She isna married, is she?"

He shook his head.

"Betrothed?"

"No."

She slid her arm around his waist and silently urged him toward the door. "I want you to be happy, but you also need to choose someone suitable."

He had always known as much, though he wondered fleetingly how she would respond if he'd fallen in love with a shopkeeper's daughter. Or worse, a lowly parlor maid. "She is Selena Delaroe, Lady Camfield's niece."

"Lady Camfield is a bit forthright, but I like her. And her niece is an exquisite young woman. I've only spoken with her a few times, but she seems like a fine person. I canna see any impediment to marriage from our standpoint."

"Good. I am hopeful the problem can be solved." During the long hours on the journey, he had considered various ways to proceed. He had a plan in mind. Now he had to pray about it and see if God—and Selena and Cameron—agreed. "Unfortunately, it is no' something I can talk about." He released her and stepped away, opening the door. "I asked her to come to Scotland. If she does, I intend to wed her the quickest way possible."

Elizabeth blinked in surprise. "An irregular marriage?"

"It was good enough for Kiernan's mother. 'Tis good enough for me." Though he had a close relationship with his parents, he hesitated. "The situation is very complex and dire enough that she could suddenly be swept from me. I pray God will grant us a lifetime together, but I will accept with deepest gratitude whatever time he gives us."

"My goodness. Such intrigue. Given my state of mind, it is a wee bit much to take in at the moment. I hope you will enlighten me at some point."

"I dinna know if that will ever be possible. But I hope you trust me enough to believe I could no' love or marry someone who wasna a good, decent person."

"I do. And I also trust God to guide you in such an important step. That isna always the same thing as following your heart. You have to be open to his leading, son. Seek his wisdom and obey him."

"That's what I'm trying to do. I truly believe he blesses our love, that he is the one who brought us together."

"I will pray about it, too." She glanced back at the bed. Patrick had not moved since Gabe entered the room. "I have a great deal of time for such things these days."

"God is our help in time of trouble. I am thankful we can turn to him in our need."

His mother smiled. "And be comforted. So am I. Now, go find some food. I'll come down in a few minutes."

Shortly before dawn, Gabriel returned to his father's bedchamber. He sent the dozing maid to her room for some real sleep. She said his lordship had not roused during the night, but Gabe noticed that he slept on his side. When he had been there earlier, his father had been lying on his back.

After making certain his father breathed normally and appeared comfortable, Gabriel walked over to the window, watching the sunrise over the distant mountains. Though he loved Inshirra, Liath Hill would always hold a special place in his heart. It was the home of his youth, a land of memories. Inshirra was the land of his dreams, a place to build into a fine estate and a home to fill with love.

For his father, Gabe knew Liath Hill held both memories and dreams. Except for excursions around Britain and time away at school, the Scottish estate had been the elder

Macpherson's home since birth. He'd inherited the land—and the title of viscount—at age eighteen. Gabe's father knew every foot of the place, the woods and heather, the burnies and loch, the fields and marsh. He knew the distinguishing characteristics of every cow and sheep, with no need to consult his records to state their ages and how many offspring they'd had.

He'd made tremendous improvements in the property over the years, along with a few mistakes now and then. Gabriel knew his father had dreamed of planting over twenty thousand trees during his lifetime—that was to be his attempt to restore a tiny part of the great pine forest of Caledonia that once had covered the Highlands. Though logging part of the timber each year was key income for the estate, Gabriel's father replaced it all and added more.

As laird, Gabe's father was acquainted with every person in the district, wealthy or poor, down to the wee bairns. Gabe expected he even knew the names of their dogs, cats, and horses. Though his father was not chief of the clan, he served as protector and provider to those who lived around him.

Sunlight shone through the window, warming Gabriel in its rays. Gazing out across the land his father loved, he silently pleaded with God to restore him to perfect health. *Please give him back his sight, Lord.*

He heard the bed creak as his father stirred. Turning around, he found his father squinting in his direction.

"Gabe?"

"Yes, Father. I'm here." Gabriel hurried to his side, wondering if he'd spoken earlier without realizing it, afraid to hope that his father had seen him.

"I thought I heard you during the night." Patrick held out his hand. He kept his face turned to the window, although Gabriel stood next to him.

"Kiernan and I arrived near midnight."

His father smiled as Gabe took his hand. Gabe was shocked at the weakness of his father's grip, but he didn't mention it.

"I'm glad you're here, lad. Glad it was you I heard last night, too. At first I thought it was Neil, which was worrisome since whomever was speaking mentioned being in love with a lady named Selena."

Gabriel laughed. "So you thought Neil had abandoned his wife for another woman?"

His father nodded slightly, then winced. "Then I decided I was dreaming. Margaret is too dear to him."

"Yes, she is. Mother said she sent word to him, but with them traveling in Wales, she didna know when he would be home."

"So she told me." He turned toward the window again, whispering, "It's a sunny day."

Gabriel's heart leaped. "Yes, it is, though early yet." He took a deep breath, afraid to ask. "How did you know?"

Patrick smiled and turned back toward him. "I see the sunlight."

"God be praised!"

"Yes. But dinna get too excited. I can see the light, and when you were standing in front of the window, I detected a darker blur. I thought it might be you because of your height." He sighed heavily. "I canna see anything but light and dark. Here, away from the window, I canna see you at all."

"But Father, it's a start. Mother said you have no' been able to see anything at all."

"True."

"And at first you could no' hear, either." Gabe did not even try to curb his enthusiasm. "Your sight will come back." *It has to*. "Are you thirsty?"

"Yes. Hungry, too. Want eggs, smoked salmon, and some oat bannocks. And coffee."

"Would you like to sit up a bit?"

"Yes." He tried to raise up but did not have the strength. "Blast, I'm as weak as a newborn."

"Let me help." Gabe put his arm beneath his shoulders and

232

lifted him, then reached around as best he could with the other hand and stuffed another pillow behind him. He eased his father back against it. "How is that?"

"It will do. Head is spinning."

"I expect we need to move you up in stages. Let you grow accustomed to each new level before hauling you upright."

His father smiled, though it seemed to take effort. "Terrace the bed."

Gabriel forced a soft laugh. His father had suddenly grown paler. He quickly poured some fresh water into a glass from the bedside table. "Here is some water." He carefully lifted his father's head and shoulders, holding the glass to his lips. He was pleased when Patrick took a good drink.

"Thank you, lad." His father leaned back against the pillows, closing his eyes.

Gabriel watched him closely. "Are you still with me, Dade?"

"Tired."

"Shall I have the eggs and salmon sent up?"

"Porridge."

"With butter and cream?"

"Yes. And coffee," he mumbled.

Gabe set the glass on the table and knelt beside the bed. "I love you, Dade."

"Love you, son." His father held out his hand. Gabriel curled his fingers around it. "Who's your lady?" He seemed to grow weaker with each word.

"Selena Delaroe. Lady Camfield's niece."

"Beautiful."

"Yes, she is, in many ways."

"She's in trouble?"

"Aye, sir." Gabriel adjusted the sheet and light blanket, smoothing out the wrinkles. His father had obviously heard some of the previous night's conversation. "Someday perhaps I can explain."

"Her brother still held in France?"

233

"Aye."

Opening his eyes, Patrick turned his face toward him and nodded minutely. "Love her?"

Gabriel sensed his father had a good idea of Selena's situation. "More than anything."

"Protect her." With those barely whispered words, his eyes drifted closed and his hand relaxed beneath Gabe's.

Gabriel frantically moved his fingers to his father's wrist, searching for a pulse. Relief rushed through him when he found the steady, strong heartbeat. At least he still lived. But was he unconscious again? "Are you warm enough, Father?" He asked the question louder than he should have.

No response.

In desperation, he shook him gently. Still no response. His father had drifted back into unconsciousness.

"Be with him, Lord Jesus," Gabriel whispered. "Anoint him with your healing. Fill him with your peace and love."

He was thankful for the words they'd shared and the counsel his father had given him even as he fought to retain consciousness. He thanked God for every second his father had been awake. "But it wasna long enough."

He had hoped—foolishly believed—the time of shadows and fear had passed. "There is so much I need to tell him, Jesus." He shook his head. "Things I need to make right between us." All the worry, fear, and guilt he had held inside came pouring out on a sob. Leaning his forehead against the mattress, Gabriel wept, silently begging God to be merciful.

Several minutes passed before he heard the floor creak. He raised his head, meeting Kiernan's misty gaze. Pushing to his feet, Gabriel wiped his eyes on his sleeve.

"How is he?"

"He was awake for a few minutes." Gabe cleared his throat and pulled his handkerchief from his coat pocket.

"Did he know you?"

Nodding, Gabe blew his nose. "He even noticed that the sun is shining."

"Thank the Lord." Kiernan rested his hand on Gabe's shoulder.

"I have been. Father could tell I was standing in front of the window. Decided it was me because of my height. He heard Mother and me talking last night, though he thought it might be Neil." Gabe managed a smile. "He picked up enough of the conversation to guess I was in love with a woman named Selena. He was relieved it was me instead of Neil."

Kiernan smiled. "I expect he was. He would no' think too keenly of Neil forsaking Margaret, especially after she's given him four children."

Gabriel looked back at the bed, another swell of emotion clogging his throat. "I thought...hoped that he would no' fade again."

"I think it will pass completely before long. The housekeeper told me that he was unconscious for much shorter periods yesterday. He wasna awake too much, but a good part of the time he slept normally. Come on down to breakfast. Your father's valet is waiting in the hall to sit with him while you eat."

Gabriel stayed with his father several hours during the day. Twice more while he was there, his father roused. Gabe's mother reassured him that he was spending more time conscious than unconscious. And she was overjoyed that her husband could detect light and dark.

During the afternoon, Gabe checked with the grieve, who oversaw the farming on the estate, and the forester to make certain all was going well. Nothing urgent needed his attention, so he spent an hour bringing his father's ledger up to date.

Near dinnertime, Angus Mackenzie returned from England. Both Elizabeth and Gabriel scolded him for not taking more time to rest, but he insisted he had to come back to see about the laird. Before he left for his own home, Angus asked to speak to Gabriel alone.

"I have a message from yer lady, sir."

"All is well?"

"Aye. Seemed to be fine. She and her aunt were going to visit Lady Camfield's son. Winston, I believe she said. Probably there by now."

Well, at least she's seeking safety somewhere. Gabriel's relief was mixed with irritation.

"I dinna think Miss Delaroe intended to stay there long."

"She planned to go back to Fairhaven?"

"No."

Gabe wished Angus would tell what he knew a little more quickly. "Did she say where else she was going?"

"No' exactly." A twinkle lit Mackenzie's eyes. "But she did ask quite a few questions about Inshirra and Liath Hill. Wondered if it was cold in the Highlands this time of year. I had the impression she was trying to decide what kind of clothes to pack."

Gabe inhaled quickly. "You think she may be coming here?"

"Canna say for certain, but that be my thinking. I told her the evenings are chilly sometimes. Heard her remind her maid to put in several shawls, a coat, and her sturdy walkin' boots."

"You said she sent me a message?" Gabe expected Angus to pull a letter from his pocket.

"Aye, but she didna write it down. Said to tell you that she would be seeking her refuge very soon. Seemed to think you would understand."

"Indeed, Angus, I do." Gabriel grinned at him, wondering what the man would think if he hopped on his father's desk and danced a jig.

CHAPTER *Twenty-Two*

NICHOLAS ARRIVED AT CAEN without mishap. A few minutes after they reached the city, the French captain offered to show him around. Nick thanked him but declined.

"I would drive you to distraction within an hour. Historians tend to spend a painful amount of time studying details, both of buildings and past happenings." He smiled and shrugged. "I will probably stay a day at each cathedral. And if by chance I run into another lover of history at the university, I could be there for a week."

The officer laughed, wished him a pleasant visit, and left with his companions for their lodgings.

Nicholas had already studied the map of Caen in the travel guide and knew how to eventually reach Adrienne Le Clare's house. He took his time, going another direction for a while, admiring the buildings and the town square to give the appearance of an interested visitor. Though he carried his bag, he stopped at the abbey of St. Etienne, where the body of William the Conqueror had once been buried.

Convinced he was not being followed, he turned toward his destination. When he came upon Rue de Charles, it did not take him long to find number 15. One could not miss it. Had he misunderstood Anton? Did the Frenchman truly mean that someone at this large, impressive house sheltered escaped English prisoners? Nicholas felt awkward walking up the steps with his valise in his hand. Perhaps he should have gone to a hotel first, then sought out Anton's friend.

He lifted the knocker, rapped on the door, and tried to appear calm. A footman answered, studying him curiously. Once again, Nick was glad he knew French so well. "Good day, sir. Is this the home of Madame Adrienne Le Clare?"

"*Oui.*"

"I am Johann Ochs, from Switzerland. A mutual friend asked me to stop by and give her his regards."

"Come in. I will see if she is at home." The footman stepped aside, glancing at Nick's clothes and the bag as he walked inside. "Wait here, please."

Nick set his valise by the door and admired the landscapes decorating the wide entryway. Some appeared to be French scenes, but most looked suspiciously English. He was no art connoisseur, but he thought all had been painted by the same hand. He was trying to read the signature on one when the footman returned.

"Mademoiselle will see you. This way, monsieur. I will put your bag in the cloak room beside the front door."

He led Nicholas past the withdrawing room to a smaller, sunlit room at the end of the hall. A young woman who looked to be near his age stood by the window, frowning thoughtfully at a canvas on an easel. She held a pallet of paints in one hand and a brush in the other. Rainbow splatters speckled her brown smock and a green streak decorated one delicate cheek. Standing in the light, threads of gold glistened in her sandy brown hair, caught up in a cluster of thick curls at the back of her head. Wispy bangs lay across her forehead, and she impatiently brushed one particularly curly lock aside, leaving a smudge of red near her temple.

Despite being adorned in paint, she was pretty. Pretty enough to leave him tongue-tied. To his surprise, the footman closed the door behind him. At the click of the latch, she looked up and smiled.

"Good afternoon, Mr. Ochs. I am Adrienne Le Clare." As he expected, she, too, spoke French. She set the brush and pallet on a nearby marble-topped table. Picking up a rag, she wiped her hands, then her cheeks and forehead as if she were used to having smudges on her face. "I understand we have a mutual friend?"

"I believe so. William Mahieu sends his regards."

Recognition flashed in her eyes. "Ah, yes, dear William. How is he?"

"Doing well."

She unbuttoned her smock, revealing a simple blue day dress made of fine muslin. "Good." She slipped off the smock and laid it on the table, glancing at him. "His leg has healed then? He is walking normally again?"

Was this a subtle test to see if Anton had truly sent him to her? "No, he must use crutches. I don't know if he will ever be able to walk without them."

She nodded and motioned for him to come toward her. "I understand. I'd like your opinion on my painting. Something does not look quite right, but I cannot decide what it is."

Nick walked across the room, thinking he should have bathed and changed before paying her a call. Unfortunately, his only other clothing was just as dirty and travel-rumpled as what he wore. She glanced at his dark gray jacket, blue waistcoat, and gray pantaloons as he neared her, increasing his regret at being so hasty to seek her aid. "Forgive me. I should have waited until I was more presentable to call on you."

"You have come a long way." She smiled, her pale blue eyes twinkling. "And you are far more presentable than some of William's friends."

He had obviously correctly answered the question about Anton's leg.

"What do you think?"

Nick stared at her. What did he think? That she was lovely, sweet, and kind. That he had not eaten since breakfast and was suddenly exhausted. That he wanted to lie down on the sofa with his head in her lap and have her sing him an English lullaby. He shook his head at such nonsense.

"Is something wrong, Mr. Ochs?"

"I am more weary than I thought."

"We shall tend to that in a moment." She turned to the painting. "What is wrong with it?"

He started. She had switched to English and spoke without any trace of a French accent. Nick narrowed his gaze, but she gave no hint of why she had changed languages. When he turned to the picture, an intense wave of homesickness swept over him. The artistic style was the same as the paintings in the entry, but instead of hills and lakes, she had painted a city street scene. One he knew well.

"York." He was unable to keep the longing and sadness from his voice.

"Yes," she said softly. "I have visited it often, but it doesn't seem quite right."

"The street…" He paused, clearing the lump that formed in his throat. "It is a little too wide." He, too, spoke in English, unable to keep up the pretense.

She studied the painting for a few seconds, then nodded. "I believe you are right. Yes, I'm certain of it. Drat. I'll have to move the buildings on one side."

Other than the street being slightly out of proportion, the scene was perfect, right down to the signs hanging in front of the shops and the items in the windows. It was all there…the linen draper's his mother visited, the hat shop his father favored, the confectionery where he and Selena bought treats as children. Without thinking, he reached toward the canvas.

She quickly caught his hand. "The paint is still wet," she murmured, wrapping his hand in both of hers and searching his face. "You, too, have been to York?"

"I grew up in Yorkshire." If he'd made a mistake and she worked for the French, he was doomed. But at that moment he did not care. "Those are shops I visited as a boy."

Adrienne drew him away from the painting, leading him to

a giltwood sofa upholstered in yellow flame stitch. She still held his hand even after they sat down.

"Are you Nicholas Delaroe?"

His heart began to pound. *God, help me.* He'd made a terrible mistake. She wasn't offering comfort. She hung onto him to keep him from running. She wasn't really Adrienne Le Clare. Or if she was, she had changed her allegiance. Could they have sent word from Verdun already? What kind of cruel joke were they playing, letting him reach the coast? Had the gendarmes discovered that Anton and Suzette had helped him? Had those good people been imprisoned because of him? *Dear God, what have I done?*

She touched his cheek, turning his face toward her. "Nicholas, I work with the British government. They contacted me and other agents a few weeks ago, saying that you might try to escape. They gave us your description and mentioned you were from Yorkshire."

"That is why you were painting York?"

She smiled. "Yes. Though at first it was an unconscious thing. I paint whatever scene comes to mind. Whenever I visit a place, I do quick pencil sketches to help me remember it later in the studio." She smiled wryly. "Obviously, I am not always quite as exact with the sketches as I should be. It did not occur to me until I started the project that I probably thought of it because of you."

"Did my sister tell them I planned to escape?" It was the only way they could have known. Perhaps his fears had been for naught. Had Selena been working with their government all along?

Adrienne hesitated slightly before answering. "I believe that is how they learned of it."

"Do you know how she is?"

"No, I'm sorry. I don't. I only know that she confided in a friend, and he, in turn, sought assistance for you from the government." She studied his face with a frown. "They said you were a détenu. Were they mistaken? You do not seem old enough."

"I was not old enough. I was sixteen, but they kept me anyway."

"How cruel." She squeezed his hand. "Well, God willing, we will see you safely home to England. But you must realize that it may take time. The coast is constantly patrolled. All small boats must be hauled up on shore at night, so it is difficult to steal one. However, we do have friends here who have ways of acquiring what we need. Sometimes they help us out of hatred for Napoleon. More often the gleam of gold sways them. I will contact them as soon as possible. They might have what we need within a few days. Or it could be a month or two."

Nick tried not to show his disappointment. "I'll be grateful no matter how long it takes. Where should I stay?"

"Right here."

"Isn't that too obvious? If you have helped very many of us, the authorities may become suspicious with so many different men staying here." His face grew warm at the implication of what he said.

"I am half French. They will think I have adopted the ways of my father's country and become like many French women these days, taking lovers and quickly tiring of them." She laughed and released his hand. "Do not worry. I have not grown decadent. I don't have any lovers. Nor have any of the other men stayed with me. I had them spirited elsewhere."

"Then why keep me here?"

"I will trust your safety to no one else. You are of great importance to our government."

He didn't like the sound of that. Perhaps Selena *was* in as much trouble as he had feared.

Adrienne's countenance softened and tenderness shaded her eyes. He had seen that expression in women's eyes before, but never directed at him. It was the look a woman gave a man when she cared for him. He had just met her. She couldn't possibly have that kind of feeling for him after a few moments' acquaintance.

No? Then why do you feel such a singular attraction to her, a unique bond?

He pushed the irritating question away. His feelings didn't matter. He was weary, not thinking straight. Besides, how could he expect an artist so adept at capturing beauty to overlook his flaws? Not just the emotional ones from his detainment, but the physical ones inflicted at Bitche. The monster that wielded the lash had taken perverse pleasure in not marking his face or any visible place. But the dozens of scars on his body were a constant reminder of the man's cruelty, as was the echo of his taunt: *"The women will flock to your pretty face, Delaroe, but your body will repulse them."* How could it not, when he could barely stand to look at it himself?

Adrienne smiled. "You are special, Nicholas. To England—" she paused, studying his face, a slight frown creasing her forehead—"but also to me in a way I do not yet understand. So you shall be my guest, as supposedly recommended by my friend William. It would be best if you continue to use your assumed name. I will try to remember to call you Johann or Mr. Ochs. But if I forget and call you Nicholas, we shall say it is your middle name. Does Mr. Ochs from Switzerland have a passport?"

"Yes, and it appears quite official."

She nodded in approval. "And does he have a profession?"

He grinned. "Yes, but he is *not* a clockmaker. Everyone I've met on the trip thinks he should be." Her laughter pleased him. "I have a fondness for history, so Mr. Ochs is a historian and sometimes tutor."

"Excellent. I, too, enjoy wandering around old buildings and dusty archives. It will not seem at all unusual for me to have a guest who likes the same thing. We will have great fun seeing the sights and losing ourselves at the university archives.

It is such a common occurrence for me, no one will pay us any mind."

Nick frowned. "Is it wise for me to roam about?"

"There is some danger to it. But I think it would be even more dangerous for you not to go out at all. My servants assist in my activities and are well rewarded for their help and their silence. Still, I am sure my neighbors noticed your arrival, though I doubt the local authorities and army will hear about your escape too quickly."

"I rode all the way from Paris in a diligence full of army officers," he said with a grimace. "I think they believed my story. We parted company at the coaching inn. I purposely wandered around the city before coming here."

"Good. If they were suspicious, they would be here already. We will take some excursions over the next few days, then load you up with books from the university. My grandmother generously contributed to their library. I am allowed to borrow anything that suits my fancy. If anyone asks about you, I'll say you are writing a short paper on William the Conqueror to present to the Swiss Historical Society.

"Then, in about a week, you will appear to leave, only to return during the night by the back entrance. There is a passageway from the carriage house to the wine cellar here. After that, unfortunately, you must be confined to the attic during the day and early evenings so you will not be seen by visitors."

Nicholas relaxed against the back of the sofa with a chuckle. "You are very good at this."

She grinned. "Yes, I am. I came here two years ago to stay with my grandmother, who was ill. When she died, I inherited this house and obtained permission to remain in France to attend to her numerous business affairs. I knew when I came here that she could not live long. I also knew that I would be in a rare position to help British prisoners. Though my father is French, my mother is English and we lived in England. I grew up in Dorset." Sadness drifted across her face. "I was betrothed to a British officer when I was nineteen, but he died in the fighting."

"I am sorry."

"So am I. He was a good man. But that was long ago. I have made a new life for myself, doing what I can to thwart Napoleon's evil." She rose gracefully and walked across the room. "You must be exhausted and famished."

"How many have you helped to escape?"

She halted a few steps from a green velvet bell pull and turned to face him. "You are the tenth. Unfortunately, only seven made it. One was captured on the way to the beach and another drowned when his boat capsized. Do you know how to swim?"

"Yes."

"And sail?"

Nick fidgeted, shifting his position. "I've sailed a few times, in a small boat with my father. Never alone. But I've read everything on it that I could find."

She frowned, tapping her finger on the back of a chair. "I hope that is good enough. There will be no opportunity for practice."

"I will not return to Verdun or Bitche. I would rather die evading capture or trying to cross the Channel."

Her jaw tightened in determination. "I will not let you die."

He smiled gently. "There is only so much you can control."

"More than you think, as long as you do nothing foolish."

"I may be many things, but a fool is not one of them." Though he spoke quietly, he was aware he did not successfully hide his irritation.

"I'm relieved to hear it." She tugged on the bell rope and flashed him a grin. "Which would you like first—food, sleep, or a bath?"

His annoyance fled. How could he stay so when she looked so delightfully mischievous? He grinned back. "A sandwich, a hot bath, and a nap, in that order, if you please. And I'd be very grateful if one of the servants could loan me a change of clothes until mine are cleaned."

"I will have Henri show you to a guest room. We should have some clothes to fit you. I keep a supply handy since some of the men arrive in tatters."

"I have other things in my bag, but I wore them on the first leg of my journey."

"You rode a coach all the way?"

He shook his head. "I walked most of the first night. In the next town, to my surprise, your compatriots hid me from the gendarmes. They helped me hire a coach, which took me to Chalons. There I caught the diligence to Paris."

"Have you slept any?"

"I took a room for one night in Paris."

"Then you are not totally exhausted."

"No. A few hours' nap will set me to rights." He stood and moved across the room, stopping next to her. "Why?"

Someone knocked on the door. "Just a minute, Henri," she called, then turned back to Nicholas. "I would like you to join me for dinner tonight." She searched his eyes. "I want you to tell me about Bitche. Everything that happened there."

"For you or the government?"

"Both."

"Does this have something to do with my sister?"

"Yes." She started to turn away, but he grabbed her arm.

When she frowned, he eased his hold. "Tell me." Indecision flickered across her face. "Please, Miss Le Clare. Whatever she has done, it was because of me."

"How do you know?"

Nick released her. "At Verdun, something was wrong, but all she would say was that she could not bear to leave me behind again."

"Again?"

"She had visited me once before." He ran his fingers

246

through his hair in frustration and worry. "And she was with me in 1803."

"When you were captured."

"Yes. Last autumn, seconds before Selena drove away, she asked me to forgive her. There was no time to question her, but I have worried greatly about what she could have meant."

"You think it means something bad?"

He shook his head. "I do not know. I had been at Bitche for some time when I was thrown back into the dungeon for no apparent reason. A few days later I was beaten and severely flogged. I couldn't understand why I was treated so badly. Up until then it had not been pleasant, but they had not dealt too harshly with me. I later learned this all happened after she arrived at the prison."

He glanced at Adrienne and caught her gaze skimming his face, neck, and hands. She was looking for signs of the lash. When he saw skepticism in her eyes, he quickly untied his cravat and unwrapped it from around his neck. She would not believe him—nor would the government—unless she had some inkling of what Selena had seen. It saddened him to know she would find him revolting, but so be it.

"I was cut to pieces, but they threw me back into the filth of the dungeon and left me there." She watched wide-eyed as he shrugged out of his coat and quickly shed his waistcoat. "By the time they brought Selena down to see me, I had been out of my head with fever for days."

He unfastened the buttons at the neck of his shirt, then the cuffs. His voice thickened with emotion. "I thought I was delirious when I heard her speak my name. I opened my eyes, and she was there. My precious, beautiful sister, kneeling in the sewage on that cold rock floor, cradling my head in her lap. She wept and touched my face with her hands."

Nick jerked the shirt off over his head, crumpling it in his hand. Adrienne's gaze fell on the white scars that covered his

247

chest like a spiderweb. She gasped and covered her mouth with one hand, her face reflecting her horror. Fighting the bile that rose in his throat, he turned so she could see the numerous thick red scars on his back. And so he would not have to watch how he sickened her.

"My face was the only place she could touch. I was covered with stinking sores and rotting flesh. Selena thought I was unconscious, but I saw her lift her head and look up at a man. Not the commandant. Someone in civilian clothes."

He cleared his throat and took a deep breath. "She begged him to set me free. She promised to do whatever he asked if he would not hurt me anymore and would let her take me from the prison." He heard Adrienne whimper softly. "I could never bring myself to speak of it. I hoped it was only the delirium."

He fumbled with the shirt, trying to straighten it to put it on. When he felt her cool hand on his back, he froze. Heart pounding, he closed his eyes. How could she bear to touch him? She traced the scars with aching tenderness, as if trying to take away his pain, his shame. Then her other hand joined the first, her fingers moving across his back and shoulders, down the smattering of scars on his arms and up again, soothing his hurt with the gentlest touch he had ever known. His chest ached and his throat burned. When he felt her soft, wet cheek press against his back, he forgot how to breathe.

"Selena is spying for Napoleon," she whispered.

No! An agonized sound burst from his throat. He inhaled with a painful shudder. "Would that God had let me die," he whispered, his voice breaking.

Adrienne slid her arms around him, holding tightly. "Nicholas, God gave men free will, and some of them do terrible things. But God is greater than wars and governments and tyrants. He wanted you to live! So much so that he allowed Selena to be used as a pawn. He will show us how to save her, just as he saved you."

Her tenderness eased his guilt and pain, and her faith

strengthened his. *By your grace, God, we will find a way.*

He couldn't help wishing that this strong yet gentle woman could make the journey with him.

CHAPTER *Twenty-Three*

WHEN SELENA ARRIVED AT LIATH HILL, Gabriel was not there.

Mariah came to meet her in the entry. "Gabriel and Kiernan rode to Inshirra yesterday afternoon. But they plan to be back by dinner today, so you will not have too long to wait."

"Then Lord Liath is better?"

"Much improved. He drifted in and out of unconsciousness for several days, a few even after we arrived. At first he could not see at all. His vision is gradually returning, though still somewhat blurry. He is sitting up in a chair right now in his chambers. Yesterday was the first time he felt strong enough to be out of bed. I know he would be pleased if you went up and said hello. Gabe's mother and Jeanie are keeping him company." Mariah grinned. "They don't know you are here or they'd be down already. I came downstairs when I saw your carriage through the window. I thought it would be amusing to surprise them."

"Are you certain it won't be too much of a surprise? I'm afraid Lady Liath will think I'm shamefully forward by coming here."

Mariah smiled and motioned her toward the stairs. "Jeanie tells me Elizabeth, Gabriel's mother, has been waiting so long for him to take a wife that she is practically turning cart-wheels."

Selena came to an abrupt halt. "Take a wife?" It was what she wanted, but not yet. And she certainly did not want Gabriel's mother to think she had raced to Scotland to force Gabriel to tie the knot.

"That is one reason you came, isn't it? Or have we all, especially Gabriel, jumped to conclusions that we should not have?"

"I do love him and would like nothing more than to be his

wife." Selena hesitated, uncertain how much Mariah or the others knew about her situation. "But I don't know if now is the right time for such an important step."

"Well, you will have a difficult time convincing Gabe. He went to Inshirra to have it aired and cleaned from top to bottom—so everything would be ready for his new wife."

"Oh dear." Selena's heart rate quickened in excitement, anticipation, and a hint of trepidation. If Gabriel had his mind set on marriage, she doubted she could resist his wonderful, sweet persuasion. Especially when she didn't want to in the first place. "I suppose I'll have to try to talk some sense into him."

Mariah laughed. "You don't sound very determined about trying to change his mind. I don't think you should." Her expression grew serious. "Difficult times lie ahead of you, Selena. Take your joy while you can. And equally important, share it with Gabriel. He deserves happiness. I believe you do, too."

"It is hard to stand firm in my resolve when I love him so."

Mariah knocked on the open door of Lord Liath's combination bedchamber and sitting room. "See who I found wandering around the front garden?"

Jeanette and Lady Liath looked toward them, both smiling in welcome. Selena noted that Lord Liath also turned his head toward the door. He frowned slightly, then touched his wife's hand.

His wife smiled at him. "It's Selena."

Longing shot through her. She wanted a relationship such as theirs, for her and Gabriel to know each other so well that they instinctively knew what the other needed.

Lord Liath's face lit up. "Welcome, my dear. Come in. You'll have to move close so I can see you better."

Jeanette hopped up from the chair on the other side of him, greeting Selena with quick hug. "Take this place. I've been pestering him all afternoon." She and Mariah moved to the settee.

Selena sat down, absently straightening the skirt of her jonquil muslin dress, and glanced at Gabriel's mother, relieved that she appeared pleased. "It is so good to see you recovering, sir."

"Feels good, too." He squinted, focusing on her face. "You are as lovely as ever. Unfortunately, my eyesight isna what it should be yet, so you'll have to excuse me for squinting at you."

"Mariah tells me it has improved dramatically."

"Indeed it has. Even blurred vision is a thousand times better than total darkness."

"I'm sure Gabriel is greatly relieved. He tried to be brave and strong, but he was terribly worried about you." Selena smiled at his mother. "I worried about all of you."

"Gabe sent you a letter by messenger. You didna receive it?"

"No. I left Fairhaven three days after he did. I took Aunt Augusta to visit her son and stayed one night before coming here."

"No doubt the messenger is following you around the country and will return in a few days." Gabriel's mother smiled. "Gabriel will be happy you are here."

Lord Liath chuckled. "That, my dear, is the understatement of the century. The lad will be overjoyed."

"No more so than I will be to see him." Selena felt warmth rush to her cheeks. "My aunt sends both of you her regards and best wishes for your recovery, Lord Liath."

"Call me Patrick, lass."

"And I am Elizabeth," Gabriel's mother said. "We dinna stand on formality with those close to us." Her eyes sparkled merrily. "Or those with whom we expect to become close."

"I am honored," Selena murmured. And she was. But she also felt a bit awkward. Both the situation and the feeling were new to her.

"Now, husband, it is time you trotted back to bed." Elizabeth touched his arm gently.

Patrick laughed. "If I were able to trot, lass, I would no' be going near that bed."

Selena stood. "Do you need assistance?"

"Thank you—" Gabe's mother smiled at her gratefully— "but we can manage."

"Lizzie, you're interfering." Patrick winked at Selena. "Perhaps I would enjoy *two* beautiful ladies helping me across the room."

Elizabeth laughed. "Of course you would, you old rogue."

"Now, this is the Lord Liath I remember." Selena smiled at them, saying another silent thanks to God. "Ever the charming gentleman."

He chuckled. "Who do you think taught Gabe?"

"Then you must be a master."

Gabriel's mother laughed again. Mariah and Jeanette joined in.

Patrick grinned wickedly. "Nice to know my efforts paid off." He stood, though not easily, and Selena quickly took hold of one arm. Elizabeth supported him on the other side. "Thank you, ladies." His tone became subdued. "You were right about one thing, wife. I need to lie down."

"And I was wrong about another." She leaned forward slightly and looked at Selena. "I appreciate your help. The way he is wobbling, we both would have toppled. Are you dizzy, Patrick?"

"Aye."

Selena held on to his arm until he sat down on the side of the bed. She wondered if Elizabeth could slip off his robe. "Do you need anything more?"

"No, dear. I can do the rest. Feel free to go lie down, ring for some tea, or anything you like."

"I would enjoy a walk. I've been cooped up in the carriage all day."

"Stroll to your heart's content."

"Thank you." Selena followed Mariah and Jeanette from the room.

Suddenly Gabe came racing up the stairs, a dashing Highland warrior in his kilt and plaid. He grabbed Selena around the waist and lifted her in the air, swinging her around with a whoop. Laughing, she rested her hands on his shoulders. "Gabriel, put me down!"

He set her feet on the floor and pulled her against him, kissing her for all he was worth. Any doubts she had about coming to Scotland vanished in an instant. She belonged in his arms, surrounded by his gentleness, strength, and love. How had she ever thought she could live another day without him?

He slowly ended the kiss and held her close. "Welcome to Scotland, my love."

She giggled against his throat. "That *was* quite the welcome."

He eased back and looked down at her with a rakish grin. "I'd do better if we didna have an audience."

Only when she heard his parents talking did she realize she hadn't shut the door to Lord Liath's room.

"Well, Lizzie, was it a good kiss?"

"Aye, it was. I believe she just said yes."

Gabriel and Selena strolled hand in hand through the fragrant pink heather, gradually going downhill toward Loch Laggan. He pointed out their destination in the shimmering birch woods before them. The loch was also visible from the house, but the woods would give them both a view and privacy.

For one of the few times in her life, she went for a walk without a hat or bonnet. She didn't care if she wound up with a hundred freckles. She wanted to feel the warmth of the sunshine and the cool mountain breeze on her face. Every few minutes she caught a glimpse of a small stream rushing through the woods—a *burnie,* Gabe called it. "No wonder you love it here. I've never been anyplace more beautiful."

"Inshirra is just as pretty in its own special way. Loch Insh is tiny compared to Laggan, but the River Spey flows along one side of my property. And the woods are bigger, older. The house is a good size for family and company. I'm sure you'll want to redecorate. Most of the furnishings are out of date."

"I'm in no rush to make another house fashionable," she said with a laugh. "Fairhaven has been enough for one summer."

"Did you have a good journey?"

"Yes, though we were followed by a government agent." She remembered the incident with the inebriated man at the inn. *Or perhaps because we were.*

Gabriel tensed, looking down at her with a frown. "You're certain it wasna Bonham's man?"

"I'm sure. He's a gentleman, not someone Bonham would hire. We noticed him at the inn the first night after we left Aunt Augusta at Winston's. He's a small, wiry gentleman, well dressed and well spoken. He stayed at the same inn as we did every night, even when there were other places nearby. He always rode far behind us, but occasionally we caught a glimpse of him. And he never passed us, even when I had Thomas drive very slowly and take an excursion to see a historic sight."

Gabe guided her down a narrow trail through the forest. "All he did was follow you?"

"Actually, he spoke to us on several occasions, beginning the third night. That evening the private dining room was already occupied, so Marietta and I ate in the taproom."

"I dinna like that." His frown returned.

"Neither did I, but it afforded us the opportunity for a better look at our mystery man. Marietta even asked the innkeeper a silly question just so she could check the guest book for his name. The gentleman was registered as John Brown." Selena looked up at Gabe with a grin. "Not a very inventive name."

He smiled back and smoothed her hair as the wind ruffled

it. "No, but then, he wanted to remain unnoticed. Sounds as if he didna succeed very well with that."

They came to a small clearing. Beyond a few scattered trees, the loch sparkled in the afternoon sunlight. Thicker woods and undergrowth surrounded the open area on three sides, sheltering them from the world and prying eyes.

"After your warning, I expected someone to follow us, so we watched for him. I did not hie off in secret or in the middle of the night. I sent Bonham's money to Ellaby with a note, explaining that I was going with my aunt to visit my cousin. I indicated I could not turn down her request without making her suspicious, and that I did not know how long I'd be gone."

"You have a way of contacting Ellaby?" He unfastened the plaid draped over his shoulder and around his chest and back, spreading it on the ground. He tossed one end of it over a log so they could lean against it and look at the water.

"Yes. I occasionally sent him messages, or in this case, a package, addressed to a different name at a house in Worcester. Thomas says it is a house of ill repute."

"That might be a way of tracking him to Bonham."

Selena nodded as he reached for her hand. "They have to meet in some fashion, though I do not know how or where."

Gabe helped her sit then dropped down beside her, putting his arm around her shoulders. "How did you begin talking to Brown?"

"A drunk had started for our table. Mr. Brown stuck his foot in the aisle and tripped him." Selena laughed, resting her head on Gabe's arm. "It was really quite amusing, though I didn't laugh until later. With a little sly assistance from Mr. Brown, the man remained on the floor for a few minutes. While I thanked the worthy gentleman, I casually mentioned that we seemed to be traveling in the same direction."

Gabriel chuckled. "You're good at that."

"What?" She tipped her head toward him.

"Plucking information from enchanted gentlemen before

they even realize they've told you anything."

"Is that a compliment?"

He gave her that adorable lopsided smile. "Yes. What did he say?"

"He calmly agreed, though I detected a bit of wariness in his eyes. He said he was going to Inverness. Then he occupied the drunk's attention with an apology until we were safely in our rooms."

"I'll have to thank him when I meet him."

"Do you think you will?" She gazed into his remarkable eyes, noting that the longer he looked at her, the darker the green became.

"Aye, we'll meet, one way or another. I assume he didna reveal the true purpose for his journey?" His gaze dropped to her lips.

Her heartbeat quickened at the heat building in his eyes. "No, though I'm sure he knew what I thought. It seemed as if he found the whole thing rather amusing. After the incident at the inn, he spoke to us briefly whenever the opportunity arose. Always some comment about the scenery or a place we had passed during the day. I felt strangely reassured knowing he was nearby, though we had no further need of his assistance."

"I'm glad he was there, too, especially since his mission was obviously only to follow you." He cupped her face with his hand, caressing her cheek with his thumb. "Thank you for having Angus tell me you were coming. It helped me no' to worry so much about you and gave me something wonderful to look forward to."

"You understood the message, then." She felt breathless, but it had nothing to do with the mountain air.

"I know what I hoped it meant, that I am your refuge, no' just Inshirra."

"You are my everything." She caressed his beloved face with her fingertips. "My refuge, my happiness, my life."

"Then marry me. I want to be your husband, Selena. To live

with you always." Gabriel pulled her into his embrace, kissing her more passionately than ever before. He kissed her again and again, whispering words of love in half a dozen languages. When he finally raised his head, she looked up at him though a haze.

"Will you marry me, sweet lass?"

"Yes, my love."

He smiled and kissed her tenderly. "I give you my promise to be a faithful husband, Selena. And to always love you." He touched his lips to hers again, deepening the kiss. When he finally pulled away, his green eyes smoldered with desire. "Become my wife, love, here and now."

That cleared some of the fog from her mind. She stared at him. "Here? Now?" She knew exactly what he meant, what he wanted. She wanted it, too, but…Selena swallowed. "In the middle of the woods?"

A tiny twinkle lit his eyes, easing some of the intensity of seconds before. "A bed of pine needles isna soft enough?"

"I suppose it is." She dragged in a breath. He made it very difficult to think coherently. "But Gabriel, we aren't married."

He gave her a teasing, knowing smile. "I asked and you said yes. You have my promise to be your husband." He leaned back, relaxing against the log. "According to Scottish law, if I promise to marry you and we make love on the faith of that promise, then we *are* married, in the eyes of the Lord and the law."

She frowned at him, eyeing him warily. "Are you certain?"

"Yes, ma'am. Every Scot of kissin' age knows the law. Especially here in the Highlands, where there isna always a minister close enough to perform a regular wedding." He smiled, lightly caressing the side of her neck. "In theory, it protects a lass from dishonor. Of course, no' all men are as true-hearted as I am. But if I renege on my promise, you can send the constable after me."

Selena scooted away from him, assuming a prim and proper

air though her cheeks were hot. "Gabriel, if we go back to the house and tell your parents we're married, then they'll know...um...what we did."

He shrugged as if it didn't concern him a bit. "True. But it is no' at all uncommon here." He grinned. "We Scots are a practical bunch. Passionate, too."

"And proud of it, apparently." She was irritated that he could throw her into chaos so easily. Perhaps she would not be so sensitive if she did not feel guilty over her behavior with the military officers during the past months. A sudden thought rocked her. Did he think she had done more than kiss those men to learn their secrets?

"Oh, aye, I forgot about your delicate English sensibilities." He sounded positively sarcastic. "And how such ladies are so easily offended—when you choose to be."

Her head spun as disbelief washed over her. He *did* think so! He expected her to give herself to him because she was unchaste. No better than a harlot. She scrambled to her feet and raced down a path toward the loch, desperately wanting to get away from him. How could she have been so stupid? He would never forget that she willingly kissed Lawrence. He probably imagined she had been with dozens of men. Why shouldn't he think she had done whatever was necessary to obtain the secrets?

Anything to protect Nicholas.

CHAPTER *Twenty-Four*

"SELENA!" GABRIEL CAME RUNNING down the hill after her. "Selena, wait." He caught hold of her arm, but she jerked away.

"Don't *touch* me!" She was amazed that she kept her voice low instead of shrieking at him. "How many, Gabriel?"

He stared at her with a bewildered frown. "What are you talking about?"

"How many officers do you think I seduced? Five, ten, fifty? Did you believe I would lie with you here in the woods because I'm a lady of easy virtue?"

Understanding dawned in his eyes, and he shook his head. "I never believed…"

When his voice trailed off, she knew he had. "I cannot marry you. I am not what you think I am. I have never been with a man. Never!" She turned away, staring at the water, determined not to cry, not to be further humiliated.

He stepped up behind her, close enough to put his arms around her, but he did not touch her. "Selena, I do no' believe you are a woman of easy virtue, but I canna say I never thought it. When you let Lawrence kiss you, I was angry and hurt. I let my imagination overrule my good sense.

"I hung on to those feelings, even nurtured them, until I followed you to meet Bonham. Suddenly the only thing that mattered was to keep you safe. Later, when I had time to think about it, I realized I'd reacted from wounded pride as much as anything else. It hurt to see you with Lawrence, but if you hadna turned me away earlier, I might have considered it in a whole different way. I might even have stayed until you went back to the party. In my heart, I knew you hadna done anything more with him or with any of the officers. The next day, he admitted you were no' impressed with him. And even less so the second time he kissed you."

"You talked to him about it?" When she faced him, he nodded. "He was working for the government? It was all a sham?"

"Yes. He was to give you false information they wanted you to pass on to Bonham. Only at the time they didna know the name he used. They thought it might help them discover who you reported to."

"You knew about this ahead of time?"

"Yes." He looked down, nudging a pinecone with the toe of his shoe. "I wasna in favor of it, but that didna matter." He glanced at her before turning to scan the hills and loch.

"So there was no need for you to follow us. You knew Lawrence would report what happened."

It seemed like a long time before he answered. Even then, he kept his gaze averted. "I'd seen the way he looked at you. I didna trust Lawrence no' to try to take advantage of you. And I still hoped we were wrong, that you were no' working for the French. I suppose I needed to see for myself if you tried to glean information from him. I didna want to take his word for it." He sighed and looked at her. "I was also very angry. I wanted to know how you acted with him. If I meant anything at all to you."

Her anger evaporated as regret swept over her. "And because of my actions, you decided I did not care for you. Gabriel, forgive me for hurting you. I turned you away because I was afraid of what Bonham might do if he found out how much I loved you. I knew he had to be watching us. I'm so very sorry that I kissed Lawrence. I told myself it wouldn't hurt because he meant nothing to me. I even convinced myself it was a sweet gesture to a man going off to war. But I felt positively horrible."

One corner of his lips turned up in a tiny smile. "When you told Bonham that you found it distasteful, I was uncommonly pleased, which seemed rather silly since you were in danger at the time. I'm certain you were right about Bonham watching us. He knew you had a chat with the major."

"He knew Lawrence was coming to Worcester. At the assembly, Bonham told me to send him an invitation after he arrived and see what I could learn from him. I assume someone had mentioned the major's expected visit at some gathering, and Bonham noted it."

"That's likely. Unless Bonham has some contact in the government or military." Gabriel frowned thoughtfully. "He must have heard it at a party. No one man could keep track of all the officers home on leave. Do you have any idea who Bonham reports to?"

"I'm not sure there is anyone above him here in England. It's merely an impression, so I can't say for certain. I've come to the conclusion that he had to have been in France with Nick, or at least in a position to watch him. Bonham knows far too much about him."

"He seems to like disguises. He could have posed as almost anyone. A French visitor or laborer, perhaps."

"It would not have taken him long to learn Nick's habits, routine, and friends. And a flirtation with a maid could have gained him access to Nick's rooms."

"Since he seems to know you well also, it would make sense for him to suggest you to his superiors, whether they are here or in France." He looked thoughtfully across the hillside. "If he does report directly to France, that will be in your favor when we catch him. You will help nab a big fish instead of a middle-sized one. Gives us more to bargain with."

"I didn't pass on everything Lawrence told me."

"Which is just as well. Makes you look better in Cameron's eyes."

"Major Cameron?"

Gabe nodded.

"I thought he might be involved."

"How did you conclude that?" He looked at her with a frown. "Did I give him away?"

"Not exactly. When I met him at Dominic's, I had a feeling I disturbed him somehow. And when I mentioned meeting him, it seemed to bother you. Under the circumstances, it made sense."

"Women's intuition." He was quiet for a minute, his expression troubled. "After the muddle I made of things this afternoon, do you still love me?"

She touched his arm gently. "Of course. I'm sorry I overreacted."

"And I'm sorry I was so…ungentlemanly."

She smiled and slid her arms around his neck. "A passionate Scot."

Gabe rolled his eyes. "I should no' have mentioned that." He drew her close. "And I should have been more in control even if I have missed you terribly. I let my love for you overrule my good sense. I didna stop to consider that you might feel that it was wrong or be embarrassed. Please forgive me."

"You know I do." She brushed back a lock of his hair that had fallen across his forehead. "Is there some other way we can be married quickly?"

A smile slowly spread across his face. "Aye, lass, there is. All we have to do is give our pledge to each other before two witnesses. And we have a whole houseful of them."

She ducked her head, suddenly remembering that she shouldn't marry him before her problems with the government were settled. "What if catching Bonham is only good enough to save me from the gallows? I might have to spend my life in prison. Or be transported. If we were married, your reputation and good name would be ruined. I could never truly be your wife or give you a family."

He gently nudged her chin up, meeting her gaze. "I want no other but you, Selena. If they transport you, I'll move to New South Wales. You would be released eventually, and we could build a home there. Or go to another country. If they throw you in prison, I'll fight until you are freed. In the meantime, you'll have every comfort I can provide, and I'll visit you as often as I'm allowed. But none of those things will happen, lass. By God's grace, we will overcome this thing."

"I desperately hope you are right."

"I'm trusting God to make it right. So I'll ask you again, my love. Will you marry me?"

Selena hesitated for a heartbeat, then again gave her life and her trust to Jesus. "Yes."

Framing her face with his hands, he lowered his head and kissed her with the utmost tenderness. "Would you like to wait until tomorrow, so we can spend our first night of wedded bliss alone in our own home?"

A warm sense of relief and well-being flowed through her. "I would like that very much."

"May your every wish be so easily granted."

The following afternoon, Selena watched with a smile as Gabriel and Kiernan clasped hands and made a seat with their arms, carrying Patrick downstairs to the withdrawing room. Elizabeth hovered behind them every step of the way, telling them every few seconds to be careful. They lowered him into his favorite chair and stepped back to let Gabe's mother get him settled.

"Are you chilled?" She straightened his woolen robe and tucked a blanket around his feet and legs.

"No, dear. I'm fine."

"Are you dizzy? Is there too much sunlight? Do you need a pillow behind your head?" She fluttered and fussed until her husband caught her hand and held her still.

"Lizzie, sweetheart, sit down and let them give their pledge. You've been pestering the lad for years to marry. Now let him do it." Patrick smiled at her as she took a seat beside him. "I feel fine. Better than I have since I was hurt." He looked at Gabriel. "And if you and your bride will stand right in front of me, I think I can see you reasonably well."

"Gladly, sir." Gabe looked at Selena. "I dinna want you to

264

miss anything, especially seeing my beautiful bride."

Awed by the love shining in his eyes, Selena caught her breath. Her gaze swept over him as he walked across the room, admiring his incredibly handsome face and his athletic body. She glanced at his legs, smiling when she remembered him saying they became scrawny if he didn't take long walks. *You must have been walking a great deal, sweetheart.*

In the kilt and plaid, he looked every bit the noble Highland warrior that he was. *How magnificent he is!* A swell of emotion brought mist to her eyes. *Heavenly Father, thank you for this fine, wonderful man you have given me. I love him so. Please help me to be a good wife to him, the wife he deserves.*

Gabe stopped beside her and offered her his arm. When she slipped her hand around it, holding tightly, he smiled in reassurance. "You're sure, lass?" How could such a strong man be so tender?

Selena still didn't believe she deserved this man or the love they shared. She half expected to wake up and find it was all a dream. Or worse, for the major and his men to burst into the room, arrest her, and drag her away from him.

A hint of worry crept into his expression. He covered her hand with his and brushed a kiss against her forehead. "I love you, Selena. With all my heart. But I'll no' push you into marriage unless it is what you want."

"It is. I'm just nervous. I've never been a bride before." With no special wedding gown, she didn't look like one, either, but she did not care. She had chosen the lilac dress she wore the first time they spent the afternoon together. And it pleased him. She could see it in his eyes.

He chuckled softly. "I'm glad to hear you have no'. This is better than an elaborate church wedding. We can make it as long or as short as we want."

"Short," she whispered as they moved to stand in front of his parents.

"No' too short." He winked at her. "I want it to seem special."

How could it be anything else?

Jeanette and Dominic sat on one side of Gabe's parents, with Kiernan and Mariah on the other. Selena had asked Marietta and Thomas to join them. They stood behind the others, holding hands. When Marietta pulled a kerchief from her pocket and wiped her eyes, Thomas put his arm around her and whispered something in her ear. Marietta smiled up at him. Selena expected there would be another marriage while they were in Scotland.

Gabriel took her hands in his, looking into her eyes with complete love and tenderness. She noticed that his hands trembled slightly. It made her feel better to know he was nervous, too.

But when he spoke, his voice was firm and clear. "Selena Delaroe, I love you with all my heart. You are my life. Nothing in this world matters more to me than you. I believe God brought you to me and that he blesses our love and this marriage. I promise to be a good and faithful husband to you, to provide for you, protect you, and stand with you through bad times and good. Before God and these witnesses, I take you as my lawful wedded wife, to love and cherish forever." He leaned over and gently kissed her forehead. "May God give us a long and happy life together."

Her heart pounding, Selena clung to his hands and drew a deep breath. How could she tell him how much he meant to her? It would take a lifetime. Through God's grace, perhaps she would have that long.

"Gabriel, you have given me a reason to live, to seek God's forgiveness and blessings. You have helped restore my faith and brought me back to the love of Jesus." When she saw the sheen of moisture in his eyes, she paused, taking another breath and clearing her throat. "I thank God with every beat of my heart for you and the love we share.

"Gabriel Macpherson, you are my love and my champion. My very life. Before God and these witnesses, I proclaim that I love you with all my heart and soul. I joyfully, and thankfully, take you as my lawful wedded husband, to love and cherish forever. I will be a good and faithful wife to you and try my best to be the kind of wife you want and need. May God grant us a very long life together."

"Amen," he whispered, brushing a lone tear from her cheek with his thumb. Then he bent down and kissed her gently.

He is my husband! Selena's knees went weak, and she felt Gabriel's arms go around her in support.

He dropped a butterfly kiss on her temple. "You're no' going to faint on me, are you, lass?"

Selena laughed and threw her arms around his neck, hugging him tightly. "I never faint! I just can't believe you're mine."

He held her close, then drew back slightly, looking down at her. Fire blazed in his eyes for a heartbeat before he banked the flame. "Believe it." He kissed her again, leaving her legs even weaker.

After a round of hugs and congratulations, laughter and happy tears, Marietta and Thomas left to see to the loading of the luggage for the trip to Inshirra. That morning, Selena and Gabriel had decided they must tell his parents what she had done and the perils they faced. But he insisted they wait until after they were married. He had already explained to her that the others were aware of the situation.

Gabriel moved two chairs closer to his parents, so his father would have a better chance of seeing them clearly. "There is something we have to discuss with you." He glanced at Kiernan, Mariah, Dominic, and Jeanie. "It might be good for you to stay, too. You might learn something new. Or have some helpful suggestions."

Elizabeth's gaze darted from Gabriel to Selena and back to her son. "This is what you spoke of the night you arrived? What you said you were no' free to explain?"

"Yes, ma'am." Gabe waited until Selena was seated, then sat down next to her, reaching for her hand. "I did not feel I could say anything without Selena's agreement. You are aware that her brother is a détenu?"

"Yes," Patrick said. Elizabeth nodded, her brow wrinkled in a worried frown.

"Napoleon has used him to force Selena to gather intelligence for France."

Elizabeth gasped. "You are a spy?"

Selena nodded sadly.

Patrick sighed and shook his head. "I feared as much when you said she was in difficulties."

"But I thought détenus were fairly well treated." Elizabeth held her hands tightly together in her lap. "I know they are no' free to leave, but the ones in the *ton* who have returned said life was much the same at Verdun as in England."

"It is at Verdun, though sometimes there are more restrictions and demands made upon them than at other times," Selena said. "Life can be very different if they try to escape or do something to incur the wrath of the commandant and are sent to one of the prisons." She went on to explain how she found Nicholas at Bitche and what transpired to coerce her into working for the French.

"I have tried to be careful regarding what I passed on to Napoleon's agent, but I have no way of knowing how much harm I have done." She inhaled shakily. "I pray I have not hurt anyone, but I may be responsible for the deaths of many."

"No, love. I told you, even the Foreign Office does no' believe you could have directly caused anyone great harm." Gabriel explained how he had been working for the British government, though he did not mention Cameron's name. The fewer people who knew the major's involvement, the better.

Patrick studied his son thoughtfully. "Are you going back to England and try to straighten this out?"

"Yes. We hope to help capture Bonham. Perhaps that will earn her enough grace with the government to gain her freedom. Though we want to spend a week or two at Inshirra.

Everyone is entitled to a honeymoon." Gabriel smiled at Selena. "She tried to convince me to wait to marry until after we knew her fate."

"I'm glad you did no'," Elizabeth said. "This way at least you will have some time together." At Gabriel's look of surprise, she smiled at Selena. "I'd wager he didna want to tell me about this until after you were married."

Selena returned her smile. "He insisted upon it."

"He thinks he knows me well, and in most instances, he does. I have always tried to dissuade him from situations where I thought he might be hurt."

"She ranted and raved for weeks before he went off to war," Patrick said with a grin. "One minute she'd be praising the lad for his bravery and the next ringing a peal over his head about the danger. Had us all in a dither."

Elizabeth made a face at her husband, causing them all to laugh. "You will learn, Selena dear, that Scottish mothers are no' afraid to express their feelings. Both good and bad. I think even if you had told me about your predicament ahead of time, I would no' have tried to keep you from marrying. Far too many people never find a love such as you share." She glanced at her husband. "I would rather my son have a few weeks or months of great happiness than no' ever know it at all."

Relief and thanksgiving swept through Selena. She had been so worried that Elizabeth would despise her when she learned what she had done. She had feared that Gabe's mother would hate her for marrying him and possibly dragging him, and his family, through the shameful mire of a public trial. "Thank you, Elizabeth. Your approval means very much to me."

Gabe stood, then leaned over and kissed his mother on the cheek. "And to me. Now, we'd best be on our way, or my bride will arrive at her new home in the dark. Father, send for me if you need me."

"Of course." He waved his hand. "But Kiernan and Dominic will take care of things here. If you wait a fortnight to go back to England, I should be up to running the estate completely on my own."

Gabriel grinned and tugged Selena to her feet, slipping his arm around her. "That gives me even more reason to stay longer at Inshirra."

"Lad, if you need an excuse, I have no' taught you very well." Patrick winked at him.

Gabe laughed when Selena blushed. "You did fine, Dade."

They said their farewells and walked outside to Selena's waiting coach. Marietta sat beside Thomas on the driver's seat. Gabriel looked up at them with a mischievous smile. "Keep your eyes on the road, Thomas."

"Aye, sir. I will." He grinned back. "Most of the time, anyway." The coachman glanced at Marietta, love shining in his eyes. "The Highland air agrees with her. Puts a blush in her cheeks and a sparkle in her eyes."

"It isna the air, Thomas. 'Tis matrimony. It's as infectious as a cold." Gabriel opened the door for Selena, helping her inside.

Selena laughed at him as he climbed in after her and sat down on the opposite seat. "I'm not sure that was a very flattering comparison."

He shrugged. "'Twas the only one I could think of." His gaze wandered slowly over her. "I'm a wee bit distracted." He waved absently out the window as the coach pulled away from Liath Hill.

When the road curved and trees hid them from the house, he said softly, "Come here, Mrs. Macpherson." Scooping her up, he settled her comfortably across his lap, supporting her back with his arm.

"Yes, Mr. Macpherson?" She gazed up at him with a happy smile.

"It occurs to me that I have no' given my wife a proper kiss."

Several minutes later, the thought crossed Selena's mind that his kiss was quite improper—and incredibly wonderful.

CHAPTER *Twenty-Five*

STANDING BACK FROM THE OPEN ATTIC window so he wouldn't be seen, Nicholas gazed restlessly toward the small park across the street. Three young children raced across the grass, playing one last game of tag in the twilight while their nannies gossiped on a nearby bench.

The long, narrow room had been his home for two weeks, and he craved being outdoors. He had read rare historical papers and ancient journals until he was sick of them. Studying the Bible had occupied some of his time, but he was too restless to stay with it for too long a stretch. A path marked the carpet where he paced up and down hour after hour, day after day.

He only left the attic to go downstairs each night, spending the late evening hours with Adrienne. To avoid suspicion, she kept up many of her usual activities—going to dinner with friends, visiting art exhibitions, painting in the afternoon. They often sat in her studio late at night, discussing England, history, or art and occasionally debating various political views. She challenged him to chess and usually won. He taught her billiards—a pleasant experience that entailed putting his arms around her several times as he showed her how to hold the cue and make the shots.

Emotionally, Nick tried to keep his distance and not grow too fond of her. He knew all too well the pain of leaving behind those for whom one cared. He needed to escape France soon…before he fell in love with Adrienne.

Her familiar knock—two taps, a pause, and another tap—evoked a happy smile. *Before you fall in love with her? Too late, I'd say.* Nick quickly squelched the thought. Under the circumstances, it was only natural for him to be attracted to her. Once he was in England, there would be many women from whom to choose.

"And I'll be the next king," he muttered. Opening the door, he questioned the warmth spiraling through him at the sight of Adrienne. He instantly detected a change from her normal attitude, an undercurrent of excitement and anticipation, and stepped back so she could come inside. "What brings you up here this time of day?"

He absently shut the door, watching her cross the room and close the window. When she turned back toward him, her eyes sparkled and her face shone. "Everything has been arranged. A boat will be waiting tonight."

Nick caught his breath, fighting a battle between excitement and sorrow. He was going home! And he might never see her again. He exhaled slowly, forcing himself to calm down, trying to quell his disappointment because she seemed so happy. She had been determined to help him, for which he was extremely grateful. He just wished she weren't so pleased that he was leaving.

"What is the plan?"

As she moved away from the window, he met her in the middle of the room. Tipping her head to one side, she studied him with a tiny frown. "I thought you would be happy."

He forced a smile. "I am, but I'm also nervous." *And being torn in two.* The depth of his hurt took him by surprise. He had expected sadness, but not such pain. Reaching for her, he gently pulled her close, resting his cheek on her soft brown hair. "I'm thrilled at the chance to go home, but I don't want to leave you."

"You aren't."

Frowning, he drew back, sliding his hands to her shoulders. "What?"

"I'm going with you." She smiled tenderly and caressed his cheek.

He wanted her to go to England—had dreamed of the possibility almost every day he'd been there—but not this way. It was sheer foolishness. Releasing her, Nick stepped away, shaking his head. "No. It's too dangerous. You could drown or be shot. Captured and thrown into prison. Or worse, executed for being a spy." Gripping the top of a straight-backed chair, he met her gaze. "You are not going."

"Yes, I am."

"No, you aren't. I'll stay somewhere else, find another way to England."

"Nicholas, I appreciate your concern, but it is imperative that I go, too. I've been blessed to help Britons escape, but over the past two months I have felt a growing sense of urgency that I should leave. Before you arrived, I requested permission from the French government to return to England, advising them that all my grandmother's business affairs were completed. Today, I received a letter forbidding me to do so. I am not willing to wait and learn why they want to keep me here."

"Isn't there a safer way?"

"None that I can think of. Nor can I risk waiting. The authorities could knock on my door any minute."

"And haul you off to prison." Nick grimaced. "What do you have in mind? Surely you don't intend to walk the seven miles to the coast."

She tossed him a saucy grin. "Why walk when we can go in style? At least, I will. You'll have to hide under the carriage seat."

"Not for long." He barely controlled a shudder. "I don't like dark, enclosed places." In truth, after Bitche, he hated them. He reminded himself that he had endured much worse discomfort, both mental and physical.

"It won't be as bad as you think. Both seats in the coach have large compartments beneath them to carry extra supplies or luggage. The back one has a removable panel between it and the boot to make space for larger objects." She winked at him. "Like handsome gentlemen."

"If they curl up in a ball." He made a face.

Adrienne laughed. "Once we are out of the city I'll raise the seat, and you can join me inside. When we leave here, you can go to the carriage house through the passage from the wine cellar. None of the neighbors will see you get in the coach, so they won't have any idea you've been here all this time."

"You are amazing."

"I'm glad you think so," she said with a pleased smile.

Nick glanced around the attic at the furniture she had brought up for him. All of the furnishings in the house were of the highest quality, though most were too ornate for his tastes. "What will you do with the house and everything your grand-mother left you?"

"There are a few small things I will take with me. A minia-ture of Grandmother when she was young and a brooch she was particularly fond of. But the rest must stay here. Most of the staff will remain as well. If anyone questions my where-abouts, they will say I decided to take a journey. The govern-ment did not forbid me to move about the empire." She laughed quietly. "They do not need to know I only chose to go such a short way on land.

"My maid will retire to the country on a generous pension. My coachman will take the carriage to Paris and sell it. He, too, has been well paid to disappear for a while." She looked at the table where Nick had spent so many hours studying. A journal and box of papers from the university archives sat next to his notepad. "Henri will return everything to the university. I gave the other servants six months' wages. They have agreed to remain here for a month, in case something goes wrong. It is unlikely we would be able to return to the house, but at least it keeps the option open. And having a few servants here will fur-ther the impression that I am on a temporary trip, not a perma-nent one." Sadness drifted across her face as she looked around the room.

"When the war is over, if Napoleon hasn't confiscated the

house, hopefully one day I can come back. My grandmother knew what I planned to do and encouraged me, even in helping the British soldiers and détenus. She did not like what France had become under Napoleon."

"I regret that you will lose so much." Nick stepped around the chair, stopping in front of her. "Do you realize how kind and generous you are?"

"I can afford to be. As the only grandchild on both sides of the family, I'm spoiled shamefully. My French grandfather was a banker and left me a fortune even before Grandmother bequeathed me the remainder. My English grandfather owns half a dozen farms and estates, of which he has given me two." Smiling impishly, she ran her fingertips along his jaw and turned toward the door. "Perhaps you should think about marrying me. You would instantly become a very wealthy man."

Nick grabbed her around the waist, halting her in midstep. "As far as I know, I'm already a wealthy man in my own right. I had a generous grandfather, too." With her back to his chest, he slid his arms around her and bent down, murmuring in her ear. "If I think about marrying you, it will be because I greatly admire and respect Adrienne Le Clare, not her money." Dropping a light kiss on her cheek, he straightened, releasing her. "Now, off with you, woman. I've never known a lady who did not have a thousand things to do before a trip."

She giggled and scampered to the door. Looking back at him, she grinned, her cheeks delightfully pink. "This time, at least, I won't have to worry about packing my clothes."

He laughed, suddenly filled with excitement and happiness. "I have a compass and I know how to navigate by the stars. The travel guide I picked up in Paris has a map of the Channel and the French and English coasts. We'll need water, food, and a bag to hold it." His smile faded. "Do you have a pistol?"

Her expression also grew serious. "Two of them. I'll take care of everything."

He had no doubts that she would.

Near ten o'clock, a light knock sounded on Nick's door. "It is time to leave, monsieur."

"I'm ready." Hours earlier, Nick had donned the clothing Adrienne sent up for him: shirt, coat, trousers, woolen socks, shoes, and a peasant's cap, which resembled a nightcap, all in black. Everything fit perfectly, which did not surprise him. As an artist, she had a good perception of sizes. His money was in a bag inside his shirt. He tucked the two loaded pistols into the waistband of his trousers and picked up the leather bag that had come with the clothing. It held the compass, the travel guide, a knife, food and water for a couple of days, and his notes on William the Conqueror. Who knew, someday he might write a historical paper worth publishing.

When the light from the footman's candle no longer shone beneath the door, Nick opened it. Since there were no curtains in the attic, he never lit a candle at night. It would not seem too unusual if the neighbors glimpsed someone moving about the room during the day. But a light in the evening could rouse suspicion.

Henri waited at the landing halfway between the attic and the floor below, shielding the candle so the light would not show through the doorway. After Nick closed the door, the footman moved his hand, illuminating the stairs for him. "Mademoiselle is waiting in her studio."

Nick followed Henri down the servants' stairs and along the shadowed hallway. The studio door was partway open, so he stepped inside without knocking, closing it behind him. The heavy tapestry drapes were drawn, blocking the view from outside. Adrienne stood in the middle of the room, wearing a royal blue, floor-length satin cloak. Instead of the usual cluster of curls, her hair was pulled up in a tightly braided knot at the top of her head. She appeared ready to go out for a late party instead of risking her life to brave the English Channel.

She gazed sadly at the large picture of her grandmother that hung above the mantel. Nick knew she had painted it six months before the elderly lady died. Her grandmother had been ill, but Adrienne had portrayed her in the best of health.

He moved quietly across the room and stopped beside Adrienne, putting his arm around her shoulders. "She was pretty, even at eighty."

"Yes, she was. I want to remember her this way, as she was on her good days and not the times when she was so ill." She looked slowly around the room, at other paintings she had done, a few only partly finished.

Attempting to comfort her, Nick caressed her upper arm. "I wish you could take them with you."

She rested her head against his shoulder. "I can paint them again. I'm taking my sketchbooks. Hopefully they will make it intact. I have several very good drawings of Grandmother." Adrienne eased away from him, turning around to look him over from head to toe. "You should pass for a fisherman." Her eyes suddenly twinkled. "Do you think I will?" She picked up a cap similar to his and put it on, pulling it down to the top of her ears and low on her forehead. Unfastening the cape, she whipped it from her shoulders with a flourish and tossed it on a nearby chair.

Nicholas stared as she slowly turned around in a circle. She was too pretty to be mistaken for a boy. From a distance, however, the large black coat effectively disguised her from the knees up. But from there down, the black pantaloons revealed the shapeliest pair of legs he had ever seen. "You should have worn trousers."

She frowned at him. "I couldn't find any to fit at the waist. They kept falling down. I didn't exactly have days to assemble my costume. Besides, I've seen fishermen wear pantaloons."

He glanced at her unhappy expression. "But sweetheart,

men don't have legs as beautiful as yours," he said softly with a smile of masculine appreciation.

She blinked and held out one foot, inspecting her limb as if she'd never noticed it. "You think they're pretty?"

At her bemusement, he shook his head. "Not pretty. Beautiful. Of course, I'm not used to seeing quite so much of a lady's leg, or at least the shape of it." He'd seen a few, but he wouldn't exactly call the women ladies. When she lost her balance, he laughed and grabbed her shoulders, steadying her. It seemed perfectly natural to slide his arms around her. "For an artist, you are amazingly unaware of your attributes."

She shrugged. "I know I'm reasonably attractive. I just never paid much attention to my legs."

"Well, if we are lucky no one else will, either, since it is dark. But whether we are picked up by a ship or reach land on our own, I'll have to stand guard over you."

Smiling, she looped her arms around his neck. "Sometimes you say the sweetest things."

"All of it true."

She closed her eyes and leaned her forehead against his chin, whispering, "I'm frightened."

Her words and the tremor that passed through her surprised him. He tightened his arms, drawing her closer. "I am, too. But when I climbed in the rented coach and started for Chalons, God told me I was going home." *Please, Lord, include her in that promise.* "And I don't think he meant in a coffin, or that I'd wash up drowned on the English shore."

"I do trust him to keep us safe, as long as I don't make a mistake."

He gently nudged her chin up and looked into her eyes. "We can only do our best, Adrienne. If we fail, I will not blame you."

"Nor I you." She paused, studying him tenderly. "Nicholas, would you kiss me? Just so I'll know what it's like in case we are caught."

He smiled and brushed his thumb across her cheek. "Don't tell me you've never been kissed."

"A few times." She lowered her gaze to the vicinity of the top button on his shirt. "But never by the man I love."

Nick's pulse quickened. "You did not love your betrothed?"

"I thought I did." She looked up at him. "Until I met you."

His heartbeat jumped to triple time. He cupped her face in his hand and lowered his head. When his lips touched hers, he could have sworn he heard a symphony. Nick moved his hand around to her back, drawing her closer, acknowledging and accepting the depth of his feelings for her. A few minutes later, he slowly and very reluctantly raised his head. "I love you, too." He gazed into her glowing eyes and released her. "Let's go home, sweetheart."

When they were out of the city, Adrienne lifted the seat inside the coach, and Nicholas hoisted himself up out of the compartment. He took several deep breaths, glad the inside of the coach was dark so she wouldn't notice how his hands shook. Being so closely confined had been difficult, but not as bad as he had expected because he kept his mind on her and the tasks ahead. Still, he felt a bit woozy, but he knew that soon would pass.

He stretched his legs and arms, then rotated his neck and shoulders. "I'm glad I didn't have to ride across the country in there. I'm not exactly shaped like a trunk."

She giggled nervously. "You don't look like one either."

"I hope not." Using touch to guide him in the darkness, he replaced the seat cover and cushion. They shifted sides and removed their supplies from beneath the other seat. "How much farther?"

"I don't think it will be too long. We're supposed to meet our contact on the road. He'll take us to the boat."

She removed her cloak and folded it, laying it on the other seat. Then she pulled on her cap. "Well, I'm set."

Nicholas put his arm around her shoulders. "You're the prettiest fisherman I've ever seen."

She laughed softly. "I should hope so. But you can't really see my face. It's too dark."

He peered out at the clear, practically moonless night. "Which is good. Hopefully no one else will see it, either."

A few minutes later, the coach stopped and the door opened. A man leaned inside and whispered in French, "A good night for a voyage."

Nicholas could not make out the man's features, especially since he had darkened his face, but the accent was typical of the area. When Adrienne nodded, Nick knew she recognized the man.

"We have half an hour before the guards come back this way," added the Frenchman, before moving out of the way.

Nick picked up their leather bags. Climbing from the carriage, he turned and helped Adrienne down the steps.

They had said their farewells to the coachman at the carriage house before they left. Near the water, sound traveled easily. It was not entirely unusual for a carriage to travel the road at night, but talking above a whisper could alert anyone else who might be out.

Bending low, Nicholas and Adrienne followed the man across the beach. He led them to a small, flat-bottomed boat pulled up on the shore, then whispered close to Nick's ear. "Use this to take you to the fishing smack. They are all empty tonight, but the one you want is on the left, away from the others." He helped Nick push the boat into the water, holding it close to the water's edge while Nick stowed their gear and carried Adrienne out to the boat.

When she was seated, Nick stepped in behind her and picked up a pole from the bottom of the boat. The man silently pushed them away from the shore. Nick wedged one end of the long pole against the sandy bottom, pushing them forward. He could just make out the silhouettes of the boats in the darkness and veered toward the one to the left of the others. Repeating the process with the pole several times quickly brought them alongside the fishing smack, which was a large sloop. They needed a boat big enough to cross the Channel, but Nick wondered how well only the two of them could handle it.

He held the flat-bottomed boat in place with the pole while Adrienne scrambled onto the deck of the other vessel. He threw her the loose end of a rope, which was fastened to the flat-bottomed boat. She pulled the rope taut, keeping the small boat next to the sloop. Nick laid their supplies on the deck and climbed aboard. She tossed the rope back into the little boat and shoved it toward the shore.

Nicholas pulled up the anchor, halting several times when the ancient chain creaked. Holding his breath, he waited for someone to shout an alarm, only to be greeted with the quiet lapping of gentle waves. Once the anchor was up, they raised the foresail and Nicholas manned the rudder, guiding the vessel out to sea. The boat was old and clumsy, but it was solid. Nick noted thankfully that it didn't leak or feel as though it would fall apart.

They never did manage to hoist the mainsail, but God smiled and sent them a gentle southwester to carry them across the English Channel. He and Adrienne took turns at the rudder, using the stars to guide them toward England.

"Why were we supposed to take this particular boat?"

Adrienne shrugged. "I paid for it. I didn't want to simply steal it and deprive people of their livelihood."

"Of course not." He doubted any of the escapees, himself included, would have thought twice about stealing a boat if it meant freedom.

They talked a while. Adrienne napped a little, and they shared the roasted beef sandwiches she'd brought. Mostly they were quiet, sitting side by side, each lost in thought. Many times during the night, Nick prayed silently for safe passage to England and for wisdom in his relationship with Adrienne. He prayed for Selena, too, asking God to spare her. He also marveled at how God had provided for his escape and even sent him someone to love. Less than a month earlier, Nick had doubted God cared about him. Now he knew differently.

He felt differently, too. His newfound faith sustained him and gave him the courage to face whatever lay ahead, whether good or bad. Glancing up at the heavens to make certain they were still on course, he asked God to strengthen his faith, to guide him through life as he now guided him home.

Home.

The word had now taken on a new meaning, one that included Adrienne. Nick still questioned his abilities and polish, but not as much as when he left Verdun. He had not decided if he was a better man than he had thought, or if she simply made him feel that way.

"I suppose I'll have to deal with the government before I go to Yorkshire," he said, glancing at her. His eyes had become so accustomed to the darkness that he could see clearly in the faint light of the quarter moon.

"Yes. The orders were to take you directly to London." She laid her head on his shoulder. "I'm sorry, Nicholas. I know you would rather go to see your parents."

"I am anxious to see my family, but it is more important that I try to help Selena. Being with you will make the wait easier."

"After we land in Portsmouth, we'll go to my parents' home in Dorset instead of going to my home. The estates are close together, but I have to be more circumspect in England."

He smiled and tickled her chin. "Can't stow me away in your attic?"

She giggled and grabbed his hand. "Not without causing a hubble-bubble. We'll recruit my parents or someone suitable to go with us to London." She grimaced. "After doing as I please for two years, I dread being under the thumb of a chaperon."

"Perhaps you can soon avoid such a plague." He rested the side of his head against hers. "Do you know someone who could help us obtain a special license? I don't know how to go about it."

She drew a quick breath. "Is that a proposal?"

"Yes. I hope you'll pardon me for not going down on one knee."

"Of course I will."

"Pardon me or marry me?"

"Are you certain you want to marry me? Our time together has been rather unconventional."

He laughed. "To say the least." He looked down at her, smiling in the first light of dawn. "My love for you and wanting you to be my wife are the only things I'm certain of right now. Everything else is unknown and a little scary. But it will be less so if you are by my side."

"I would be honored to marry you, Nicholas."

Keeping one hand on the rudder, he leaned down and kissed her gently. "Soon."

When he straightened, she sighed, snuggling her head against his shoulder and neck. "As soon as possible."

After the sun came up, he took the compass and the map from the bag, using them to keep on the course he had plotted weeks earlier. As the day progressed past midafternoon without sighting land, Nick wondered if he had miscalculated, or if there was something wrong with the compass. Could they be sailing up the middle of the Channel instead of across it? Then he checked the position of the sun and knew they were going in the right direction. He reminded himself that with only the foresail hoisted, they naturally went slower than he would have liked.

Adrienne lay on the deck nearby, sleeping peacefully. He watched her for a while, admiring her smooth skin and delicate coloring, smiling when she quietly mumbled gibberish. Marriage to this brave, intelligent, and lovely woman would never be boring.

He was glad she could rest. He'd had a few hours' sleep that morning. Though tired, he knew he could function for several more hours. She awoke about an hour later and took her turn at the rudder while he dozed.

Late in the afternoon, he spotted the Isle of Wight far in the distance. "England." Adrienne scrambled to her feet for a better view. He, too, stood straighter, his gaze pinned to that tiny dot of land.

There were times, more than he cared to admit, that he'd despaired of ever seeing his homeland again. It was a common feeling among those imprisoned in France. He supposed it was the same for the French prisoners in British hands. But it did nothing to lessen the impact of his first glimpse of Britain. Unable to speak, he wanted to laugh and weep at the same time. *Thank you, Jesus! Thank you, heavenly Father!*

He held Adrienne tightly with one arm, not realizing tears rolled down his face until she tenderly wiped them away with her fingertips. She, too, cried with joy and thanksgiving. He squeezed her once more, then lifted his arm from around her. Swiping his eyes on his coat sleeve, he turned his attention back to steering the boat.

During much of the night, Nick had kept the wooden seat beside the rudder folded up, preferring to sit on the deck, out of the chilly wind. Even though his arm had been above his head, it hadn't been too difficult to steer the boat. Through the day, they had switched back and forth between sitting and standing. Now he lowered the narrow seat and perched on the edge, relishing the sight before him.

Land. Beautiful, green, beloved England.

At least he imagined it was beautiful and green. They were still too far away to detect any distinctive features. But in his mind's eye, he saw hills and dales, stone houses with thatched roofs and flowers along the front walks…children laughing and playing, mothers humming, men working inside and out…a butcher chasing a dog away from his door, yelling at him—in English.

When Nick chuckled, Adrienne looked at him. "What is so amusing?"

"I was just thinking how wonderful it will be to hear everyone speaking English." He grinned at her. "And I wondered if dogs naturally understand whatever language is being spoken."

She laughed. "You're tired."

"Can't be. I'm too happy to be tired."

Half an hour later, Adrienne stretched her arms and wiggled her legs. "What a beautiful day for sailing." She assumed a haughty air. "Life has been so dull of late." She pretended to yawn, patting her hand against her open mouth. "Would you care to take a little jaunt down the coast, my dear? Clear the cobwebs from your handsome brain?"

Nick laughed and stretched his legs out in front of him. "How do you know my brain is handsome?"

"Darling, if it is inside that beautiful head, it has to be."

"Men aren't beautiful." He smiled indulgently as she pranced in a small circle around a hatch.

She stopped and met his gaze. "You are."

How could she make him feel ten feet tall with only a look? "And you are not only beautiful, but also incredibly sweet. I love you."

"I love you, too." She smiled and started around the hatch again.

"Are you bored, my dear?"

"A little. Mostly, I'm tired of sitting." Suddenly she stopped, planting her feet wide to brace against the waves. "Ship off the starboard bow, captain. Or maybe it's the port bow. That direction." Adrienne pointed toward the right, then shielded her eyes with her hand. "I think they're changing course—oh my!" She spun around, looking at him with a worried frown. "Nick, they're coming right toward us."

He stood, keeping his hand on the rudder. "This close to shore, it has to be English." He peered at the ship but could not determine which flag flew above it. "Doesn't it?"

"Usually."

Her pale face chilled his soul. "But not always?"

"Occasionally, overzealous French captains patrol dangerously close to shore, hoping to thwart smugglers and enforce the blockade."

"Or capture escapees." *God, please don't let us be caught this close to England!* Nick's mind raced. If he stayed his course, there was a slim chance they could outrun the two-masted brig.

A very slim chance.

CHAPTER *Twenty-Six*

NICK PRESSED HIS LIPS TOGETHER. If it was a French ship, their best hope was to get so close to shore that the captain dared not follow them. If they were captured, one man and two pistols would be useless against such a large crew. Nick could only hope the captain was an honorable man who would protect Adrienne. He certainly wouldn't be able to.

God, please, don't let this happen!

Frustrated and angry, he wanted to pound something. However, he refrained. He didn't want to frighten Adrienne more. Nick glanced toward the setting sun. If they could stay away from the other ship past twilight, the darkness might help. The wind shifted slightly, and he studied the sky, which was quickly becoming overcast.

"I think we may be in for a storm." Adrienne moved to his side, resting her hand on his shoulder.

Nodding, he adjusted the rudder to compensate for the wind change. "It will become dark faster, which could work to our benefit. But if it starts raining, it will be difficult to see the lights on the coast."

Suddenly, she dug her fingers into his coat. "It's British! I see the flag." Laughing, she hugged him.

Relief poured through him. "Hallelujah!" Releasing the rudder handle, he put both arms around her. He meant for the kiss to be quick. He truly did. But they had experienced too many emotions in such a short time. The instant his lips touched hers, he forgot everything but her—beautiful, wonderful, brave Adrienne. He cherished her, savored her, and indulged in the sheer pleasure of holding her.

When the rudder smacked him in the leg for the third time,

he reluctantly raised his head. "I think I'm going to enjoy being married to you."

Her face turned pink, but she grinned. "I think it will be quite nice." She glanced toward the front of the boat. "We've strayed off course, captain."

Nick looked around and laughed. "If I don't tend to business, we'll wind up back in France. Shall we go meet our escort?"

"If we don't, they might think we are smugglers and open fire."

He grabbed the rudder, carefully turning the fishing smack in the general direction of the oncoming ship.

Adrienne stepped out of his way. "Did you bring Mr. Ochs's passport?"

"Yes." Nick reached inside his coat and pulled the forged document from an inner pocket.

"I think it would be best if he disappeared."

Flashing her a grin, he tossed the fake passport over the side. "Good idea. Since I have no legitimate papers, they will probably have plenty of questions and some doubts as it is. No need to risk complicating matters any further."

She leaned against the railing, appearing more relaxed than she had since leaving Caen. "We won't have any problem once we're in Portsmouth. I'm well acquainted with the authorities there, both civilian and military."

Nicholas winked. "Notorious, are you?"

"Not exactly." Smiling, she reached over and pulled off his black cap, ruffling his hair. "Though when I arrive dressed like this, I will be." Adrienne removed her cap also and threw them both into the water. "Remind me next time I need a disguise that those things are rather annoying."

Thinking of how her cap kept sliding down over her ears, he laughed. "That's only because yours was too big."

"I had to use what I had on hand." She dropped gracefully onto the deck, leaning against the side, and stretched her legs out in front of her. "I hope we don't cause too big a stir in town. As the granddaughter of a marquis, I try to behave with some decorum here in the home district." Making a face, she muttered, "I have to take down my hair. This braid is giving me a headache." She began deftly pulling the pins from her hair.

Nick stared at her. "Your grandfather is a marquis?"

She tipped her head and looked at him, working her fingers through the braid to loosen it. "The marquis of Woodsford. Didn't I tell you? I thought I mentioned it."

"Well, you didn't." He knew she was part of the aristocracy, but since she had never mentioned her grandfather's title, he assumed the connection to a lord was distant. By the rules of Society, it was of no consequence. His grandfather had been a viscount, so Nick was fairly close to being her equal. But even as a lad, he had heard of the marquis of Woodsford, a powerful member of the House of Lords.

His heart sank, along with his spirits. How could she have neglected to tell him something so important...and devastating?

Adrienne lowered her hands, studying him. "Does that pose a problem?"

"I can't marry the granddaughter of a peer."

"Why not?" She frowned at him and went back to work on the braid. "You're a member of the *ton*. My family might protest if you weren't, but they would relent eventually simply because I love you."

Nick shifted his gaze away from her, noticing he had veered off course again. It was harder to hold the boat steady in this direction. Grumbling under his breath, he adjusted the rudder, pointing them back toward the ship. "Breeding isn't everything." Glancing at her perplexed expression, he grimaced. "I'm neither cultured nor educated. Can't carry a decent conversation. In a crowd, I'm a looby." When she shook her head, he glared at her. "Adrienne, I'm four-and-twenty and green as grass. I'll be an embarrassment to your family."

"Nicholas, you are better educated than most gentlemen I know."

"Didn't go to the university."

"Possessing knowledge is what is important, not how a man acquires it. As for culture, you may not be up on the latest dances—"

"Don't dance at all!" he interrupted, frowning. Another shortcoming to add to the list.

Adrienne smiled sweetly. "We'll remedy that. I'll teach you. Just as I'll keep on instructing you about art." She scrambled to her feet, facing him. "You are extremely well read in numerous areas and unequaled in your knowledge of history. You could teach the professors at Oxford or Cambridge."

Her hair blew across her face, distracting him. Until now, she'd always worn it pinned up, and he hadn't realized it was so long, almost to the middle of her back. It billowed about her face and shoulders in dozens of tiny waves. "Your hair is beautiful." He gently brushed it away from her lips and cheek.

"It isn't normally this wild. Braiding it makes more waves."

Nick buried his fingers in it, rubbing the silky strands. "I like it this way. Wild and free, like you."

"It will be a mass of tangles if I don't tie it down." She turned to face the wind and pulled a ribbon from her pocket. Sliding it beneath her hair, she tied the unruly locks back from her face. "There, that's better. I won't have to keep spitting it out of my mouth." When he chuckled, she perused him thoughtfully. "Now, where was I?"

"Bolstering my self-confidence," he said with a rueful smile.

"Precisely. You are intelligent, as well as an interesting and entertaining conversationalist."

He shrugged. "I hold my own with you. Don't do too badly with a small group of men, either. But I clam up at parties or in a crowd. Especially around women."

"Good." She caressed his arm. "I don't want other women

trying to steal you. Besides, you'll have me to smooth your way at social functions. I intend to be very unfashionable and not leave your side. Actually, I find the London Season tedious. I didn't bother with it the two years before I went to France. I much prefer smaller functions, particularly country ones."

"Like late suppers for two?" Nick smiled, remembering the nights they'd sat before the fire in her studio, nibbling on cold meats and cheese, laughing and talking.

"If I had my choice, I'd spend all my time alone with you." Leaning against his shoulder, Adrienne kissed him on the cheek. "Nicholas, don't ever doubt yourself. You are the finest man I've ever known. You are brave and loyal, strong in heart, mind, and body. I trust you with my life and my heart."

"No man could ask for more." He curled his hand around the back of her head, caressing her cheek with his thumb. "I'd kiss you, but I'd rather not have an audience. We're about to be overrun by a British brig. I need to tend the sail."

She shifted to the side. Maintaining his hold on the rudder, he stepped out of her way, and she moved to take his place. Turning the rudder over to her, he winked. "Keep 'er on course, mate."

"Aye, aye, captain."

Nick quickly lowered the foresail and secured it. Then he placed the two pistols on top of the hatch in plain view. When Adrienne stepped up next to him, he slipped his arm around her shoulders. They waited as the larger, two-masted, square-rigged brig, *Mutine*, drew alongside.

"*L'Afrodille*, prepare to be boarded!" called an officer from the deck above.

Nick chuckled. "We just crossed the Channel in a daffodil." He glanced down at Adrienne, laughing at her smug smile.

A sailor threw down a line, and Nick tied it to the fishing smack. When they threw down another, he went forward, securing that part of the boat, too. He returned to Adrienne, watching as two men slung a rope ladder over the side of the brig. Four sailors scrambled down it, deftly jumping onto the deck of the sloop.

Two of the men, armed with pistols, guarded them as the other two quickly searched the ship. When they kept glancing at Adrienne's legs, he again put his arm around her, resting it protectively at her waist. If he had wanted to slip something by them, he would have needed no other distraction than this beautiful woman.

"No one else on board, sir," called one of the sailors. He picked up the pistols from the hatch cover and motioned for Nick and Adrienne to climb up the ladder.

"I'd like to take our gear." Nick nodded at the two leather bags lying on the deck. "It is all we have."

The sailor seemed surprised that he spoke English. "We'll bring them."

"Thank you." Nick steadied the ladder as Adrienne climbed up. He waited until two men assisted her over the railing, then quickly climbed up after her. The same men helped him onto the deck, then escorted them a short distance to meet the captain and two other officers.

"Monsieur, are you aware that you are in English waters?" The captain spoke passable French.

"Yes, sir, thanks be to God." Nick replied in English. When he glanced toward the coast, a sudden swell of emotion clogged his throat. Unexpected tears stung his eyes. He felt Adrienne slip her hand in his. Holding it firmly, he cleared his throat and gathered his composure. "And you cannot imagine how good it feels. I am Nicholas Delaroe of Yorkshire. I am—" He paused. "I have been a détenu." His throat tightened, and he cleared it again. "By God's grace and this lady's help, I am finally free."

"I assume you have nothing to verify your identity." The captain's face creased in a mild frown.

"No, sir. I do not."

The captain fixed his gaze on Adrienne. "Does the lady speak English?"

"I should hope so, Captain, since I grew up in Dorset." She gave him a fetching smile. "I am Adrienne Le Clare, the marquis of Woodsford's granddaughter. Fortunately, I do have a passport. An English one." Nick released her hand, and she unfastened the first few buttons on her coat, taking the passport from the inside pocket and handing it to the officer.

As the captain read it, Nick scanned the ship. Several lanterns had been lit, including one near them. Every man on deck watched the proceedings. Even the cook had wandered up to throw some slop overboard. He stood with the bucket tipped over the rail, its contents long since dispatched to the fish.

Suddenly a midshipman came up from below deck, buttoning his coat. As he passed a lantern, Nick noted that his hair was uncombed and his skin pale. He appeared to be around nineteen. The man moved toward them slowly, walking as if he were unwell, but he never took his gaze from Adrienne's face. "Miss Le Clare, it is you!"

"Mr. Jackson, how nice to see you again!" Adrienne held out her hand to the young man.

Taking hold of it, he gallantly bent down to kiss it—and almost toppled on her before Nick caught him.

"Mr. Jackson, are you unwell?" Adrienne peered into his ashen face as Nick helped him straighten.

"'Tis the megrims, ma'am. Been plagued with blinding headaches since I left Bitche." The young man turned cautiously toward his captain. "I beg your pardon, Captain Halston, for coming on deck in this condition. But Miss Le Clare is the lady who helped me escape France. Found me a safe place to hide and a boat, too. I always hoped I'd meet the Angel of Caen on this side of the Channel. Never had a chance to say a proper thank-you."

"Angel of Caen?" Surprise flickered across her face.

"Yes, ma'am. That's what the men you've helped call you. I doubt there's a man among us who doesn't say a prayer for you most every day. We were terribly afraid you would be caught."

"I was, too. When I was denied permission to leave the country legally, I decided to take a more adventurous route."

The midshipman glanced at Nicholas and smiled. "Something tells me that wasn't the only reason you came home."

Adrienne laughed. "Quite right, Mr. Jackson. As of this morning, I became betrothed to Mr. Delaroe."

"Please accept my best wishes, ma'am, and my congratulations, sir."

Smiling, Nick nodded, touched by the young man's unabashed admiration for Adrienne.

"Thank you." Adrienne smiled gently. "Now, please, go see to your poor head."

"Yes, Jackson, go below," ordered the captain. He nodded at the midshipman, his expression kind. "You've thanked your Angel, and saved her and Mr. Delaroe from further annoying interrogation."

Jackson looked at Adrienne once more. "I can't thank you enough for all you did for us." He glanced at Nick. "Take good care of her, sir."

"I intend to."

As the young man made his way toward the stairs, the captain turned back to Nick. "Have you been detained since the war resumed?"

"Yes. Eight very long years."

The captain held out his hand. "Mr. Delaroe, welcome aboard our floating piece of England."

Grinning broadly, Nick shook his hand. "Thank you, sir."

A cheer went up from the crew.

Laughing, Nick settled his hands at Adrienne's waist and picked her up, swinging her around in a circle. When he set her feet on the ground, he pulled her into his embrace and kissed her.

The crew roared their approval.

When he released her, Adrienne laughed, even though she blushed furiously.

The captain chuckled. "Would you like to go below, ma'am, and rest? My cabin is at your disposal."

"I'm too excited to rest. I've been away from England for two years myself and will take great delight in watching the lights of the city as we go into port." She leaned toward the captain, speaking softly. "But, if you could find me a pair of trousers to wear, I wouldn't mind going below long enough to change. I've been advised these pantaloons are somewhat...distracting."

"I wondered if it might be a new Parisian fashion." The captain's eyes twinkled merrily. "I expect we can find something to fit, though my men will be greatly disappointed. Unfortunately we will not be able to go into port until morning. We have already missed the tide."

Nick felt a stab of disappointment and saw it reflected on Adrienne's face. He considered trying to continue on their journey in the fishing smack, but changed his mind the instant a drop of rain hit him on the nose. "Then we will be most grateful for your hospitality, sir. If the weather were better, we might give it a go in *L'Asrodille*, but not with a storm upon us."

"A wise decision. Though it does not appear to be a severe storm, I could not in good conscience let you try it on your own." The captain glanced at the sloop. "You have done well to come this far with only the two of you for a crew."

Adrienne laughed softly. Nick noticed several of the men smile and turn their heads to listen to the pleasing, feminine sound. "Especially since neither of us has done much sailing."

"Then I commend you doubly. I trust we can make you comfortable, even as we continue on our patrol. Lieutenant

Mercer will show you to my cabin, Miss Le Clare, and find what you need." Captain Halston nodded to one of the officers. "Also advise the cook that we will have guests for dinner, Mr. Mercer." He turned to the other gentleman. "Prepare the smack to be towed, Lieutenant Finch. Set sail as soon as you are ready."

"Aye, sir."

"Mr. Delaroe, if you care to follow Lieutenant Mercer, I'm certain he would lend you his quarters to freshen up."

"I would appreciate that, captain."

After a pleasant dinner with the captain and his officers, Adrienne decided to try to sleep.

Nick sought out Mr. Jackson. They traded stories of their escape attempts and how they wound up at Bitche. As Nicholas suspected, he and Jackson had been in the prison at the same time. He remembered a young midshipman by that name who had arrived the same day Nick was thrown back into the dungeon. They had been in the same crowded cell, along with twenty other men.

In the darkness of the dungeon Nick had never seen the other man's face. The one time there had been enough light to put faces with names, Nicholas had been incapable of seeing anyone beyond his sister.

After Nick's release and recovery, he had been told that Jackson had also suffered a severe beating. The men had been quite concerned about him since the lad had received some severe blows to the head.

Jackson shifted on his bunk. "I'm glad to know you survived, Mr. Delaroe. I never saw anyone else beaten and whipped like you, and I was in and out of Bitche three times."

"I understood that you endured a harsh beating of your own." Nicholas rested his arm on the upper bunk across from the midshipman.

The lad waved his hand in a dismissive manner. "The commandant was unhappy because I'd almost escaped on the way back to prison. But he was preoccupied with you. After your release, he remembered that he was furious with me. I'm certain being hit in the head is what caused these cursed headaches. But I don't have them so often anymore."

He paused, a faraway look in his eyes. "As long as I live, I'll never forget your sister coming into that cell. She is the most beautiful woman I've ever seen." He turned toward Nick. "Brave, too. Most women couldn't have stood it. She knelt down on that floor without a thought for herself."

Nick hesitated, then met Jackson's gaze. "Did you hear what she said to them?"

"Not all of it. Begged for your life, she did. The civilian bent down and said something. She answered, but I couldn't understand either of them. Then he said she could take you out of the prison. She left and in a while, they carried you out. It took courage to try to escape again after what you went through."

Nick shrugged. "As you well know, being at Bitche is enough to drive a man to find a way to escape." Jackson grinned, and Nick leaned against the bunk with a smile. "As far as I know, though, you still hold the record for persistence. Six tries, wasn't it?"

Jackson laughed quietly. "Took me that long to do it right."

CHAPTER *Twenty-Seven*

As THE SHIP SAILED INTO PORTSMOUTH harbor early the next morning, Nicholas and Adrienne stood by the railing, their arms around each other. Hopes, fears, elation, thanksgiving— they all swirled through Nick. He had dreamed of this moment a thousand times in a hundred forms. But until two days earlier, he had not dared dream he would share it with anyone, let alone with the love of his life.

"Thank you, Lord God," he whispered, resting his cheek against Adrienne's hair.

"Amen." She pressed her hand against his side.

They gathered up their bags, waiting impatiently until the ship docked. Many of the men came by with smiles and good wishes. Others stopped their work to shake Nick's hand and bow to Adrienne. Judging from their subtle comments, Nick suspected Jackson had told them of his ordeal at Bitche.

As the gangplank was lowered into place, Captain Halston turned to them with a smile. "It was a pleasure having you aboard, Miss Le Clare."

Adrienne laughed. "Believe me, sir, the pleasure has been mine. Sailing on the *Mutine* is more comfortable than a French fishing smack. Faster, too." She surprised him by standing on tiptoe and kissing his cheek. "Thank you, captain. May God protect you and your men."

"Thank you, miss." The captain's smile grew even wider.

Nick held out his hand. "Captain Halston, we are forever in your debt."

The officer shook Nick's hand. "All in the line of duty, sir. It was an honor to have you aboard. On behalf of myself and my crew, we wish you the best."

Nick murmured his thanks.

A sharp whistle blew and the men stopped wherever they

were, standing at attention. The captain nodded, and a sailor opened the gate to the gangplank. "Permission granted to leave the ship, Mr. Delaroe. Welcome home."

Nick nodded and turned toward the opening. He hesitated, taking a deep breath, suddenly afraid he would wake up and find it was all a dream. Then Adrienne touched his arm.

When he looked at her, she smiled gently. "It's real. You succeeded this time."

"Because of God—" he smiled—"and because of you." Heart pounding, Nick squared his shoulders and exited the ship, walking down the gangplank in long, measured strides. In the back of his mind, he heard his father admonishing him to keep a stiff upper lip. "Hard to do, Papa," he whispered.

He stepped off the gangplank and moved a short distance onto the dock. Myriad feelings swept over him, almost overpowering him in their intensity: gratitude to God and Adrienne and all who helped him; sorrow for those he left behind; joy; and most of all, an overwhelming sense of relief.

"I'm free." He was barely able to comprehend it. One battle in his private war with Napoleon had been won. Now he could help Selena fight another.

Nick closed his eyes and listened, filtering out the creak of the ship and rattle of carriage wheels to focus on the people. A dozen conversations went on around him—happy, sad, cheerful, strained. All around he heard workmen's shouts, jovial teasing here, an argument there—and not one word of French among them.

He sensed someone in front of him. Opening his eyes, he met Adrienne's gaze.

Her delicate brow wrinkled in a frown, and worry filled her eyes. "Nicholas, is something wrong?"

A smile started at one corner of his lips and slowly spread across his face. "I'm just listening, sweetheart."

"To what?"

"The blessed sounds of England."

In the rented coach, Nicholas and Adrienne shed their coats, which were much too warm for a summer day on land. All the way from Portsmouth to Bere Regis, the town near Adrienne's home, they shifted from one window to the other, to see all the sights. Nick tried valiantly to keep his gaze from straying too often to her shapely form. Though the task was difficult, it would have been nigh unto impossible if she had not traded the pantaloons for trousers.

He had never been to Dorset, but greatly admired the gently rolling hills and wide valleys. It was dairy country, with lush green pastures separated by small woods, making the scenery particularly picturesque. Adrienne kept up a running commentary of tales about the area and her family.

As they drove up the lane to her family home, she could barely sit still. "They are going to be so surprised and happy. My parents will adore you." She leaned out the window, clearly anxious for her first glimpse of the house.

Nick became more nervous by the minute. Why should her parents even like him? They knew nothing about him and had no reason to believe anything he said. Nor could he prove it. Not right away. As far as he knew, he had plenty of money and could support her comfortably, even luxuriously. But he had heard of more than one gentleman whose funds had been poorly managed during his detainment. His father had always dealt wisely in business affairs, but some things were beyond even a prudent man's control. Nick could be a pauper and not be aware of it.

When the carriage pulled up in front of the grand house, which was even larger than Nick's boyhood home, Adrienne reached for the door handle. He caught her hand. "Let me go first so I can help you down."

She grinned and moved back out of his way. "If I'm unlady-like enough to arrive in trousers, what will jumping out of a carriage hurt?"

"Your ankle?" He grinned back, enjoying her happiness and excitement despite his own misgivings. The instant the carriage drew to a halt, he opened the door and hopped out. When he turned to lower the steps, she was already leaning out the door.

"Just lift me down."

He complied, chuckling as she raced up the steps to the house. During the carriage ride, he had taken the ribbon from her hair and tucked it in his pocket. If he had his way, she would loosen that glorious mane whenever he was around. And he might even buy her a pair of pantaloons to wear when they were alone. He gathered up their bags, tipped the coach-man, and followed at a more sedate pace.

The footman opened the door just as she reached it. He stared at her for a second, then grinned broadly. "Miss Adrienne! Welcome home!"

"Thank you, Hobbs." She looked back at Nick and motioned for him to hurry up. "Don't be so slow. A turtle could move faster."

"Yes, ma'am." Nick trotted up the steps, nodding to the amazed footman. The servant's gaze darted to Nick, then back to her, taking in their black shirts and trousers—especially hers. If the man didn't quit ogling her, Nick thought irritably, he would be forced to plant him a facer.

Hobbs glanced at the carriage as it started back down the drive. "You don't have any luggage?"

Nick held up the small leather bags. "These are all we brought with us."

"We escaped France in the dead of night." Adrienne's smile was filled with pride. "And sailed across the Channel in a fishing smack."

The footman's mouth dropped open, his awed gaze moving from Adrienne to Nicholas.

"Are my parents home?"

Hobbs slowly nodded, then collected himself and backed out of the way so they could move inside. "Yes, miss. Your mother is tending to her rose bushes. And your father is down at the stables."

"Would you go tell Father I'm home, please? We'll find Mama."

The footman grinned. "Yes, ma'am." He shut the door behind Nick and raced down the hall.

"If you want to seek out your mother by yourself, you can stick me somewhere." Nick glanced into the nearby withdrawing room. "I'll study the paintings or something."

"I will not leave you here by yourself. Mother would scold me for being so rude. Besides, I can't wait for her to meet you. And you her. I think you'll like my parents."

"I'm sure I will." He laid the bags on a carved gilt table nearby and offered her his arm. "Lead the way."

Adrienne hustled him down the hallway, through a pleasant sitting room, and out a door leading to the gardens. He instantly spotted a slender woman not too far from the house. She wore a green frock, wide-brimmed yellow hat, and work gloves. Whistling a cheerful tune, she cut the faded roses from a bush and dropped them into a basket at her feet.

When her mother picked up the basket and started toward another row, Adrienne called to her. "Mama, your roses are as beautiful as ever."

Mrs. Le Clare whirled around with startled shriek. When she saw her daughter, she dropped the basket and clippers and rushed toward her. "Adrienne!"

She released Nick's arm and ran to meet her mother, hugging her fiercely.

Mrs. Le Clare held her close. "Oh, my darling girl, I am so happy to see you." She kissed her on the cheek, then stepped back, looking her over. "But what on earth are you wearing? Surely a man's shirt and trousers aren't the vogue in France for gently bred young ladies." Before Adrienne could answer, her mother noticed Nicholas. Her eyes widened as her gaze raked over him. She slanted a cautious glance at her daughter. "And who is this gentleman?"

"Mother, I would like you to meet Nicholas Delaroe from Yorkshire. Nicholas, this is my mother, Alice Le Clare."

Nicholas bowed respectfully. "It is a pleasure to meet you, Mrs. Le Clare. Your daughter speaks highly of you and the rest of the family."

"I'm glad to know she still holds us in good regard. Welcome to our home, sir."

Nick inclined his head. "Thank you, ma'am."

"Nicholas was a détenu," Adrienne said. "He helped me escape France."

Nick smiled at Mrs. Le Clare, hoping he didn't look as ill at ease as he felt. "Actually, ma'am, it was the other way around. Adrienne helped me escape. She arranged a safe hiding place and secured a boat to cross the Channel. She has done the same for several prisoners of war and détenus."

Her mother studied Adrienne's countenance, then his, and lifted an eyebrow. "But Mr. Delaroe, she did not cross the Channel with any of the others."

He smiled, glancing at his beloved. "No, thankfully, she did not. Otherwise I would still be wandering around France, hiding in thickets. Or walking across France to the penal depot with a gun at my back."

Mrs. Le Clare pulled off her work gloves, holding them in one hand. "So you crossed the Channel by yourselves?"

Was that disapproval in her tone? Nick restrained a frown. "We made part of the journey in a French fishing smack, until we were picked up by a Royal brig. The captain delivered us safely to Portsmouth this morning. Then we immediately hired a coach to bring us here."

Adrienne moved beside Nicholas, surprising him when she slipped her hand into his.

303

"Adrienne, dear, I can see why traveling with Mr. Delaroe would be rather appealing." Her mother's gaze flickered to their joined hands. "But why did you feel compelled to steal away from France in such a dangerous manner?"

"I was denied permission to leave the country. I was afraid the authorities suspected I had been helping Britons escape. I dared not stay a day longer. Leaving under cover of darkness, with Nicholas to see me safely here, was my best option."

"So you journey home shamefully dressed, clinging to a stranger." The deep, angry voice came from behind Nicholas and Adrienne.

Nick clenched his jaw. Adrienne seemed to pale as they turned around. A scowling gentleman stood there, his legs wide apart, fists resting on his hips, looking more than ready for a confrontation. He had the same pale blue eyes as Adrienne—but his burned with a father's wrath.

Adrienne lifted her chin. "It was a disguise, Papa. I had my hair tucked up under a peasant's nightcap and wore a coat so I passed for a fisherman."

Le Clare met Nick's gaze. "Impossible."

"That's what I tried to tell her." Nick shrugged lightly, waiting for her father to get around to him.

"You only objected to the pantaloons," Adrienne muttered.

Her father's eyebrows shot up. Seconds later, his face took on the appearance of a thundercloud.

Nick barely stifled a groan. He could well imagine what her father was thinking—that Nick was on far too intimate terms with his precious daughter. His only daughter. And the marquis of Woodsford's only grandchild. "I fear Miss Le Clare is bordering on exhaustion, sir." That was a stretch, though he knew she was tired. "It was quite an adventure, and she was very brave, but we've had little rest in the last few days."

Her father's gaze honed in on Adrienne's tired, pale face. He glanced back at Nick with a dark frown, but when he again turned to Adrienne, tenderness softened his expression. "Ah, *chérie,* forgive me for upbraiding you. I am delighted to see you." He opened his arms wide. "Come give your papa a hug."

She complied, resting her head against his chest and wrapping her arms around his waist. Nick noted a tear in her eye. "*Tu me manques,* Papa."

"I missed you, too. I am very glad you are safely home." He patted her on the back and kissed her forehead. "Now, go with your mother and let her pamper you. After you've rested we will have a nice, long talk."

Adrienne nodded, then yawned. "There is much to tell you."

Her father looked over her head, meeting Nick's gaze. "I'm certain there is. We'll have a chat at dinner."

"That will be nice." Adrienne stepped away from her father and smiled at Nick. "I'll have a room made up for you right away."

"Thank you. I'll be in soon." If Le Clare didn't challenge him to a duel first.

Adrienne glanced at her father, then back at Nick and nodded. "I'll see you this evening."

"I look forward to it." Nick smiled tenderly. "Rest well."

When the women were out of hearing, Le Clare turned to Nicholas with a frown. "I did not catch your name, sir."

"Nicholas Delaroe."

"You are a British officer? A prisoner of war?"

"I was a détenu, held at Verdun. When Britain went to war in 1803, I was traveling with an older cousin in France."

The thunderclouds in Le Clare's expression eased slightly. "And your family?"

"My father owns a large estate in Yorkshire. His brother is Viscount Stillington. My aunt is the dowager countess of Camfield. Though I currently own no land, my grandfather left me a sizable inheritance. I have been gone for eight years, but it is reasonable to expect my fortune is still intact."

Le Clare's gaze shifted to Adrienne, who paused at the door

and looked back at Nicholas before she disappeared inside the house. "My daughter seems quite enamored with you." He turned a steely gaze on Nick. "Am I correct that you hold her highly in your affections?"

"I love her, sir."

"I see. So you escaped from Verdun, found your way to Caen, and made contact in some way with Adrienne."

"A Frenchman in a town near Verdun hid me from the gendarmes. A British officer had been kind to him when he was wounded and captured by the Russians. Now he does what he can to help Britons trying to escape. He told me about your daughter and how to find her." Nick glanced toward the house with a hint of a smile. "Though he neglected to mention that she was young and beautiful."

Le Clare followed his gaze. "And too independent. Since it is highly unlikely you fell in love with her on the short voyage across the Channel, I would like to know how you developed such a strong attachment for my daughter."

Nick hesitated, not wanting to cause Adrienne trouble with her parents. Nor did he want to lie to her father. "She hid me in the attic of her house for three weeks. I know it was highly improper, but she felt it was the safest place for me to be."

Le Clare's scowl returned. "She mentioned helping other Britons escape. Did she hide those men in her home, too?"

"No, sir. I was the only one. Upon my word of honor, nothing untoward happened between us."

"Nevertheless, you have compromised her."

Nick met the older man's gaze directly. "Sir, I would be honored and blessed to marry Adrienne."

"That is fortunate, Delaroe, because you most certainly shall."

CHAPTER *Twenty-Eight*

A FEW HOURS AFTER GABRIEL and Selena returned to Fairhaven from Scotland, Miller tapped on the open office door. Gabriel looked up from the desk and smiled. "Come in. How does your new role suit you? Have the other servants accepted your elevated status?"

Miller smiled wryly as he walked into the room. He stopped and closed the door behind him. "For the most part. Though I'm glad Miss Dela—excuse me, Mrs. *Macpherson*, was here for a few days after moving me up to butler. It gave the rest of the staff time to adjust. Truth is, sir, everyone, except for perhaps Mrs. Pool, detested Hardwick so much they're more than happy to work with me, even though I'm still learning my way. Mrs. Pool has even surprised me. Seems like she's trying to be nice. And she isn't as harsh to the other servants as she used to be."

"Good. Selena was hoping the woman would mend her ways after Hardwick's abrupt departure. Have there been any problems? Anything I should know about?" Gabe leaned back in the chair and motioned for Miller to sit across from him.

"Several people called the first week until word went around that the ladies were out of town." Miller sat down in the leather chair. "They were all ladies and gentlemen who had been here before. But two things have been worrisome."

Miller frowned, meeting Gabriel's gaze. "When Mrs. Macpherson and Lady Camfield left on their trip, I stayed out front for a few minutes afterward. No particular reason except to enjoy the sunshine and consider how I would handle things in my new position. I watched the coach go down the lane and turn onto the road. Then a few minutes later, low and behold, a man on horseback came out of the woods halfway down the lane and followed the coach. It worried me, so I ran to the stables and told Morley. He saddled Fireball and rode after them but didn't see anyone following them."

Brown would no' be caught by a groom. Even Selena had not spotted him right away.

A few days after Gabe and Selena went to Inshirra, his forester mentioned meeting an Englishman named Brown in the nearby village. Gabe sent a footman to invite the man to dinner, but Mr. Brown had already departed the area—going south toward England instead of northward to his supposed destination of Inverness. Perhaps learning they were married and at Inshirra was all he had needed to know. "I appreciate your concern, Miller. And Morley's, too."

"For a while after that, I thought I saw someone hiding behind every tree and bush. I finally overruled my imagination, but then I actually did see someone watching the house. Spotted him from one of the upstairs windows. He came by every day, though seldom at the same time. He'd stay in the woods about an hour, then leave."

This did not surprise Gabriel either, though it was a bit more worrisome than Miller's first revelation. Cameron might use such a method to watch for their return. So could Bonham.

A dull red tinged the butler's cheeks. "I know you would have confronted him, sir. I thought about trying it but never could decide the right way to go about it. I'm not a coward, but I've never done anything like that. And I'm not a very good shot."

"I would no' expect you to do such a thing." Gabe shook his head, thankful the servant had not tried something so foolish. It could have gotten him killed. "It was wise no' to confront him alone, Miller. Dinna feel badly about it." He made a mental note to give the man some shooting lessons. "That type of thing comes from experience. Dinna forget I spent twelve years in the Gordons." Plus he had been trained from short-pants days to protect and to lead.

Miller nodded. "Thank you for understanding, Mr. Macpherson. Being a footman is all I've ever done. I thought maybe the man was planning a robbery, so the other men and I slept downstairs in different parts of the house. I even recruited O'Conner's two oldest boys. That way we'd hear someone if they tried to break in."

"Excellent." Gabe admired the man's ingenuity. When he thought of Selena's jewelry, he was grateful for Miller's diligence.

"Mayhap I was just skittish, but I felt it was necessary. Thankfully, nothing happened."

"Caution is usually sensible, Miller. I appreciate your efforts, and I know Selena will, too. Have you seen him today?"

"No, sir. Not yet."

Gabe tapped his finger on the arm of the chair. If only he could be certain the man Miller had seen was one of Cameron's men—and not Ellaby. After his encounter with Bonham, he doubted the French agent would spend his time lurking in the woods himself. "Was it always the same person?"

Miller nodded. "Tall and skinny. He practically could hide behind a tree without anybody noticing."

"My height?"

"At least. Maybe a little taller."

That ruled out Bonham or Ellaby. "If you see him again, advise me immediately."

"Yes, sir." Miller stood. "I'm glad you're back, Mr. Macpherson. And, if I may say so, sir, we're all pleased as can be that you and Miss Delaroe married. It was plain to see how much you loved each other."

Gabriel laughed and stood also. The staff's approval was not necessary, but it could certainly make life more pleasant. "Obviously, we were no' nearly as discreet as we should have been." He walked around the end of the desk toward the door.

"Well, sir, I suppose it's hard for people to keep their faces from lighting up when they see the one they love."

"Quite true." Gabe smiled at the butler. "I think I'll go find my wife and watch her eyes sparkle when she sees me."

Miller grinned and opened the door for him. "I expect they will."

Gabe went upstairs to Selena's bedchamber. He had taken the room next to hers, though there was a larger one down the hall. Remodeling that part of the house was high on his priority list. He met Marietta coming out the door. "Is she still up here?"

"Yes, sir. She's tapping on the wall." The maid grinned and left the door open for him.

"Looking for an escape route, love?" He had an idea his lovely wife had similar plans to his.

Selena turned to him with a bright smile. Her beautiful violet eyes sparkled like flawless amethysts. "We need a door between our chambers."

Gabriel slid his arms around her waist and pulled her close. "I could knock a hole in the wall."

"A door would be better." She put her arms around his neck, toying with the hair lying along his high collar. "Then we could have privacy when necessary. Not that I mind having you help me dress." She smiled. "But when your valet joins you, I would prefer not to wander around in front of him in my stays and petticoats."

"I'd prefer you dinna, either. So a door it will be." He kissed her thoroughly, delighting in her eager response. Several minutes later, he slowly raised his head. "How I pity all those lords and ladies who marry for lands and money."

"We have both."

"Aye, but we also have love, and that's much more important."

"Yes." She sighed softly, gazing up at him with a dreamy expression. "Sometimes I still can't believe I'm married to you."

"Shall I pinch you so you'll know you're awake?"

"Don't you dare." Laughing, Selena wiggled out of his arms.

"Did you come up here just to tease me, or was there some other reason?"

"Both." Gabe told her about the man Miller had seen in the woods. "If we spot him, I'll go have a little chat."

"What if he is working for Bonham?"

"Then we'll soon discover it." Gabriel was not afraid to confront Bonham or one of his men. He relished the idea.

They didn't have long to wait. They were in Selena's sitting room—now his, too, she proclaimed—when Miller came up to find him. The butler knocked lightly on the open door. "The man we discussed is back, sir. Only this time it looks like he's riding up to the house. Must have seen that you're home."

"Thank you, Miller. I'll be right down." Gabe stood and started out of the room, but Selena caught his arm.

"I'm coming, too."

"Maybe he just wants to sell me a horse to replace poor old Fireball."

"Highly doubtful."

Gabe shrugged. "Wishful thinking."

Selena playfully swatted his arm as they walked down the hall. "Fireball loves you. He'd be crushed if he thought you were going to replace him."

"I didna say I was going to do away with him. He can live here and grow fatter and slower, but it's embarrassing to ride such a nag." Gabe opened the door to his bedchamber.

Selena followed him into the room. "You didn't seem to mind when you were estate manager."

"I didna want to complain for fear I'd be sent packing."

"What a clanker." Selena chuckled, but sobered quickly as Gabe withdrew a small pistol from a box on his dressing table and loaded it.

"It is highly unlikely that I'll need this, but I believe in being prepared." He doubted Cameron expected him to simply turn over his wife, but he did not intend to take the chance. Or risk the even remoter possibility that the man approaching the house did indeed work for Bonham.

Selena took a deep breath. "Do you think he might arrest me?"

"He can try." He cupped her chin in his hand and slowly kissed her. "But he willna succeed."

As they went down the wide staircase, the landing window offered a clear view of the lane and the man riding toward the house. He kept the horse at a leisurely walk. "Well, he's on a fine steed," said Selena. "Far above the likes of Ellaby."

"Judging by the way he rides, he's cavalry. Or was." Gabe rested his hand on Selena's shoulder. "Prepare yourself, love. I expect we'll have a visit from Major Cameron very soon."

At the bottom of the stairs, Gabriel caught Miller's eye. "We'll wait for our guest in the drawing room. Show him in when he arrives."

Miller nodded, then peeped out the window by the front door.

In the drawing room, Gabriel positioned Selena on a sofa facing the windows. He stood behind her, placing the pistol within easy reach on a table in back of the sofa. He knew Miller would guard the hallway. By facing the windows, Gabe could see if anyone else approached from outside.

A few minutes later, Barnes, the footman, showed a tall, thin man into the room. The man nodded to Selena, then Gabriel. "Thank you for seeing me. I'm John Lambert, an acquaintance of Major Cameron."

"Welcome to Fairhaven, Mr. Lambert." As always, Selena played the perfect hostess, though Gabe knew she had to be nervous. She motioned toward the armchair across from her. "Please make yourself comfortable."

Gabriel bit back a tiny smile. They had not discussed where the man should sit, or even if he should. That particular chair, however, was the most uncomfortable one in the room. Selena readily admitted her mistake in buying it simply because she liked the design in a catalog. The white velvet seat cushion wasn't bad, but the ornate scrollwork up the middle of the open mahogany back could prove tedious, especially to someone with a knobby backbone.

"Thank you, ma'am." Lambert sat down, looking at Gabriel. "Cameron wants to see you." He glanced at Selena.

"He is welcome to call anytime." Gabriel watched the other man carefully. Lambert gave the impression of being totally at ease, but Gabriel doubted he missed the smallest detail.

Lambert shook his head. "He is staying nearby and wants you to visit him." He looked at Selena again, his appreciative gaze lingering. "He specifically said to bring your lovely wife."

Gabe tensed. His old commander knew him well. The major would assume that Gabriel had told her everything. "I'd prefer that he come here."

Lambert smiled lazily and shifted his weight in the chair, leaning to one side. "He expected you would." His demeanor changed subtly, his tone firmer. "But I must insist that you go to him. Right now, in fact. You both will be free to return here whenever you wish."

Why would Cameron insist they go to him? If Bonham was having the house watched, his man would certainly take note of everyone who visited. A call from Gabriel's former commander might arouse some suspicion. Gabriel and Selena paying an afternoon call on someone else, however, might not be so notable, depending on where the major was staying.

Gabe glanced at Selena, catching the fear in her eyes. "Do I have Cameron's word on that?"

"Yes."

Gabriel walked around the sofa so he could see Selena's face. "Cameron willna go back on his word, love. They willna try to keep you."

She took a deep breath and held his gaze. "Then we shall go with Mr. Lambert and see if our plan meets with the major's approval."

Lambert's eyes narrowed. "What plan?"

Selena rose and slipped her hand around Gabriel's arm. "Please take no offense, sir, but I prefer to discuss this with Major Cameron first."

"No offense taken, ma'am." Lambert stood. "He is visiting the Le Clares east of Worcestershire."

"Georges and Alice Le Clare?" Selena looked surprised.

"Yes. Do you know them?" Lambert cast a derisive glance at the mahogany chair.

"I've met them, though it was some time ago. Their daughter, Adrienne, and I had our coming-out the same year. I saw her at various social functions for a few years, but we never really became closely acquainted." Selena looked up at Gabriel. "Mrs. Le Clare is the marquis of Woodsford's daughter." She shifted her gaze to Lambert. "I assume they are staying at his estate?"

"Yes, ma'am."

"Then I know where it is. If you will excuse me, gentlemen, I'll fetch a bonnet."

"Of course, my dear." Gabriel squeezed her hand before she slipped away. "I'll have the gig brought around."

"I'll be down shortly." With a tight little smile to Lambert, she quickly left the room.

Gabriel stepped to the door and called to Barnes, instructing the footman to order the gig brought to the house. Then he returned to the drawing room, shutting the door behind him. "What does Cameron have in mind?"

"I don't know. My assignment has been to watch the house and take you to him when you returned." Lambert clasped his hands behind him. "One of the major's men followed your wife to Scotland." A tiny smile touched his face. "I expect you knew that."

"Yes, a Mr. Brown. It seems he saved her from some unpleasantness at one of the inns. I'd hoped to meet him and express my appreciation. But he disappeared a few days after we went to Inshirra."

"His orders were to report back to Cameron if she went to you. The major did not believe she could do us any harm in the Highlands, or as a new bride."

Perhaps Cameron's heart is softening after all. Gabriel stepped behind the sofa and retrieved his pistol.

Lambert's eyes widened minutely. "I'm glad I didn't anger you."

"I'm glad you didna, either. These days I try to be prepared for anything. Sometimes it is hard to distinguish between friend and foe."

The other man nodded slightly. "Especially when your loyalties are at odds with each other. When Cameron first explained the situation to me, I thought you were a fool. But upon meeting your wife, I've revised my opinion. She is exquisite."

"I agree." Gabriel pocketed the pistol in his coat. Filled with unwavering determination, he walked toward the door. "I intend to make certain she stays that way."

CHAPTER *Twenty-Nine*

As they drove to the Woodsford estate, Selena absently rolled the strap on her reticule between her fingers. *Please, God, see us through this. Guide us, and Major Cameron, to find the best way to resolve this whole situation.* She glanced at the lines of worry on Gabriel's face. He'd tried so hard to reassure her, but doubt and concern hovered in the depths of his eyes.

Had she been wrong to marry this man she loved so much? Would she only bring him heartache and humiliation? *Please, Lord, don't let him be hurt because of me.* Still, she had to do the right thing. She was accountable for her actions and she had to make recompense in some way. *Help me to be strong, Lord!*

Selena laid her hand on Gabe's arm.

He immediately met her gaze, his brow creasing in concern. "Yes, sweetheart?"

"I love you."

His expression softened and tenderness warmed his eyes. "I love you, too."

"Forgive me for involving you in all this."

The corner of his mouth lifted in a wry smile. "If I remember correctly, I involved myself. Jumped in with both feet and the humble attitude that I could resolve everything and charm my way into your heart in about a week."

Selena smiled and stretched up to kiss him on the cheek. "Well, you did charm your way into my heart."

"But it took longer than a week."

"Actually, it didn't. All during your interview, I kept telling myself I'd be a fool to hire you—I was far too attracted to you for my own good. But I simply could not turn you away. Even then, I sensed that you would make a difference in my life."

Gabriel grinned for the first time since Lambert had knocked on their door. "Didna suspect how much, did you?"

"No." She laughed and slipped her hand around his upper arm, squeezing lightly. "I knew what I wished, what I longed for, but I thought I was strong enough to simply be friends."

"There is nothing simple about friendship. It requires caring for someone despite their mistakes and faults, perhaps even because of them. 'Tis the foundation for love."

"Sometimes I fear I was wrong not to send you away." She sighed and released his arm. "I do not want to bring you pain."

He guided the horse around a deep hole in the roadway, then glanced at her. "I will never regret loving you or marrying you, Selena. I do not embrace pain or sorrow, but if that is what God allows to come to me, I will still rejoice because I've been loved by you. Even now, my heart cries out to God to keep you with me always. But if that is no' to be, I will thank him and praise him for the love we share and for every minute we have together. The Scriptures say that all things work together for good for those that love the Lord Jesus. We do. And I trust God to keep that promise."

"I do, too." She took a deep breath. "I just hope that God's idea of good is the same as ours."

Gabe reached down and covered her hand with his. "So do I."

When Gabriel, Selena, and Lambert arrived at the Woodsford estate, the footman showed them into a private sitting room, advising them that he would find Major Cameron. Though restless, Selena sat down on the gold brocade sofa, knowing neither of the men would sit until she did. Lambert lounged comfortably on a well-cushioned chair. Gabe prowled the room, stopping now and then to study some of the landscapes or gaze out the window.

A few minutes later, Adrienne Le Clare breezed in. "How nice to see you again, Selena. I know you are here to visit the major, but I couldn't let the opportunity pass without giving you my best wishes." She smiled mischievously. "And to meet the man who finally won your heart."

Selena had not remembered Adrienne as being so pretty. The woman seemed radiant. Her eyes glowed with a soft light, and her smile was that of a woman whose joy simply bubbled over.

Adrienne looked like a woman in love.

Selena smiled and shook her hand. "Thank you. I'm pleased to see you, too. I'd like you to meet my husband, Gabriel Macpherson. Gabriel, may I present Adrienne Le Clare."

Adrienne held out her hand to Gabriel. "Mr. Macpherson, it is a pleasure. I've heard many good things about you from the major."

Gabriel shook her hand, bowing slightly. "I'm honored to meet you, Miss Le Clare. And glad to hear Cameron has told you good things." He glanced at Selena with a smile. "He knows tales that are no' so flattering."

"We've heard a few of those, too." Adrienne laughed, nodding a greeting to Lambert as she took a seat in a chair across from Selena. She was obviously used to seeing the man, but from the expression on Adrienne's face, Selena surmised he was not the object of her affection.

Adrienne turned to her. "I'll have to share the stories with you sometime. To hear the major tell it, your husband and Lord Branderee were full of mischief and managed to get themselves into one scrape after another."

"That I can believe." Selena forced a smile, hoping it looked more sincere than it felt. The drive over had been difficult enough, but to sit about waiting for the major and attempting small talk was unbearable. Cameron gave his word that they could leave. *Gabe trusts him.* The words became a litany running through her mind. *Please, God. I don't want to die or go to prison.*

Her gaze fell on her husband as he stared out the window, his brow knit in a deep frown. *Please, dear Lord, don't take me from him. Guide us.*

"I'm sure Major Cameron will be here shortly," Adrienne

said. Her expression softened when Selena looked at her. "I know this is difficult for you, especially having to wait."

Before Selena could respond, Gabriel turned to Adrienne, his eyes narrowing. "You are familiar with our situation?"

"Yes. I have been working for Major Cameron the past year, though I have been in France for two years. I went to care for my father's mother when her health began to fail. Papa dared not go back. Though he is French, he has lived in Britain almost thirty years. Both he and Grandmother feared that Napoleon would force him to remain in France. After my grandmother died, I stayed in Caen to see to her business affairs. I also worked for the British Foreign Office, passing on information when I heard something useful and doing what I could to help Britons escape."

A sudden, wild hope surged through Selena. Adrienne Le Clare helped Britons escape France? Major Cameron had promised Gabe he would try to help Nick. *Dear Lord, could it be…?* She met Gabriel's gaze and saw the same hope in his eyes. He joined her on the sofa, reaching for her hand as Adrienne continued.

"I made arrangements with the Foreign Office before I left for France. They understood that I would not participate in any espionage efforts until after my grandmother's death. I didn't want to endanger her safety."

The door opened and Major Cameron entered. "Gabriel, it's good to see you." He and Gabe shook hands, then Cameron turned to Selena with a polite bow. "Mrs. Macpherson, I believe marriage agrees with the lad."

"It agrees with both of us, sir." Selena did not attempt a smile. Her gaze drifted to Gabriel. "These past weeks have been the happiest of my life." She looked back at the major. "Thank you for allowing us to have this time together."

Surprise flashed through his eyes, then an element of grimness settled over his features. "Regrettably, happiness is oftentimes elusive."

Selena's heart lurched.

"You are no' going to make this easy, are you, Cam?" Bitterness colored Gabriel's voice.

"It isna an easy matter." Cameron glanced at Lambert and motioned toward the door. The man rose and walked from the room without a word.

Adrienne stood also. "If you will excuse me, there are matters to which I must attend. You know where to find me, Major." Her gaze traveled from Gabriel to Selena. "Have faith," she murmured, then left the room.

When the door closed, Cameron took the chair Lambert had vacated. "May I call you Selena?"

"Yes." She tightened her grip on Gabriel's hand.

"I assume Gabriel told you about me and his involvement with our investigation?"

"Yes, he did."

"I could no' go away and leave her unprotected," Gabriel said firmly. "At the time, I didna reveal your name or anyone else's. But I did tell her everything we knew about her."

"I see." Cameron pursed his lips thoughtfully. "As an agent for the crown, I do not approve of your actions. They border on treason. But as a man, I understand your need to protect the woman you love." He sat up straighter, leaning forward slightly. "Very well. Selena, what Gabriel told you is basically all we know about the operation. We still have no idea who Bonham is or whom his contacts may be. Which means, unfortunately, that you are the only suspect we have. If you are arrested, it is likely the courts will convict you as a traitor."

Selena's mouth went dry, and her heart pounded wildly. *Please, God...* "I know Gabriel has told you how much I regret what I have done. If I must pay for my crimes, then I will accept that fate." She heard Gabriel's sharp intake of breath. "Even lying in my husband's arms, I have nightmares. I am tormented by the fear that I have sent men to their deaths." She pulled her hand free from Gabe's firm grasp and picked up her reticule, which she had placed on the table beside the sofa.

"From the beginning I knew I would be held accountable for my actions. If not caught, I always intended to turn myself over to the authorities once my brother was safely home. I kept a list of the information I passed on." She withdrew a sheet of paper from the bag and handed it to him, then laid the reticule back on the table. "I also included things I was told but did not relay because they seemed to be more unusual, and therefore possibly more significant."

Cameron took the paper with a puzzled frown. "You did this, knowing it could mean a death sentence?"

How could she make him understand? "Believe me, I have no wish to die nor to spend my life in prison. But I do have a conscience. And, despite all I have done, a sense of honor." She took a deep, trembling breath. "But my reasons for the list are not entirely noble—"

Her voice broke, and she paused. Gabriel put his arm around her shoulders and recaptured her hand in his. His strength gave her the courage to go on. "I hope you can look at those messages and tell me the damage I've done. I—I need to know if our men died because of me. If they did, then perhaps…I should pay with my life."

"No!" Gabriel embraced her protectively. "You dinna have to die to make recompense!"

Casting a worried glance at Gabe, Cameron leaned against the back of the chair and began to read. When he finished, he folded the paper and returned it to her. "I compliment you on your discernment. A few of the things you did not tell Bonham would have been crucial, possibly disastrous to our men." He smiled gently. "Otherwise, I see nothing that Napoleon would not have already known or would not have learned from other sources, usually multiple ones. I think I can safely say you cannot be blamed for the death of a single man."

"Thank God!" Sheer relief made her head spin. The tears she'd held in check for so long now overwhelmed her, flowing down her cheeks. She turned with a soft cry and buried her face against Gabriel's shoulder.

Thank you, God! Oh, thank you!

Gabe rubbed her back, murmuring gentle, loving words of comfort punctuated with tender kisses on her hair. After a few minutes, she managed to compose herself. She sat up, gratefully taking the handkerchief Gabriel pressed into her hand. She wiped her eyes with trembling hands and—though she knew Aunt Gussie would have been mortified—blew her nose. "Thank you, Major."

"You're welcome, my dear. But we are no' out of the woods yet. You could still be arrested and tried for treason."

"You would do that?" Gabriel asked sharply.

Leaning against him, Selena felt his whole body tense.

"No' unless I'm forced to. I dinna run the intelligence office—yet. But I can be most persuasive and I intend to assist you all I can."

Gabe relaxed and lightly caressed her shoulder. She met his gaze, and he nodded. It was time to tell Cameron their plan.

Gabe turned to meet the major's steady stare. "Selena and I want to help you catch Bonham."

"I suspected as much. Do you have something in mind?"

"We thought we'd have an impromptu ball to announce our marriage. Invite everyone Selena knows. Conveniently, there is little on the social calendar at the beginning of next week."

"So Bonham should be on the list." Cameron nodded thoughtfully, looking at Selena. "He may no' have any use for you anymore since you are married."

"Perhaps not. But he is not a man who likes to be thwarted." A chill crept down her spine. "If he is still in the area, he will not forgo the opportunity to personally chastise me."

"That could be dangerous." Cameron shook his head.

"She will be carefully watched, by me and as many others as I can trust. Kiernan, Mariah, Dominic, and Jeanie came back, too. We can work out some kind of signal, so if he does reach her without our realizing who he is, Selena can let us know."

Cameron thought for a moment, then nodded slowly. "I'll consider it. I like the idea of using a party to flush him out, but I'm no' sure you should risk using Selena as bait." He stood. "Mariah made the trip again? Is that wise?"

"She didna think it would bother her. They are no' going as far each day as we did." Gabriel smiled for the first time since Cameron entered the room. "Mother says Mariah is as strong and healthy as any Highland lass."

"Well, then there's no problem. She can deliver the bairn in the morning and go back to tending the sheep in the afternoon."

Cameron moved around the chair and walked over to a door connecting to another room. "I can have several men here by then. Adrienne would also be good to watch for him. She is intelligent and quick-witted. She made the arrangements for nine Britons who successfully fled France. Three détenus and six military men." He looked over his shoulder with a smile. "The last one caught her eye and, so it would seem, her heart. The French government would not allow her to leave the country legally, so she and her betrothed escaped on their own. They crossed the Channel a fortnight ago in an old fishing smack. You'll need to add them to your invitation list."

He opened the door. "You may join us now, Adrienne."

He turned around, meeting Selena's gaze, and she frowned. His smile was a mixture of pleasure, satisfaction—and unexpected gentleness. "I dinna think he will refuse the invitation."

Selena's heart lodged in her throat. She took a deep breath and reached for Gabriel with trembling hands, afraid to hope. The shadow of a man fell across the doorway.

"I promised I'd see what could be done to help your brother escape." Cameron spoke quietly. "I sent word to our agents to watch for him and assist him in every way. God did the rest."

Nicholas stepped into the room, and Selena went weak. For

323

a second, she couldn't move. Then, with a cry, she shot off the sofa, tears of joy rolling down her cheeks. He met her in the middle of the room, enveloping her in a loving embrace.

"Hello, little sister." His voice thickened, and he pressed his face against her hair.

She hugged him furiously, then leaned back and framed his wet face with her hands. Tears pooled in his eyes, but he looked well. "Oh, Nick…" Then her throat clogged and she couldn't say anything else. He pulled her close.

"I know. Sometimes I never thought I'd make it, either."

They held each other a few minutes more, then Selena eased away. She looked at Cameron, shaking her head. "'Thank you' doesn't seem adequate, Major."

"It's enough for me. Adrienne is the one who spirited your brother out of the country."

Selena turned to her, struggling to take it all in. Nicholas was here, safe and sound. He was home. And he was in love! "Now I know why you looked so happy earlier. Not only did you rescue my brother, you're going to marry him! How wonderful for both of you."

Adrienne laughed. "I take it you approve?"

"Of course." Selena gave her a hug, too. When she turned around, Gabe was introducing himself to Nicholas and shaking his hand. Then, as she watched, one of her fondest dreams— one that she'd nearly despaired of—came true: her wonderful, loving husband pulled her dear, shy brother into a hearty embrace, slapped him on the back, and welcomed him home.

CHAPTER  Thirty

"YOU ARE INCREDIBLY LOVELY, sweetheart."

An hour before their ball was to begin, Gabriel stood in the doorway between his bedroom and Selena's. His apprehension about the evening fled at the sight of his beautiful wife. That this glorious creature was his still amazed him. How had he ever won her heart? He walked slowly around her, admiring her silk gown, or more accurately, the way she looked in it. That particular shade of purple made her eyes vibrant, not to mention complementing her soft, lovely skin and shiny black hair.

She gave him a pert smile. "Thank you, sir. Please take note of the modest décolletage."

Gabriel smiled, running his fingertip along the double band of wide velvet ribbon at the neck of her gown. Matching ribbon trimmed the hem, waist, and edge of the cap sleeves. "I did. Has it always been so? Or did you fear disapproval from a jealous husband?"

Selena laughed. "I had the seamstress add the ribbon. She altered several other gowns in similar ways. Judging by the light in your eyes, I assume it meets with your approval?"

"Aye, lass, it does. There is only so much of your beauty I am willing to share with other men." He ran his knuckle along her jaw. "What jewelry do you wear with purple?"

"Mulberry," she said absently, gazing up at him in a way that tempted him to lock the door and forget about the party.

"You're going to wear mulberries around that lovely neck? Will they no' leave a stain?"

She shook her head with a smile. "The color of the dress is called mulberry, not purple. As to jewelry, I haven't decided."

"What about diamonds?"

325

"They would be lovely if the necklace dipped down on the gown. The diamond necklace I have is shorter and lies at the base of my throat."

"See how this one looks." Gabe pulled a narrow wooden box from his coat pocket and handed it to her.

Her face lit up. "What is this for?"

"The party is to celebrate our marriage, is it no'? It seemed appropriate to give my lovely bride a gift, especially since I didna on our wedding day."

She wiggled her fingers in front of his face, showing him the simple gold wedding band. "You gave me a ring later. It is my most treasured possession." She brushed a kiss across his lips. "You're so sweet." Opening the box, she gasped softly. "Oh, Gabriel, it's beautiful."

Gabe tried not to appear smug. His wife would soon learn that he had an eye for beautiful jewelry. For beauty, period. Hadn't he chosen her? "Shall I put it on?"

"Yes, please." Selena kept staring at the necklace. The design was simple: a long gold chain with a two-inch gold crescent set with eight diamonds. The matching earrings were crescent-shaped with two diamonds each.

Gabe chuckled and kissed her forehead. "Then take it out of the box."

She blinked, then laughed. "Of course. You'll have to forgive me. This is the first time a gentleman has given me such a gift."

"I should hope so," he said dryly, stepping around behind her.

She set the box on her dressing table and removed the necklace, handing it to him over her shoulder.

He put the necklace around her throat and fastened it, meeting her gaze in the mirror. The gold chain sparkled against her skin and the diamonds flashed brilliantly against the purple silk. He rested his hands at her waist. "Perfect."

"Yes, it is." She turned toward him, sliding her arms around his neck. "Thank you."

"You're welcome." He leaned down and kissed her, barely resisting the urge to linger far longer than he should. "Dinna forget the earrings."

"As if I could."

"I'll go see if Nick is ready. We need to hide him in the office before any of the guests arrive."

"Before you go, I have something for you, too." She turned back to the dressing table and picked up a smaller box, handing it to him. "It isn't quite as impressive as your gift, but I think it will suit you."

Smiling with pleasure, Gabe opened the box. A cravat pin made of a single, large emerald set in gold twinkled up at him. "It's lovely, sweetheart. And yes, it suits me perfectly." He leaned down and kissed her again. "Thank you."

"I picked an emerald because of your eyes." She sighed softly. "I do love your eyes."

The tone in her voice and her dreamy look were almost his undoing. Would his knees always go weak when she gazed at him that way? "That's all?"

"No, dear. I love you totally. And I must say you look dashing. Half the women will probably swoon at your feet."

"Only half?" Gabe winked at her in the mirror as he pinned the emerald through the folds of his cravat. He straightened and examined his reflection. His black coat, crisp white shirt, white satin waistcoat, and red, green, and blue tartan kilt were perfection. He looked every inch the lord of the manor. He studied the fur sporran hanging from his belt to make certain the small pistol inside it was not visible, then touched the handle of the sheathed dirk at his side. The emerald sparkling from the folds of the snowy cravat added an elegant touch he decidedly liked. He turned, grinning at her. "*Now* I look dashing."

"Indeed." She adjusted a tiny fold in the cravat. "Go see to my brother. I'll be down soon." She took a deep breath, releasing it slowly. Apprehension crept across her countenance. "I pray this scheme works and Bonham is captured."

"So do I. If he comes, I believe he'll give himself away, especially when Nick makes his grand appearance." Cameron had suggested they make a special announcement, informing everyone at the same time that Nicholas was safely home, then introduce him. "It should shock Bonham into a blunder."

"May God will it so."

"Aye." He touched her face. "Fear not, love. He is with us. We will not fail." Gabe only wished he felt as confident as he sounded.

On his way downstairs, Gabriel stopped by the room where Nicholas was dressing. He could hear him pacing the floor. When he knocked, Nick instantly opened the door.

Gabe grinned at the look on the younger man's face. "Nervous?"

"Quaking in my boots." Nick joined him in the hall.

"I thought the aristocrats in Verdun had a social life much like here at home."

"They do. There are enough British wives and families in residence to keep the men civilized. But the single men far outnumber the single ladies."

"So the older, more polished gentlemen monopolized them."

"Precisely. I'm all at sea when it comes to *ton* parties. I'm afraid I'll turn red and stutter and stammer and make a fool of myself." Nick took a deep breath and blew it out quickly. "Especially since I'll be on display, so to speak."

"Hopefully not for long. As soon as we nab Bonham, you can slip away."

"That can't happen too soon for me," Nick said.

Nor for me, Gabe echoed silently.

Gabe left Nick to pace in the estate office where the other

guests would not see him. A few minutes later, Adrienne and her parents arrived, and she went to keep her beloved company during the long wait. Gabe smiled as she hurried down the hall. He knew how hard it was to be away from the one you loved for even a moment. His smiled faded. If their plan didn't work, he and Selena would be parted far longer than that.

God, be with us.

He heard a sound at the top of the stairs and turned to see Selena descending with Aunt Augusta, who had come back to Fairhaven for the occasion.

Augusta paused at the bottom of the stairs and inspected Gabriel from head to toe. "Well, scamp, good thing you hired some burly footmen for the occasion."

"Why is that, auntie?"

"When the ladies get a glimpse of you, we'll have swooning women all over the place. Someone will have to haul them outside and throw them in a pile."

Gabriel laughed, picturing a pile of elegantly dressed, limp bodies, arms and legs going every direction. "I dinna think we will have much of a problem. But I thank you for the compliment and would like to mention that you look enchanting this evening."

"Of course I do." Augusta glided off to the kitchen, muttering about lobster salad and collared eel.

"I need to make one last check in the ballroom and the other rooms that will be open to our guests." Selena started down the hall.

Gabe quickly caught up with her. "I'll go with you. Dinna have anything else do to."

When they reached the ballroom, Selena drew up short and nodded toward a small, wiry man dressed as a footman standing outside on the terrace. "That is Mr. Brown."

"I think I'll go introduce myself." Gabe gave her a wink and walked out the garden door. "Mr. Brown?"

The man turned to him with a hint of a smile. "Actually, the name is John Brownstone." He held out his hand. "Good evening, Mr. Macpherson."

Gabe shook his hand. "Good evening. I'm sorry I missed you in Scotland. I sent one of my men to the village to invite you to dinner, but you had already gone."

"How unfortunate." Brownstone grinned. "It would have made for an interesting evening."

Gabriel laughed quietly. "I merely wanted to thank you for coming to my wife's assistance at the inn."

"She probably could have handled the boozer by herself, but I was happy to oblige." Brownstone's gaze strayed toward the ballroom. Selena waved at him and he smiled, giving her a brief nod. "Cameron warned me to be on my guard and not fall under her spell." He looked back at Gabriel. "An impossible task. But he also told me to look after her, to feel free to intervene if there was any trouble."

"So I should thank him also."

Brownstone nodded. "Yes, though I'll admit I would have done it anyway. I have no stomach for seeing any woman come to harm. I expect the major would do the same."

"He has on many occasions." Gabriel pulled out his watch and checked the time. "The party will soon begin."

"Let us hope that when it's over we have something to celebrate."

"By God's grace, we will." Gabe went back inside, stopping to chat with the members of the orchestra. Then he wandered to the drawing room, where Cameron and Mr. and Mrs. Le Clare were waiting. Kiernan, Mariah, Dominic, and Jeanie all arrived a short time later.

Gabe hovered near the doorway, anxious for Selena to return. As he had done so many times in their lives, Kiernan stood beside him.

"Is everything set?" Kiernan glanced down the hall at the rather large footman standing beside the ballroom doorway.

"We're ready. Cameron has men scattered all over the house

330

and grounds in the guise of footmen and grooms. After our special guest makes his appearance, any man who seems the least bit suspicious will likely find himself escorted to the estate office and interrogated."

Kiernan chuckled. "You may cause a few raised eyebrows."

"So be it. I dinna care how many people we scandalize as long as we catch Bonham." Gabe took a deep breath, his worry returning tenfold as he watched his precious wife walk out of the ballroom. "And God keeps Selena safe."

"He's a good friend to depend on."

"I'd hate to be facing this without him." Gabe smiled at Selena as she approached, hoping to reassure her. "Well, love, have all the flowers wilted?"

"Not a one." She put her hand around his arm when he held it out to her.

He was relieved to feel nary a tremble. *Such a brave lass.* "Your Mr. Brown's name is actually Brownstone."

"Good thing it isn't gallstone."

Gabe laughed and turned her toward the door. "If so, he likely would change his method of determining an alias."

"Or find a new name altogether."

They joined the others in the drawing room, with Augusta coming in soon afterward.

A few minutes later, Miller stuck his head around the door-frame. "The first carriages are coming up the drive." His voice jumped an octave in his excitement.

"Calm down, Miller." Selena motioned for him to come into the room as Augusta shook her head and Cameron chuckled.

"Yes, ma'am." His voice squeaked.

"This is easier than your old job. You don't have to fuss with hats and wraps. All you do is read their names from the invitations and announce our guests in a deep, loud voice. You can do it. I heard you announce Lord Branderee and Lady Mariah as I was coming down the hall. You were fine."

"But I'm used to them coming here." He glanced at Kiernan

and Mariah. "I know how to pronounce their names."

"I don't believe there is anyone on the invitation list with too difficult a name. If you are uncertain of one, simply ask for the correct pronunciation. Now, relax and be dignified."

Dominic tipped his head toward Jeanie. "Aren't those contradictions?"

She whacked his arm with her fan and told him to hush.

"Go back to your post, Miller," Selena said.

The butler bowed and obeyed, squaring his shoulders and marching from the room.

Selena sighed. "Is everyone as nervous as I am?"

Kiernan gave her an encouraging smile. "Only your butler."

Gabe disagreed. The undercurrent of tension in the room was much greater than the normal worry caused by even such an important social event as a ball. "I believe we're all a bit on edge. Which is probably no' a bad thing. It will keep us alert."

At the sound of a coach pulling up in front of the manor, he offered Selena his arm. "Come, lass. 'Tis time to trap a viper."

Selena decided the ball guests were divided into two groups. One swore they had been completely taken by surprise at her marriage to the handsome Scot. The others were just as adamant that they had heard wedding bells in the air at the breakfast party.

"Should have known you'd go off and marry a foreigner," Mr. Stoddard grumbled.

Selena wondered what he would do now that he couldn't trail around after her. Though the way he and some of the others in her old retinue crowded around her, she wasn't altogether certain they intended to stop. At least not until Gabriel put his foot down. She would have been at his side right then if the cook hadn't thrown a tantrum because one of the fake footmen dropped a bowl of pudding.

A young man laughed at Stoddard. "Scotland isn't a foreign country."

"Might as well be. Ways are foreign. Men in skirts. Humph!"

"If I were you, I wouldn't let my husband hear you call it a skirt. It's a kilt. A fine and noble tradition." Selena edged away, impolitely wiggling through a group of people to keep the hangers-on from following her.

Selena stopped beside Mariah and Jeanette. Mariah peeked back at Stoddard and the others. "Having trouble convincing your admirers that you no longer want their attention?"

"Yes." Selena rolled her eyes. "They can be so silly. Gabriel once said they scuffled among themselves to show me their latest tricks." Selena spotted him across the room, near the windows.

"An apt description." Mariah glanced at an ornate gold clock on the wall and sobered. "It will soon be time."

Selena looked around, noting the positions of the British agents, as well as Cameron, Kiernan, and Dominic. The men had spread throughout the crowd, guarding the doors and windows. At ten o'clock, Le Clare would announce his daughter's engagement and Nick's return home. If all went well, Bonham's volatile personality would betray him. In light of the expected joyful reaction from everyone else, it would only take a hint of displeasure on his part to arouse suspicion. She hoped he would try to slither out the door and be soundly caught.

"I doubt the guests will be gossiping tomorrow about the excellent orchestra," Jeanette said.

"Pity." Mariah listened to a few bars of the current piece. "They are quite good."

"I'll pass on your compliment."

"As if you don't have other things on your mind," Mariah said quietly as Selena moved toward Gabriel.

As she had done that night a year earlier at the London ball, Selena met Gabriel's gaze across the crowded room. She felt the same jolt of awareness, the same sense that this man would change her life forever. Looking into those gentle green eyes as he searched her soul, she relived that moment when two lonely hearts touched, brought together by the power of the Master's hand.

When she had not seen him again during the rest of the Season, she'd wondered if he had been an illusion, a product of loneliness and a fertile mind. Tonight, in his kilt, he looked much as he had then, only the fire in his eyes burned even brighter. She still could not believe she had not recognized him when he first came to Fairhaven. Surely that, too, was part of God's wonderful plan.

A woman reached out to tap Selena's arm with her delicate fan. "Lovely party, my dear," she said when Selena paused and turned to her. The lady stared at Selena's necklace with a calculating gleam in her eyes.

"Yes, delightful," another woman nearby joined in, glancing at Gabriel. "Your husband is such a handsome man."

Selena murmured her thanks and kept walking, nodding and smiling to her guests, making a comment here and there. She stopped when people moving onto the dance floor blocked her way. She was still in Gabriel's line of vision.

Just then, she saw Le Clare weaving through the crowd toward the low stage they had built for the orchestra.

Selena's heartbeat quickened, and she took a steadying breath, slowly scanning the room as a new song began.

God, be with us…

Calm settled over her, and she let out a sigh. He was.

Two lines of dancers moved toward each other, a blur of colors and sparkling gems. Joining their partners, each couple gracefully spun around before forming the lines again. The conversations of those watching the dancers merged into a hum, ebbing and flowing like the tide.

A gentle breeze blew through the open doors and windows, keeping the room comfortably cool and dissipating some of the more powerful perfumes. But not all of them. The lady next to her reeked of some nauseating concoction for which she probably had paid a ridiculous sum. Selena eased her way through a closely packed group of guests, pausing when the noxious odor no longer assailed her nostrils. Under normal circumstances, she would never have invited more than a hundred to the ball. She detested the popular fashion of inviting twice as many people as a ballroom could comfortably hold, but there had been two hundred invitations to the outdoor breakfast. Unless she included them all, she could not be certain Bonham was on the guest list.

A new fragrance drifted on the breeze—a man's lavender cologne with a trace of something else that subtly set it apart from the common brand. *Bonham!* Selena glanced to either side of her but saw no one she knew particularly well. She listened to the nearby conversations.

A lady in back of her laughed softly, murmuring something Selena could not hear.

A man laughed. "You look puzzled, my dear."

Selena froze. It was the same voice, and the exact phrase Bonham had used that night in the woods when he abandoned his raspy tone. She turned just far enough to look behind her. Two older, corpulent gentlemen were discussing the price of corn. Mr. Jones, formerly of her entourage, was there with a young lady whose name she couldn't remember. Mr. Hopkins and his Miss Brown were with them. Next to them, two matrons tittered, one of them commenting on Gabriel's bare knees.

Jones couldn't possibly be the spy. He was too short, too plump. Nor could she imagine quiet, shy Mr. Hopkins as the lecherous Bonham. She looked away, not wanting to be caught staring. But as she listened, she frowned. Hopkins was neither quiet nor shy with Miss Brown. He flirted provocatively with the young lady.

Perhaps he is in love. Love often makes men more daring.

Even as she offered this reasoning, Bonham's words drifted back to her: *I am two people.* What better disguise for a cruel,

blackmailing traitor than that of a quiet, unassuming gentleman? Someone who could go practically unnoticed in a crowd
of admirers and thus be privy to her social schedule and many
of her conversations.

Selena glanced at Hopkins again. No, surely she was wrong.
With everyone other than Miss Brown, he was withdrawn and
timid. Suddenly he moved his hand, and she caught the glim-
mer of a gold ring on his little finger. She gasped, her gaze flying to his face. As if sensing her perusal, he looked directly at
her. In a heartbeat, his pale, gray eyes became shards of ice.

He knew she had recognized him.

Selena tried to move away, but as Le Clare stepped onto the
stage, the crowd shifted, blocking her in every direction. She
looked toward Gabriel but could no longer see him. Nor could
she see any of the other men who were supposed to watch for
Bonham and, if necessary, protect her.

Suddenly, Hopkins stood right behind her. He put his arm
around her waist, holding her firmly against him. The other
guests stretched and shifted to see what was happening across
the room, engulfing Selena and her captor in the process.
Excited murmurs filled the air.

Hopkins leaned down until his lips touched her ear. "How
foolish you are, my dear. Regrettably, you must pay for your
folly."

God! Help me!

Selena desperately searched the room, but she could not see
Gabriel. She was certain he would maneuver until he could at
least see her, which meant she needed to stay where she was.
Not that she had any choice in the matter.

She drew a steadying breath. She had to keep Hopkins—
no, *Bonham*—occupied until Gabriel spotted them. "I can still
work for you."

"Now, you mock me, chérie. Your jealous husband would
not allow such flirtations."

"He is not as jealous as you think." *God, forgive me for the lies, but I don't know what else to do!* "He was far more interested in my money than me."

Hopkins snorted and tightened his arm. "You expect me to believe that?"

"You said yourself he was badly in need of funds." *Gabe, where are you?* "He deceived me. He will return to Scotland soon, but I will not go with him."

As Le Clare began to speak, the crowd moved once more, opening up a path toward the garden door.

"I'll decide later whether or not I believe you. For now, I will take my leave, and you will accompany me."

Selena felt something cold and sharp press against her side. When she looked down, she caught a glint of light off a thin, long bladed knife.

"Do not make me kill you, Selena. It would be such a waste."

"There would be dozens of witnesses."

He glanced toward Le Clare and began to edge toward the door, shoving her along in front of him. "Who aren't paying a bit of attention to us. They are too busy straining their ears to hear. The man needs to talk louder."

"Wouldn't need to if you'd be quiet," a man complained as they walked behind him.

Le Clare said something else, and the room erupted with cheers and applause. The commotion startled Hopkins, and Selena felt the blade prick her skin. When she gasped, he pulled the knife back slightly.

Hopkins mumbled in her ear. "What is all the uproar?"

Then an awed hush fell over the crowd. Selena saw Nick walk across the floor with Adrienne at his side. Though his cheeks were flushed and his smile self-conscious, he was incredibly handsome in his dark blue coat and buff pantaloons. In spite of her fear, her heart swelled with pride and thanksgiving.

Thank you, Lord, for bringing him safely home.

Adrienne wore an icy blue gown of gauze over a darker blue satin slip. She appeared fragile and delicate, a far cry from the strong woman Selena knew her to be.

Hopkins went rigid. *"No!"*

At his shout, those around them drew back, leaving the two of them in the middle of the room with Nicholas and Adrienne. Nick gently pushed Adrienne into a cluster of guests and turned toward Hopkins. His expression hardened, and his eyes grew dark.

Selena detected another movement out of the corner of her eye.

"Release my wife, Hopkins." Gabriel's command echoed around the room as he stepped into view. Standing with his feet braced for action, a pistol aimed at Hopkins's head, he blocked the way to the garden door. "Or should we call you *Bonham?"*

Hopkins faced Gabriel, dragging Selena in front of him. "Stay back, or I'll cut her."

"Like you cut me, Catroux?" Nicholas inched toward them. Selena was startled to see the hatred burning in her brother's eyes.

Hopkins swerved back toward Nick, his breathing harsh, his fingers digging into Selena's side. "It was such a pleasure, feeling the whip cut into your flesh. Does the fine lady know about your scars, Delaroe?"

"She knows...and loves me still."

"You lie!"

"And you're a traitor." Gabriel had closed the distance between them until he was only a few yards away. He now held a dirk in his hand instead of a pistol. He moved the knife back and forth in front of him, catching the light with the long, wide blade.

Selena felt Hopkins tense. *He fears the blade more than a bullet.* And why shouldn't he? It was his preferred weapon.

"And a blackmailer." At the sound of Kiernan's voice behind him, Hopkins spun around, again taking Selena with him.

Anger welled up inside her. Rage at the cruelty and torture her brother had suffered, at the guilt and indignities she'd been forced to endure, at the pain and destruction this man so carelessly sowed...

Enough! She would no longer be dragged around like an old cloth doll. Gritting her teeth, she kicked Hopkins in the shin with the heel of her shoe.

Hopkins shouted an oath and jerked his arm tighter about her waist.

Selena dug her nails into his arm. "I won't do you any good if I faint, you idiot."

Hopkins swore again but quit squeezing the air out of her.

A dozen men surrounded them now, all slowly moving closer, tightening the circle. Selena noticed Cameron was among them, but he said nothing. Brownstone was by his side.

"Did it ever occur to you that Selena might be feeding you false information?" Dominic's voice was filled with disdain.

"What?" Hopkins spun around again and came face to face with Gabriel.

In a heartbeat, Gabe touched his dirk to Hopkins's throat. Then he smiled—a quirky, impish little smile that would cause one to question his sanity—and drawled, "'Tis a braw blade, is it no? And lairger than yers."

Hopkins froze, and Gabe's smile vanished. A cold, hard light gleamed in his eyes. "Release my wife," he said softly. "Or die."

Selena felt Hopkins shiver, and his knife clattered to the floor as he released her. She stepped forward, leaning against her husband's strong body when her legs began to shake.

Gabe put one arm around her, crushing her to him, supporting her. But he kept the knife against Hopkins's throat. "I should kill you now and save the government the trouble."

Then he slowly lowered the dirk. "Fortunately for you, God frowns on cold-blooded murder. But I'll no' weep when you hang."

As Cameron's men hauled Hopkins toward the garden door, Gabriel slipped the dirk into the sheath and embraced Selena. "Forgive me, lass, for not reaching you before he did. If he had hurt you—" His voice broke, and he kissed her forehead tenderly. "You are my life, Selena."

She held him tight: "And you are mine. And my protector, my champion." When the excited hum of a hundred conversations penetrated her dazed mind, she looked up at him. "Send all these people home."

"Aye, love. 'Tis the best idea anyone has had lately." He guided her to the orchestra stage. When a violinist hopped up, offering her his chair, she accepted gratefully.

It took a few minutes for Gabriel to get everyone's attention. "Ladies and gentlemen, I must ask you to please leave."

"But we haven't had any supper, young man," shouted an elderly gentleman.

Gabriel glanced at Selena, and she nodded with a tired smile. "Let them eat. It's all set out by now anyway."

He frowned and faced their guests again. "Very well. Stay and eat, then go home. But you'll have to find your own way to the supper table." Gabe stepped down from the stage and scooped Selena up in his arms.

She was drained, too tired to protest. Nor did she want to. She put her arms around his neck, resting her head against his shoulder. As he strode across the room, Selena picked up snippets of conversation. By the time they walked through the doorway, she had pieced together the rumor flying around the room—that she had been pretending to spy for France to protect her brother, but had been working for the British government at the same time, passing on false information.

Kiernan and Dominic were waiting for them at the foot of

the stairs. "Nick and Adrienne are in your upstairs sitting room," Kiernan said as he and Dominic walked up with them. "Along with the Le Clares and Mariah and Jeanie."

When they reached the second floor, Cameron lounged casually against the wall.

"I can walk the rest of the way, Gabe." Selena looked at Cameron as Gabe set her feet on the floor. "I heard a strange rumor downstairs just now. That I had also been working for the English."

Cameron shrugged, then straightened. "One can always count on rumors to change the facts a wee bit. I believe the proper wording was that you had been helping the British government by passing on false information."

"But Cameron, I only did that once, with the information Major Lawrence gave me. And even then I didn't tell Bonham everything."

"Ah, but lass, Lawrence wasna the first one." The major glanced at Gabriel. "I didna quite tell Gabe all of it. There were two others before Lawrence. According to the log you showed me, you told the French exactly what we wanted you to."

"Can you convince your superiors not to prosecute Selena?" Gabriel rested his hand on her shoulder.

"It should no' be a problem, especially since the foreign secretary promised me a promotion if we caught Bonham." Cameron winked at Selena. "I'm now second in command in the section. When I explain how you helped us in the past— with no mention that you did it unwittingly—and how you risked your life to help us capture the true spy, they will have no inclination to try you. They'll probably give you a medal."

Her body went weak as intense relief swept through her. Gabe let out a whoop. Circling her waist with his hands, he picked her up and spun her around. Laughing, Selena protested. "Put me down, my love. I've already gone in too many circles tonight."

He complied, but supported her with a strong arm around her waist. He clamped his other hand on Cameron's shoulder. "Thank you, my friend."

"I know there were times you doubted me, lad. You could no' help it. But I always hoped it would turn out this way."

Selena leaned her head against Gabe's shoulder and sighed, tears of joy misting her eyes. "The nightmare is over."

He nudged her face up with his knuckle and kissed her gently. "Aye, dear lass. And the sweet dreams begin."

Epilogue

Inshirra
August, 1815

SELENA LAY IN THE SWEET PINK heather of the mountain glen. Gabriel dozed beside her in the sunshine of a lazy afternoon. They had stolen away to spend time alone before a houseful of company arrived at the end of the week. Gabe's parents and hers; Aunt Augusta; Nick and Adrienne with their two little girls; Dominic and Jeanie with their two boys and a girl; and Kiernan and Mariah and their little boys all were coming. Even Cameron and his new bride would be there.

She watched an eagle high overhead, admiring its beauty and soaring flight. She often wondered how many people truly appreciated freedom. Perhaps they did not realize its importance until it was taken from them—or until the threat of losing it hung over their heads.

After Napoleon's first abdication the previous year, the military prisoners of war and détenus had returned home, some tasting freedom for the first time in twelve years. The French emperor had briefly regained power, only to finally be defeated by Wellington at Waterloo. Napoleon was now on a ship bound for St. Helena, a small rocky island where he would spend the rest of his days.

Bonham had been convicted of treason and hanged. Ellaby was never found. Cameron speculated he fled to America or some other foreign land as soon as Bonham was arrested.

In the four years since Nick's return from France, he and Adrienne had traveled from Scotland to Ireland and to every district in England. He diligently managed their profitable estates and periodically increased his holdings, but he could not stay in one place too long. He refused, however, to travel beyond Britain. Never again would he set foot on foreign soil.

Selena sighed, thinking how peaceful her life had become. Or as peaceful as it could be with three-year-old identical twin boys to keep up with. Though she and Nick had been very close, the bond between little Patrick and Alexander was uncanny. They acted alike, thought alike, even finished each other's sentences.

Her father had tolerated her presence at Nick and Adrienne's wedding, and showed a grudging admiration for Gabriel even then. Through God's grace, she kept trying to restore their relationship, but his forgiveness had been slow in coming.

Then, one day, her mother shocked them all by stomping her foot and shouting at her husband to grow up and stop blaming Selena for his mistake. She then informed her stunned mate that she intended to stay at her sister's until he made peace with his daughter. She packed her bags and left that very afternoon. It took him a week to come around.

The relationship between Selena and her father had been tenuous at first, but he slowly lost the icy shell he'd developed while Nick was in France. It disappeared completely when the twins were born—and they named one of the boys after him and one after Gabriel's father.

Gabe leaned up on one elbow, looking down at her. "Was that a happy sigh or a sad sigh?"

"I'm a contented Highland wife." She traced the line of his jaw with a sprig of heather. "I oversee an excellent garden and a fine dairy, and have learned to spin and weave wool from our own sheep."

"And made me a nice tartan in the process."

She nodded with a smile. "Made you a passable tartan. The first duty of a Highland bride."

"But are you happy, my love? Do you miss England? We dinna have much of a social whirl here."

"Aye," she said, bringing a smile to his handsome face, "but we have good friends and loving families, both near and far. They provide all the social activities I need." She sat up, gazing down the mountainside at the glistening waters of Loch Insh. "I enjoy going to Fairhaven and I'm pleased with all the progress we've made there. But this is my home now, and I love it here. When we are gone I soon long to return."

Gabriel's smile warmed her to her toes. "Once the Highlands have hold of you, they draw you back. No matter where you go, nor how fine the land, in your heart you'll hear their call." He gently pulled her down to him and brushed a kiss across her lips. "But I'll tell you a secret, lass. Even the Highlands canna warm a man's lonely heart. Only the love of a woman can ease that ache."

She rested her arms against his chest, gazing into those beautiful green eyes she loved so much. "Are you happy, Gabriel?"

He rolled her back into the heather, bracing himself up on one arm so he could look down at her. "Aye, lass. Sometimes I think I'm happier than a man has a right to be. I once thought we might have to flee to the ends of the earth to keep you safe. I even considered a slow boat to China."

"Such a long, boring trip."

"It would no' have been boring." Imps danced in his eyes as he tickled her.

Selena giggled, trying to move away from his hand. "I love you."

He gently caressed her side. "I love you, too, sweet lass."

At his kiss, her soul sang a melody as old as time, praise to the loving God who joined two hearts as one and gave them their Highland home.

More Romance Fiction from Palisades and Sharon Gillenwater

Antiques
by **Sharon Gillenwater**

Deeply wounded by his late wife's infidelity, Grant has avoided all women. Then he meets Dawn, an antiques dealer who won't marry a man who doesn't share her faith. Can they find a love that will endure?

88070-801-8

A Christmas Joy
by **Sharon Gillenwater, Peggy Darty,** and **Amanda MacLean**

Three holiday-romance novellas in one! In Sharon Gillenwater's contribution, *Love Wanted*, Colin McCrea seeks the mysterious woman who captured his heart. Also: Sadie Grayson's ideals are tested by a former sweetheart, and Heather, a model, finds out what she really values.

88070-780-1

Love Song
by **Sharon Gillenwater**

As famous country singer Andrea Carson faces a life-threatening illness, Wade Jamison shows her that she also needs inner healing. But can she convince him that their love can survive the demands of her career?

88070-747-X